Collective Action under the Articles of Confederation

Rather than focusing on why the states did not contribute to the national government under the Articles of Confederation, *Collective Action under the Articles of Confederation* asks why the states did contribute. Why did states pay large portions of their requisitions to the federal government when problems of collective action and the lack of governmental incentives imply they should not have? Using original data on Continental troop movements and federal debt holdings within each state, Dougherty shows that states contributed to the national government when doing so produced local gains. Such a theory stands in stark contrast to the standard argument that patriotism and civic duty encouraged state cooperation. Material incentives and local interests bound the union together and explained the push for constitutional reform more than the pursuit of mutual goals.

Keith L. Dougherty is an assistant professor of political science at Florida International University and a recipient of a 1998 Fulbright Scholarship. His research interests include American political development, federalism, and constitutional design. Several of his works on the Articles of Confederation have appeared in *Public Choice* and the *Journal of Theoretical Politics*, as well as in edited volumes.

Collective Action under the Articles of Confederation

KEITH L. DOUGHERTY

Florida International University

CAMBRIDGE
UNIVERSITY PRESS

PUBLISHED BY THE PRESS SYNDICATE OF THE UNIVERSITY OF CAMBRIDGE
The Pitt Building, Trumpington Street, Cambridge, United Kingdom

CAMBRIDGE UNIVERSITY PRESS
The Edinburgh Building, Cambridge CB2 2RU, UK
40 West 20th Street, New York, NY 10011-4211, USA
10 Stamford Road, Oakleigh, VIC 3166, Australia
Ruiz de Alarcón 13, 28014 Madrid, Spain
Dock House, The Waterfront, Cape Town 8001, South Africa

http://www.cambridge.org

First published 2001

Printed in the United States of America

Typeface Sabon 10/12 pt.   *System* QuarkXPress [BTS]

A catalog record for this book is available from the British Library.

Library of Congress Cataloging in Publication data
Dougherty, Keith L., 1965–
Collective action under the Articles of Confederation / Keith L. Dougherty.
p.   cm.
Includes bibliographical references.
ISBN 0-521-78209-0
1. Federal government – United States – History – 18th century.   2. State rights.
3. Constitutional history – United States.   I. Title.

JK316 .D68 2001
320.973′09′033 – dc21   00-031264

ISBN   0 521 78209 0   hardback

To my father Paul and to David Lalman,
for the fundamentals of writing, politics, and constructive thought

Contents

List of Tables and Figures   *page* ix

Acknowledgments   xi

1   **The Mystery of State Contribution**   1
    The Confederative Design   3
    Explanations for Poor Compliance   7
    State Compliance and Private Gain   13
    Overview of the Book   15

2   **National Interests and State Sovereignty:**
   Objectives of the Confederation   17
    Philosophical and Legal Origins of the Articles 18
    Goals of the Confederation   25
    Conclusion   32

3   **Collective Action and the Provision of Public Goods**   34
    The Voluntary Provision of Pure Public Goods   35
    Actual State Payments   42
    Joint Products   45
    Conclusion   49

4   **The History of State Compliance**   51
    The Revolutionary Years, 1775–1780   52
    The Morris Years, 1781–1784   59
    Waning Years of the Confederation, 1785–1789   77
    Conclusion   82

5   **State Contributions and Private Interests**   84
    An Empirical Evaluation   85
    Manipulating Private Benefits   98
    Conclusion   101

6   **Reacting to Rebellion**   103
    Significance of the Shays Requisition   105
    Two Unrests   107
    Governmental Responses   115
    Discussion   124
    Conclusion   127
7   **A New Constitution**   129
    More Efficiency   131
    Institutional Solutions   132
    The Pragmatics of Reconstitution   153
    Conclusion   160
8   **Conclusion**   162
    The Federalist Debates   163
    A Confederation Based on Virtue   173
    Lessons from the American Confederation   179

Appendix: Olson's Collective Action Game   183
Glossary   193
References   197
Index   207

List of Tables and Figures

TABLES

3.1 The Requisition to Suppress Shays' Rebellion   38
4.1 Old-Money Requisitions, 1775–1779   54
4.2 General Requisitions, 1780–1788   79
5.1 State Compliance with Requisitions for Soldiers,
    1777–1783   89
5.2 Regressions of State Contributions and the Distance of the
    Continental Army   92
5.3 State Compliance with Requisitions for Money,
    1784–1789   95
5.4 Regressions of State Contributions and the Public Debt   97

FIGURES

3.1 Quarterly Requisition Payments and Compliance   43
3.2 Frequency of State Payments, 1782–1789   44
4.1 Federal Expenditures and Soldiers in Continental Pay,
    1775–1783   63
5.1 Compliance (in Regular Soldiers) and the Distance of the
    Continental Army, 1777–1782   91
5.2 Monetary Compliance and the Public Debt, 1782–1789   96
A.1 The Provision of Public Goods in an Institution-Free
    Setting   185
A.2 Reaction Curves   187
A.3 Rational Provision of Public Goods under the Articles   191

Figures, Tables and Finances

Acknowledgments

Any work of this magnitude owes rounds of gratitude to a great number of people. Joe Oppenheimer coauthored an argument that initiated my research into the Articles of Confederation and helped me see the topic from creative angles. Piotr Swistak offered the important broad strokes that gave the project structure, vision, and organization. I am indebted to him for both his insight and his idea of investigating several of the institutional designs proposed. David Lalman showed me the importance of detail. He taught me how to write and how to think clearly. He never gave me his opinion, but he always guided me through the consequences of my reasoning. The depth of his contribution will not be forgotten. With a supportive smile, Eric Uslaner continually pushed me toward greater simplification, and Whitman Ridgway guided me through the historical literature. I thank them all for their time and feedback.

I am also indebted to Michael Cain for his work on the two papers that we coauthored on the Articles of Confederation. His earlier assistance grounded the study and built its foundation. Our discussions led to a great many arguments presented throughout the work, including the argument for why the framers reconstituted the federal government.

Rita Simon and John Stack mentored me and taught me how to successfully write papers for publication. I am also indebted to Kathryn Doherty, Marek Kaminski, David Klubis, Daniel Simon, and Kirsten Wood for patiently reading chapters, offering suggestions, and simplifying the work. They were the linemen of my advisors who may never realize the thanks they truly deserve. Mary Gallagher and Betty Nuxoll, coeditors of the *Papers of Robert Morris*, guided me toward source documents that were invaluable to the data analysis. Anjali Ilayperuma and my mother Bonnie provided endless emotional support that was deeply appreciated.

Finally, but not least important, Mancur Olson wrote the theory underpinning Chapter 3 and read a prospectus of my work. His optimism and enthusiasm for the subject was inspiring. Unfortunately, he never read the completed manuscript. He died in February 1998 at a loss to his students and to the social sciences. To Mancur, and to all the others, I offer my sincerest thanks.

1

The Mystery of State Contribution

It is essential to the idea of a law, that it be attended with a sanction: or, in other words, a penalty or punishment for disobedience. If there can be no penalty annexed to disobedience, the resolutions or commands which pretend to be law will, in fact, amount to nothing more than advice or recommendation.

– Alexander Hamilton[1]

Congress faced a hidden enemy throughout the Revolutionary War. In addition to fighting the British, Congress struggled with its own inability to raise resources from the states. Without adequate men, money, and supplies from the states, members of Congress could not provide Continental troops. As John Sullivan observed in 1780, "they send Regulations to the States, some comply some do not; and the Consequence of this is too Obvious to need Explanation." Some 10,000 American soldiers died in camp from starvation, wounds, or disease. Food and supplies were so scarce that a band of soldiers resorted to eating their dog near Lake Champlain; others at Valley Forge tried to gain sustenance from the soles of their boots. The problem of providing for the army and raising new recruits was so severe that as early as 1776 George Washington wrote, "I think the game is pretty near up."[2]

When the war ended, state support for the federal government declined to even lower levels. Requisition payments dwindled out of existence in the summer of 1786 and Congress became incapable of providing the security, diplomacy, and open commerce upon which the

[1] Federalist 15, Rossiter, *Federalist Papers*, 110.
[2] John Sullivan to the President of New Hampshire, November 15, 1780, Burnett, ed., *Letters of Members*, 5: 447; George Washington to John Augustine Washington, December 18, 1776, Washington, *Writings*, 6: 398. Casualty figures come from Peckham, *Toll of Independence*, 131–132.

nation relied. Lack of revenue prevented Congress from fully paying its foreign and domestic debts, from forcing the British to comply with the 1783 Anglo-American peace treaty, from reacting to the Spanish blockade of the Mississippi River, from enforcing treaties with the Indians, and from averting the piracy of the Barbary states.[3] These problems did not produce imminent peril, but they demonstrated that the union was ill prepared to pay off its debts, stave off foreign invasion, and protect its shipping. Such problems might have been avoided if Congress had received the resources it requested from the states.

Even though Congress was poorly funded during the American confederation, it was never penniless, at least not for long. States did not pay all of the money requested by Congress, but they did pay some. Whenever the situation became dire, one or more states always seemed to pull through for Congress. These last-gasp contributions helped Congress win the War of Independence and provided over two fifths of the money it requested from the states between 1781 and 1789. The latter allowed it to reduce domestic debts by one fifth.[4]

The fact that states withheld their resources is not that surprising. The American confederation, like so many confederations and international organizations, was designed to produce nonexcludable goods for regional governments through a system of requisitions. Nonexcludable goods were goods that could not be feasibly excluded from one state if they were to be provided for another state. Requisitions were an appropriation of state resources for the purpose of supporting the central government, similar to an unenforced tax on regional governments for national goods and services (these and other definitions are listed in the glossary in the back of the book). The United Provinces of the Netherlands (1579–1795), the old Swiss Confederation (1291–1798), and the German Bund (1815–66) all depended on requisitions to raise men, money, and supplies. Modern international organizations such as the United Nations, European Union, and Organization of African Unity have used this institution as well. These confederations and international organizations do not enforce their requests for resources from their member states. They merely divide the cost of common goods and

---

[3] Brown, *Redeeming*, 17–19.

[4] These figures are based on United States, *Statement of the Accounts of the United States of America, during the Administration of the Superintendent of Finance* and *Statement of the Accounts of the United States of America, during the Administration of the Board of Treasury* (hereafter referred to as *Statement of the Accounts*). Similar figures can be found in *American State Papers*, 1 (finance): 56–57.

Special thanks to Mary Gallagher, coeditor of the *Papers of Robert Morris*, for helping me locate the first two of these most valuable records.

request the money needed to pay for them.[5] Regional governments and nation-states are supposed to pay out of legal obligation, not because of punishment for noncompliance or reward for compliance. This leaves the decision to contribute ultimately in the hands of state officials. Since central governments provide goods that benefit all states and state officials are usually responsible to their local constituents, we would expect regional governments to free-ride and not provide their share of requisitions. The same is true for the American confederation. Even though regional governments demand the goods provided by a central government, they have no incentive to unilaterally contribute to these goods, and the resources obtained from requisitions should be meager. Given what we know about unenforced taxation, confederations and international organizations that rely solely on requisitions for men, money, and supplies should fail.

Since requisitions were voluntary, their failure should be of little surprise to modern scholars. The real mystery is why the states paid any money to Congress, and why other confederations and international organizations which depend on requisitions succeed at all. In other words, why did the states pay sizable portions of their requisitions when our best understandings of unenforced taxation suggest they should not? This book answers that question for the American confederation. In doing so it also sheds light on the successes of other confederations and international organizations.

THE CONFEDERATIVE DESIGN

The framers of the American confederation recognized the importance of acting collectively to provide for their collective interests. No state could carry out a war against Great Britain individually nor pay off debts common to all states on its own. Their borders were too ill defined and their enemy too strong for the thirteen states to maintain their affairs privately and independently. What the states needed was a "perpetual

---

[5] Not all of these confederations maintained unenforced taxation systems throughout their existence. Neutral governments of the German confederation were authorized by the Schlossakte of 1820 to use force against regional governments that did not pay their requisitions (Article 33). Likewise, Article 19 of the U.N. charter allowed the General Assembly to revoke a state's voting power when the state is more than two years behind in its payments. The latter sanction could be waived whenever the Assembly was "satisfied that the failure to pay [was] due to conditions beyond the control of the member" (quoted in Lister, *The European Union*, 137). The credibility and size of these threats must be noted before a requisition system can be accurately described as "unenforced" taxation. Other confederations that have adopted systems of requisitions include the restored Swiss Confederation (1815–49) and the Commonwealth of Independent States (1991–).

union" (Article III) to bind them together into a "league of friendship" (Article II) and mutual assistance. The Articles of Confederation established this league and organized the American states from 1781 to 1789. Although this system was officially enacted in 1781, its institutions were more or less in place by the inception of the second Continental Congress in 1775. Congress issued its first requisition for money that year and its first requisition for men in 1777 when it also passed the Articles of Confederation to the states for ratification. For this reason, I refer to the entire period from 1775 to 1789 as the American confederation. The underlying structure of the requisition system did not change during this time.

To promote interests common to all states, the Articles of Confederation established a Congress that determined, allocated, and administered the demands of the confederation. The Articles empowered Congress to provide national defense, to preserve open commerce, and to foster international diplomacy. These goods produced nonexcludable benefits for nearly all the states and could not be provided fairly nor effectively without national organization. To pay for their cost, Congress requested money from the states in requisitions.[6]

When Congress passed an act, it appropriated the money needed to pay for the act from the national treasury. The treasury was then replenished by annual requisitions on the states that varied according to estimated expenditures for the following year. After the amount needed was determined, Congress asked each state to pay a set proportion of the total and to return its portion by a specified due date. As directed by Article VIII:

all charges of war and all other expenses that shall be incurred for the common defence or general welfare, and allowed by the United States in Congress assembled, shall be defrayed out of a common treasury, which shall be supplied by the several states, in proportion to the value of all land within each state, granted to or surveyed for any person. . . . The taxes for paying for that proportion shall be laid and levied by the authority and direction of the legislatures of the several states within the time agreed upon by the United States in Congress assembled.

---

[6] Almost all congressional revenues came from requisitions on the states, public bonds, or loans from abroad. Since public bonds and loans depended on future revenues, these forms of finance actually depended on requisitions. Other revenues came from the creation and selling of a national bank, the printing of unbacked currency, and the sale of western lands. Although the latter list provided important income, those revenue sources were short-lived and cannot be considered a stable source of revenue during the confederation (see Ferguson, *Power of the Purse*, and Jensen, *The New Nation*, for a more careful delineation).

Article VIII provided clear constitutional authority for Congress to requisition the states and legally required the states to comply.[7] Since Congress had no means to enforce its requisitions, however, implementation of national policies depended on the willingness and ability of thirteen separate state legislatures. Jonathan Arnold and David Howell, delegates from Rhode Island, summarized their view of this process in a letter to their governor:

> The Continental treasury is to be supplied from the several states agreeable to Article eight, by successive requisitions. When a new requisition is made, the purposes for which it is to be appropriated are to be pointed out to you; and it is to be accompanied with particular estimates. You are at the same time, to be informed what has been done, with your last quota, and on a full consideration of the representation so made to you, you are to grant your money like freemen.[8]

Despite legal obligations, many believed that the states maintained the authority to independently decide whether to pay their requisitions. In effect Congress determined the size of a requisition, while the states judged how much of it to pay.

The system reflected an early conception of republican government that was prominent at the time. American Whigs believed that a republic required sacrifice of individual interest for common interests. "In a monarchy each man's desire to do what was right in his own eyes could be restrained by fear or force," wrote historian Gordon Wood. "In a republic, however, each man must be persuaded to submerge his personal want into the greater good of the whole."[9] Monarchs were tyrannical, according to Whig theory, because they could wield unlimited power, not because of their hereditary selection. If popularly elected rulers were given coercive power, they might ignore the will of the people and abuse their power as monarchs had done. With such a conception of government, coercion was not acceptable. Patriotism and love of country were the only way of assuring that laws would be obeyed. The whole structure of the Articles of Confederation depended on it. Virtuous individu-

---

[7] The obligation to pay requisitions is further advanced by Article XIII, which asserts, "Every State shall abide by the determinations of the United States in Congress assembled, on all questions which by this confederation are submitted to them. And the Articles of Confederation shall be inviolably observed by every state." Requisitions for men followed a similar procedure (see Articles VI, VII, and IX, in particular).

[8] Jonathan Arnold and David Howell to Governor Greene, October 15, 1782, Staples, ed., *Rhode Island in Congress*, 397.

[9] *Creation of the American Republic*, 68. As used here, "Whig" refers to late eighteenth-century Americans who believed in ideals of republicanism as described by Gordon Wood, 46–75. Also see Bailyn, *Ideological Origins*, 160–229.

als would obey the decisions of state officials and virtuous state officials would preserve the greater good of the union.

To ensure that state officials empathized with their neighbors and acted as a whole, delegates frequently met to discuss their common concerns. Describing a similar plan, Ben Franklin wrote, "[T]he colonies would by this connection learn to consider themselves, not as so many independent states, but as members of the same body; and hence be more ready to afford assistance and support to each other."[10] The authors of the American confederation hoped that a creed of partnership and common obligation would encourage state compliance. They further reasoned that states would prefer to pay for federal expenses voluntarily than to empower the national government with the authority to tax. If the states failed to pay their requisitions, Americans would have no choice but to adopt coercive measures and force the states to comply or raise revenue directly from the people. Since coercing the states and direct taxation were equally deplorable and deemed abhorrent ever since the Stamp Act, the authors of the Articles of Confederation presumed that states would want to pay their requisitions. They believed that as long as congressional delegates spent the nation's money on goods and services that were in the true interests of the states, the states would pay the requested funds.

Civic virtue seemed so promising that it inspired a young James Madison to observe that "a spirit of Liberty and Patriotism animates all degrees and denominations of men. Many publickly declare themselves ready to join the Bostonians as soon as violence is offered them."[11] Sacrificing for the common good appeared frequently in the early months of the war. Both states and individuals appeared to rise to the common cause. Many believed this harmony sprang from a virtuous people and that virtue would continually bind the confederation together.

But the harmony was short lived. Shortly after the war began Congress received little of the money it requested from the states and was unable to fully supply the troops under General Washington's command. As historian Andrew McLaughlin pointed out, "the pivotal problem, the immediate and unrelenting problem, was how to get revenue for the

---

[10] In this quote Franklin described why the states should have complied with the system of requisitions outlined by the Albany Plan. The same understanding governed the system of requisitions under the Articles (Reasons and Motives on Which the Plan of Union was Formed, July 1754, Franklin, *Papers*, 5: 401–402).

[11] James Madison to William Bradford, November 26, 1774, Madison, *Papers*, 1: 129. See also John Page to Thomas Jefferson, April 26, 1776, Jefferson, *Papers*, 1: 288; James Madison to William Bradford, June 19, 1775, Madison, *Papers*, 1: 151–153; and Letter XII, Dickinson, *Political Writings*, 1: 272–273.

pressing needs of the confederation."[12] Although the states had promised to pay their requisitions in signing the Articles of Confederation, they frequently did not pay their debts to the national government and never authorized an alternative method of raising revenue until the Constitution. This left the confederation incapable of carrying out its immediate tasks and undermined the very security of the union.

EXPLANATIONS FOR POOR COMPLIANCE

Early Americans offered several explanations for why the states did not pay their requisitions. Although they disagreed about the exact reason, all arguments predicted low levels of payment. The Federalists argued that the Articles of Confederation created low levels of federal revenue between 1775 and 1789. The Anti-Federalists, in contrast, argued that poor economic conditions prevented states from fully complying with requisitions. Both arguments have been supported by modern research.

After the confederation had waned and the history of poor compliance was fully known, the Federalists argued that the Articles of Confederation did not give the states adequate incentive to contribute to the union. In *Federalists* 15 through 22, Hamilton pointed to the insufficiencies of the union and cited Congress's lack of revenue as evidence that the system had failed. In Federalist 15 he argued:

If . . . the measures of the Confederacy cannot be executed without the intervention of the particular administrations, there will be little prospect of their being executed at all. The rulers of the [states], whether they have a constitutional right to do it or not, will undertake to judge of the propriety of the measure themselves. They will consider the conformity of the thing proposed or required to their immediate interests or aims; the momentary conveniences or inconveniences that would attend its adoption.[13]

Even though the Articles gave Congress the power to request money through requisitions and a forum for states to address their common concerns, they gave Congress neither the power to enforce its requests nor any guarantee that states would act according to the whole. Since state leaders did not have the "knowledge of national circumstance essential to a right judgment," they acted according to local interests and

---

[12] McLaughlin, "The Articles of Confederation," 57. Also see McLaughlin, *A Constitutional History*.

[13] Rossiter, ed., *Federalist Papers*, 111. For similar arguments, see Charles Pinckney's Speech, January 16, 1788, South Carolina, *Debates Which Arose in the House of Representatives of South Carolina*, 3–9; John Marshall, Convention Debates, June 10, 1788, and James Madison, Convention Debates, June 10, 1788, Jensen, *Documentary History*, 9: 1120 and 1144–1146, respectively.

neglected their legal obligations to the union.[14] This prevented them from acting collectively and from fully providing the goods demanded by the union.

Hamilton believed the lack of enforcement power created Congress's financial woes. Continuing with these institutions, he warned, would ultimately lead to the dissolution of the union or a reorganization of states into regional republics. The warning bolstered popular support for a stronger central government and ultimately the Constitution.

Hamilton's theory, and that of other Federalists, was consistent with the modern theory of public goods. Economists have long argued that the pursuit of self-interest in private good markets brings about mutually advantageous outcomes. But economists have also recognized that in public good markets, the pursuit of self-interest can cause individuals, or in this case states, to fail to act collectively.[15] This is what Hamilton and other Federalists were trying to say. Even though the states gained from raising the army or reducing the debt, individual states could gain even more by withholding their contributions and letting other states provide these goods on their behalf. The states would have little incentive to contribute to their common interest despite their common demands. Combined with weak institutional arrangements, the natural tendency to withhold requisitions explained the low levels of payments from the states.[16]

The reason that states do not have incentive to contribute to public goods stems from the nature of the good itself. As defined by economists (and as used here), public goods are those goods which are both nonexcludable and nonrival.[17] Nonexcludable means that no state can be feasibly excluded from the benefits of consuming the good. For example, it would be difficult if not impossible to exclude a state from the benefits of deterring foreign aggressors. If one state deterred foreign aggressors, all states would receive the benefits. This makes military deterrence a nonexcludable good. Nonrival, on the other hand, implies that the consumption of a good by one state does not reduce the amount available for other states to consume. For example, when one state benefits from deterrence, it does not reduce the benefits from deterrence available to

[14] Federalist 15, Rossiter, *Federalist Papers*, 111.
[15] Samuelson, "The Pure Theory"; Olson, *Logic*; Sandler, *Collective Action*; and Ostrom, *Governing the Commons*.
[16] At least two sets of authors have described the decision to pay requisitions as a public goods problem. See Dougherty and Cain, "Marginal Cost Sharing," and Jillson and Wilson, *Congressional Dynamics*.
[17] Neither property implies that states benefited from a good by the same amount nor that states must receive positive benefits from a good. They merely imply that public goods are collective in nature.

others. Since deterrence is both nonexcludable and nonrival, it is a public good. When a good is public, every state can benefit from the good's production, whether it pays for it or not. Under such circumstances, each state has an incentive to withhold its contribution and let other states provide the good on its behalf.

Private goods, in contrast, are both excludable and rival. They are excludable when one actor can consume a good to the exclusion of others and they are rival when an actor's consumption reduces the amount available for others to consume. A hamburger, for example, is a private good because consuming it prevents other individuals from consuming it and also reduces the amount of hamburgers in supply by one unit. In the case of the American confederation, transferring wealth from residents of all states to residents in one state may also be a private good as well. Each dollar received produces benefits for the residents of that state that cannot be obtained by residents of other states. It also reduces the benefits available for transfer by one dollar. If wealth transfer is both excludable and rival, it is a private good.[18] Throughout the book, I use terms such as "private benefits," "public aspects," and "private interest" to refer to the excludable and rival aspects of private and public goods, not governmental or nongovernmental ownership as they are frequently used by historians and political scientists.

Since the time of Adam Smith, economists have argued that trade of private goods produces mutually advantageous, or "efficient," outcomes because private goods are excludable. Actors have to pay for private goods in order to obtain them, and the price mechanism ensures that they are efficiently supplied. Likewise, states that want private goods produced by a central government would have to contribute the resources needed to produce that private good. Without such resources, central governments will not be able to supply them.

This is not the case with public goods. Since public goods are nonexcludable, a state can obtain a public good whether or not it contributes to its purchase. In other words, a state can gain the benefits of a public good without paying for its costs. Realizing this, each state has an incentive to withhold contributions in hope that other states will pay for the good on their behalf. If a state anticipates that no other state will contribute, they still have no incentive to contribute on their own. Doing so

---

[18] Wealth transfer can produce nonexcludable benefits when donators benefit from the transfer – as may be the case with many welfare payments. At this point, I am simply trying to illustrate the differences between public and private goods. I am not trying to make any definitive claims about the nature of wealth transfers. I later argue that paying public debts during the confederation was a type of wealth transfer that produced both public and private benefits. In other words, wealth transfer was simultaneously a public and a private good.

would only waste valuable resources without producing the desired result – an adequate army or a paid-off debt.

A quick glance at the confederation suggests that Congress attempted to supply public goods and that states should have withheld their requisitions as public goods theory would predict. When the authors of the confederation limited Congress to tasks which they believed advanced the interests of all states, they inadvertently gave it the responsibility of providing goods that were public in nature. Congress maintained the authority to provide national defense, to preserve open commerce, and to foster international diplomacy. All of these goods were nonexcludable and nonrival.[19] However, the most important duties of Congress and clearest examples of public goods were the national war effort and reducing federal debts. Congress spent roughly 95 percent of its expenditures on the Continental army during the Revolution and 88 percent of its budget toward the war debt after the Revolution.[20] Every dollar paid by a state raised another soldier for the nation's defense or reduced the federal debt by an additional dollar. These payments benefited all states to the exclusion of none. At the same time, providing these benefits did not reduce the amount of goods that other states could consume. Since the primary functions of Congress were martial and most of its subsequent expenses went to other nonexcludable and nonrival goods, congressional goods and services can be thought of as public goods. These goods required state funds in order to be produced, but as the theory of pure public goods predicts, states should not be expected to contribute toward their production.

Perhaps the Federalists had a similar theory in mind when they complained about the ineffectiveness of the union. The Federalists recognized that without institutional mechanisms to induce cooperation, "self-interested" states would not pay their requisitions in full. Their arguments about poor institutional design suggest that states had few incentives to pay their requisitions. This explains why states did not render their quotas in full.

---

[19] Other responsibilities assigned to Congress by the Articles include: coining money, settling disputes between states, fixing the standards of weights and measures, and maintaining an efficient postal service. All but the last were nonexcludable and nonrival goods.

[20] The first percent is the average amount of congressional money spent on military items from 1776 to 1781 (United States, *Statement of the Receipts and Expenditures of Public Monies during the Administration of the Finances by Robert Morris* – hereafter cited as *Statement of the Receipts*). The second percent is the average, annual estimated expenditures budgeted for the national debt from 1784 to 1789 (United States, *Journals of the Continental Congress* (hereafter *JCC*), 26: 186–196; 29: 765–771; 31: 459–466; 33: 569–583; 34: 432–443).

The Anti-Federalists, in contrast, had a different explanation for why the states did not pay their requisitions. "[N]on-compliance is to be attributed more to inability of the people, than to their unwillingness to advance the general interests," wrote William Grayson. According to the Anti-Federalists, factors external to the Articles of Confederation prevented states from paying their requisitions. The problem was not one of constitutional design, but of limited state resources. As Melancton Smith wrote:

> indeed it is my decided opinion, that no government in the difficult circumstances, which we have passed thro', will be able to realize more than two thirds of the taxes it imposes. I might suggest two other considerations which have weight with me – There has probably been more money called for, than was actually wanted, on the expectation of delinquencies; and . . . The war left the people under very great burthens, and oppressed with both public and private debts.

The Anti-Federalists seemed to agree that states made substantial contributions to Congress given their circumstances, but they disagreed about why the states did not pay in full.[21]

The "Federal Farmer" argued that states did not fulfill their requisitions because requisitions were apportioned according to unjust principles and Congress consumed state attentions with repeated requests for the power to assess federal imposts. These factors limited the ability of states to comply. But the chief argument made throughout Anti-Federalist writing was that states lacked the resources requested. As Luther Martin wrote, "the States have shewn a good disposition to comply with the Acts, of Congs. weak, contemptibly weak as that body has been; and have failed through inability alone to comply." The Whig conception of government was not at fault; the political-economic environment of the time caused Congress's financial woes. If Congress wanted greater revenues, the Anti-Federalists believed it would simply have to wait for more favorable circumstances. Presumably a better environment would produce almost complete compliance with requisitions.[22]

[21] William Grayson, Convention Debates of Virginia, June 12, 1788, Jensen, ed., *Documentary History*, 10: 1190; Speeches of Melancton Smith, June 27, 1787, Storing, ed., *Complete Anti-Federalist*, 6: 172.

[22] Luther Martin's quote comes from Madison's Notes on Debates, June 27, 1787, Farrand, ed., *Records of the Federal Convention*, 1: 437. Melancton Smith and the Federal Farmer both claimed that states paid 66 percent of the money requested. Figures from *Statement of the Accounts*, however, suggest that states paid roughly 40 percent between 1782 and 1789 (see Chapter 3). For Anti-Federalist views of why states did not pay their requisitions, see William Grayson, Virginia Convention Debates, June 12, 1788, Jensen, ed., *Documentary History*, 10: 1190; Speeches of Melancton Smith, June 27, 1787, Storing, ed., *Complete Anti-Federalist*, 6: 172; Federal Farmer XVII, January 23, 1788, Allen and Lloyd, eds., *Essential Anti-Federalist*, 86–87.

Historians Robert Becker (1980) and Roger Brown (1993) have examined a variety of tax and legislative records that support the Anti-Federalist claim that limited state revenue prevented the states from fully complying.[23] Becker suggests that states limited their requisition payments by continuing to tax regressively after the Revolution had begun. Regressive taxation placed the bulk of taxes on the poor and middling classes, who could not pay the taxes demanded of them. Combined with a postwar depression, regressive taxation produced little revenue for the states and prevented them from transferring their wealth to the federal government.

Brown agrees with Becker but goes one step further. "Rather than parochialism or indifference," Brown argues, "the simple inability to collect these taxes explains why the states did not provide Congress with the hard money it asked for."[24] Brown argues that specie was scarce and that many small farmers, artisans, and craftsmen could not pay their taxes because they did not have enough disposable income after the war. He further argues that citizens demanded tax relief out of necessity. As a result, politicians sensitive to tax relief took majorities in the legislatures of Connecticut, New York, Georgia, and North Carolina. Legislators in the other nine states backed off hard taxation policies to avoid electoral defeat. According to Brown, this across-the-board retreat from heavy taxation resulted from low levels of wealth within the states, and it indirectly explained why the states did not raise all of the funds requested by Congress.

The line of the debate was drawn. The Federalists argued that the system of requisitions was flawed and supported their claim based on the history of requisition payments. The Anti-Federalists referred to the same payments and argued that states were prevented from complying in full. Both camps predicted very little revenue from the states, but neither fully explained why the states contributed part of their resources.

Unlike the Federalists, the Anti-Federalists presumed that contributing was the natural condition.[25] State politicians were supposed to act virtuously and would have fulfilled their quotas, they thought, if they had the wealth needed to do so. But they failed to consider the possibility that states which did not self-abnegate for the common concern

---

[23] Becker, *Revolution, Reform, and Taxation*; and Brown, *Redeeming*. Also see Studenski and Krooss, *Financial History of the United States*. Although most historians have not addressed the issue directly, limited state resources seems to be the dominant explanation for why states did not comply with requisitions (e.g., see Rakove, *Beginnings of National Politics*, 173).

[24] Brown, *Redeeming*, 141.

[25] See e.g., Louis, Letter XI, Dickinson, *Political Writings*, 2: 228–235.

would have no reason to contribute to the confederation. This led them to the wrong starting point. The Anti-Federalists, and some historians, should have assumed that states would withhold their requisition payments as predicted by the pure theory of public goods, rather than assume that states would fully pay their requisitions in the absence of financial constraints. Starting from this perspective takes established economic theory seriously while still considering various limitations on state wealth.

The confusion appears to stem from interpreting poor institutional design and resource constraints as mutually exclusive arguments. Despite Anti-Federalist claims to the contrary, it is quite possible that the Articles of Confederation failed to encourage requisition payments *and* the states were unable to comply in full. Establishing the latter does not deny the former. It merely suggests that any limitations in a state's ability to pay augmented the institutional problems of the union – a point with which I wholeheartedly agree.[26] Together, or apart, the arguments of lack of incentive and inability to pay suggest low levels of compliance from the states. The nation should have received very few or no resources, and it should have lost the War of Independence.

But taking these theories seriously presents a puzzle. The states won the War of Independence and contributed more resources than the theory of public goods or limited state resources would predict. States contributed 53 percent of the men levied for the Continental army from 1777 to 1783 and 40 percent of the money requisitioned for the federal treasury from 1782 to 1789. The real mystery of the confederation is, Why? Why did the states pay such sizable portions of their requisitions when they had no institutional incentive and limited ability to comply?

STATE COMPLIANCE AND PRIVATE GAIN

Following a few clues offered by contemporaries, I suggest that states contributed for reasons that went beyond civic virtue. States contributed to the national treasury when it advanced local interests. In other words, states were not faced with a problem of providing pure public goods at all. They were attempting to purchase joint products and the private aspects of these joint products encouraged their partial compliance with

---

[26] Brown's argument against the Federalist is based on his finding that states lacked the resources needed to pay (see 141–155 in particular). As I argue here, the fact that state resources were limited does not imply that the Articles of Confederation worked well or the Federalists were somehow misguided. Both institutional problems and resource constraints could occur simultaneously and both could explain the failures of the American confederation.

requisitions. Joint products are collective goods with multiple aspects of publicness – in this context, goods that contain both private and public benefits.[27] Since states usually have to pay for private goods in order to attain them, the pursuit of the private benefits derived from congressional goods and services gave the states reason to comply. The combined forces of public and private benefits explain the modest levels of payment made during the confederation. Private benefits encouraged states to pay, while public benefits gave them no reason to contribute. The history of state compliance in general and state reactions to Shays' Rebellion in particular substantiate this argument. Empirical evidence on Continental troop movements and ownership of the public debt further support this explanation in a manner that is fully consistent with the collective action problem that typified the American confederation.

Determining why states paid their requisitions resolves a major point of contention in the Federalist debates and offers an explanation for the stability of unions with similar structure. If states contributed to advance local interests, then early Whig assumptions that states would sacrifice local interests for the needs of the union may have been misguided. States contributed to advance their own interests and these incentives encouraged them to contribute to the union despite, not because of, the Articles of Confederation. Such incentives helped the states win their independence from Great Britain and explain why they were able to pay off sizable portions of the national debt. The union was bound by private material interest, not the structural incentives of the Articles of Confederation.

The Federalists had a convincing explanation for why states would not contribute to the confederation, but they never explained why states did. Discovering that states contributed to obtain the private aspects of joint products completes the Federalist argument. States contributed to protect local lands, to free families from occupation, and to prevent the British from quartering in their homes. These private benefits bound the union together more than civic duty or a sense of the common good, and they explained the partial contributions from the states. Such an explanation is consistent with Hamilton's claim that state decision makers ignored their constitutional obligations and considered "the conformity of the thing proposed or required to their immediate interests or aims."[28] State decision makers did not have to be partially self-sacrificing when they contributed to the union and partially localistic when they withheld their contributions. Using the theory of joint products they could have been consistently localistic and still contribute to the union consistent with state behavior. Such a claim reflects the

---

[27] See Sandler, *Collective Action*, 11.   [28] Federalist 15, Rossiter, *Federalist Papers*, 111.

Federalist argument that state politicians sought the immediate interests of their states in deciding whether to contribute. The theory of joint products completes the Federalist argument in a way that is fully compatible with the Federalist view of human nature and the failures of the American confederation.

Attributing the confederation's success to the excludable aspects of congressional goods may be useful for other confederations as well. Private benefits may encourage payments in other confederations and explain why poorly designed confederations partially succeed. This is in line with the New Institutionalist literature on the effects of government institutions on economic performance and modern understandings of confederative designs.[29] Attributing the success of the union to factors outside the institutional framework offers a general hypothesis that may explain the success of requisition systems in general and explain how states overcome deficiencies in institutional design.

OVERVIEW OF THE BOOK

This book is divided into eight chapters. The next chapter introduces the basic structure of the American confederation and the principles behind its design. It illustrates two distinct reasons for adopting the Articles of Confederation and helps to explain why the authors of the confederation chose to fund collective goods through the system of requisitions. The third chapter outlines the collective action problem expected from a system of voluntary taxation. It suggests that neither the provision of pure public goods nor the Articles of Confederation could explain the amount contributed by states. The theory of joint products, however, is consistent with state contributions made throughout the confederation.

Chapters 4 to 6 evaluate the theory generally, systematically, and specifically. Chapter 4 puts the system of requisitions into context. Historical examples illustrate both the collective action problem and the motivations behind state compliance. State actions between 1775 and 1789 suggest that states pursued local interests in lieu of common concerns. These pursuits hindered the union in nonexcludable contexts and encouraged cooperation in excludable contexts.

Chapter 5 presents statistical evidence indicating that states paid their requisitions when paying gave them local gain. States contributed more men to the Continental army when the army was close enough to bestow private benefits on a state than when it was farther away. They also contributed more money to the national treasury when their citizens stood to benefit from such payments. Such evidence corroborates the joint products argument at a general level.

---

[29] North, *Institutions*; Sandler, "Theory of Alliances."

Chapter 6 illustrates the same relationship in a specific case, where the theory of joint products appears to have failed. States attempted to raise an army to suppress Shays' Rebellion through a special requisition, but they did not respond to the special requisition consistent with the distance measures developed in Chapter 5. Nonetheless, they did contribute consistent with the theory of joint products. Virginia hoped the army could be used to subdue an Indian uprising within its territory, while Massachusetts and other New England states raised local forces of their own. The remaining states free-rode on the requisition, as the theory of joint products would predict.

Chapter 7 suggests that resolving the collective action problem was the primary motivation for institutional reform in the 1780s and the primary motivation for the Constitution. Several amendments and institutional designs were proposed, each of which would have improved the effectiveness of the federal government with some tradeoff in state sovereignty. The Constitution was proposed by the nationalists in 1787, not because it was the only solution to the collective action problem, nor even the best solution, but because it was the most likely proposal to pass ratification by the states.

The final chapter concludes the analysis, illustrates how the Federalists used failures of the confederation to justify a new constitution, and introduces the implications for other confederations and international organizations. Before we draw such conclusions, however, we must first explore the organization of the American confederation and why its authors adopted its seemingly naive design.

2

National Interests and State Sovereignty: Objectives of the Confederation

The Safety and Happiness of Society are the objects at which all political institutions aim, and to which all such institution must be sacrificed.

– James Madison[1]

The Articles of Confederation, like any constitutional document, resulted from a compromise between diverse political interests. Conservatives such as Carter Braxton, James Duane, and James Wilson were reluctant to secede from British rule. However, when war became imminent, they supported the Revolution and pushed for a strong central government to protect private property and to regulate trade. On the other hand, radicals such as Samuel Adams, Thomas Burke, and Richard Henry Lee made an early push for independence. They deplored centralization and supported unification only to thwart British rule.[2] Working from these differences, the American revolutionaries compromised on a confederation that promoted common state interests while preserving state sovereignty. The resultant Articles of Confederation outlined this compromise and framed America's first federal government from 1781 to 1789. Although the Articles were officially enacted on March 1, 1781, many of its institutions were in place from the beginning of the second Continental Congress in 1775.

Securing independence and mutual protection were the primary reasons for confederating. In 1775, Samuel Adams declared that each

---

[1] Historical Hall, Madison Building, Library of Congress, Washington, DC.

[2] Jensen, *The Articles*, 13–14. Jensen argues that two political factions drafted the Articles and slowly decentralized the structure of the union as the drafting process continued (for more, see Rakove, "Legacy of the Articles"). Others claim that the drafting process resulted from delegates representing the interests of their states or more pragmatic needs of the union. See Freedman, "Why Constitutional Lawyers," and Rakove, "Collapse of the Articles," for each argument, respectively.

colonial legislature "is and ought to be the sovereign and uncontrollable Power within its own limits or territory."[3] Congress received authority from the states, while the states received authority from the people. This made the central government an administrative body at the center of a permanent state alliance rather than a national government managing national affairs.[4]

This chapter discusses the philosophical and legal origins of the confederation and the reasoning behind its institutional design. In doing so, it attempts to explain why early Americans adopted this seemingly irrational system of requisitioning the states. The chapter also describes the two goals of the confederation: promoting common state interests and protecting state sovereignty. It was these goals that shaped the institutional design of the confederation and made it partially successful. Even though the system of requisitions did not encourage states to contribute to common goods, it did protect state sovereignty.

PHILOSOPHICAL AND LEGAL ORIGINS OF THE ARTICLES

For the radical Whigs of the eighteenth century, a republic was more than a structure of government based on representation. It was a spirit of government where individuals gave up "all private interest that is not consistent with the general good" to find "happiness in the welfare of the whole." Representatives in a republic saw the common "rights, interests and dangers" of their people, and advanced the communal good of the multitude.[5] They did not pander to specialized interests or promote their own views. Virtuous representatives promoted the general interests of the people and represented their will more out of conscience's sake than out of the threat of electoral defeat. Similarly, virtuous citizens adhered to the decisions made by their representatives because their representatives expressed their own desires. There was no conflict between common and personal liberty in the Whig conception of a republic, because the people "as a body" were "never interested to injure themselves." Communal interests promoted the interests of all individuals and there was no room for one part of a constituency to act against another.

A republic was bound together by love, rather than fear of punishment. But if any representative or citizen acted against the common good,

[3] Samuel Adams to Elbridge Gerry, October 29, 1775, Adams, *Writings*, 3: 229.

[4] The Conservatives, who were the precursors of the Nationalists, argued that sovereignty rested in the American people as a whole rather than in the states. Although they skillfully advanced their position, it was inconsistent with the form of government outlined by the Articles. Congress had no direct authority over the people, and delegates clearly represented the states (Jensen, *The Articles*, 9–14).

[5] Hart, *Liberty Described*, 11; Letter XII, Dickinson, *Political Writings*, 1: 275. For a summary of the idea, see Wood, *Creation of the American Republic*, 46–90.

they would suffer the punishments of "heaven itself."[6] Whigs assumed that people, when set against their rulers, were a homogenous body with a collective interest distinct from the aggregation of their individual interests. This made the idea comprehensible.

The beauty of the Whig conception of government is that it freed democracy from the irony of coercing the people when the people were supposed to rule – or at least this was how many Whigs viewed it. In a republic all power emanated from the people. The people held the power to tax and their representatives created the rules that advanced their common interests. Rather than coerce the people into compliance, a virtuous citizenry adhered to the laws and paid taxes voluntarily, avoiding the contradiction of coercing the people to comply with their own interests. No outside body – such as the British or the Confederation Congress – could be given the authority to levy taxes or pass legislation inside a republic. Doing so would disrupt the whole system. As Rhode Island delegates Jonathan Arnold and David Howell wrote:

> the weight of Congress rests and bears on the several states; the states bear only on the several counties, in some states, and the counties on the towns . . . in all, on the individuals, – the broad basis of power, – which reared and supports the whole fabric.[7]

Arnold and Howell recognized that government responded to the power that funded it. To be truly free the people would have to willfully concede to the decisions of their representatives without coercive threats from those whom they elected. This made each republic sovereign in its internal affairs.

The idea was similar to the theories of Montesquieu and later Tocqueville.[8] Few Americans believed that an expansive republic, distinct from a confederation of states, was feasible in 1776. They believed that republican government could exist only at local levels. If individuals were to discuss their concerns and to form a truly common interest, they would have to interact in small communities. More expansive republics, such as those the size of the thirteen states, would produce more disparate interests and produce professional politicians distant from the people. Finding the common interest of millions of people would be too difficult and a large republic based on virtue could not last long. A better system would leave democracy to the states and create a confederation of states that handled the external affairs of each democracy.

---

[6] Quincy, Observations on the Boston Port Bill, *Memoir*, 323, quoted in Wood, *Creation of the American Republic*, 61; Hart, *Liberty Described*, 13.

[7] Jonathan Arnold and David Howell to Governor Greene, October 15, 1782, Staples, ed., *Rhode Island in Congress*, 394–398.

[8] Montesquieu, *The Spirit of the Laws*; Tocqueville, *Democracy in America*.

The American confederation and its Whiggish traditions originated from multifaceted debates between American political leaders and members of the British Parliament. The central theme of this debate was the British right to tax in the colonies. Other issues such as liberty and the authority of law were also debated, but these topics were less pertinent to requisitions.[9] Americans argued that colonial legislatures represented the people and they possessed the sole right to tax.

"No taxation without representation" was a common cry in America's push for independence.[10] It was central to America's perceptions of natural rights and inspirational for colonial opposition to British rule. Following the leads of John Locke and Edmund Burke, Americans believed that republican government gained its authority from the people and that the people, or their representatives, held the sole authority to tax. All other bodies exercised arbitrary rule and violated democracy itself. As James Otis argued, "the Parliament of Great Britain has an undoubted power and lawful authority to make Acts for the general good"; however, it "cannot take from any man any part of his property without his consent in person or by representation."[11]

Few Americans contested Parliament's authority to make laws.[12] However, most questioned its ability to represent Americans, hence its authority to levy taxes in North America. According to the Whig view, Americans were not represented by Parliament because they could not elect British parliamentarians. Therefore, any assessment of taxes from Great Britain was considered arbitrary and undemocratic.

The British, in contrast, believed that even though colonists were not part of the British voting constituency, British Parliamentarians still

---

[9] The development of national ideology in the United States and its influence on American political institutions has been studied at length. See Reid, *Constitutional History: The Authority to Tax, The Authority to Legislate,* and *The Authority of Law;* Rakove, *Beginnings of National Politics;* Bailyn, *Ideological Origins;* and Wood, *Creation of the American Republic.* Others have argued that political economic events shaped ideology (Appleby, *Liberation and Republicanism in the Historical Imagination;* Matson and Onuf, *A Union of Interests*) and that American political leaders actually manufactured ideology to serve their interests (Morgan, *Inventing the People*).

[10] See, e.g., Hopkins, "A Vindication of a Late Pamphlet."

[11] James Otis, "The Rights of British Colonies Asserted and Proved," July 1764, in Beloff, *The Debate,* 63 and 68.

[12] Daniel Dulaney and John Dickinson jointly argued that duties on trade for the purpose of regulation were constitutional but duties on trade for the purpose of revenue were not. This reconciled Parliament's authority to legislate with its lack of authority to tax. Since the distinction was first made in British common law, Dulaney and Dickinson's stance involved legal posturing as well as a way of reconciling the American argument (see Beloff, *The Debate*). For a different opinion, see letter I, Dickinson, *Political Writings,* 1: 143–150.

represented the colonists through virtual representation. Parliamentarians did not speak merely for their constituents. They spoke for imperial interests as a whole and could represent the empire as a whole. This disagreement over representation justified America's stance against the Stamp and Townshend acts and created a new conception of representation that ultimately defined the Articles of Confederation.[13]

The idea of taxation by consent was not created by the Americans; it was first part of British constitutional law. The first written document to address constitutional rights, the Magna Carta, included a clause central to the doctrine of taxation by consent. The Magna Carta declared that "no scutage or aid should be imposed unless by the common counsel of the realm."[14] Members of the House of Commons later clarified the doctrine after King James I imposed taxes in the fifteenth century. The lower house declared, "[Y]our subjects have inherited this freedom, that they should not be compelled to contribute to any tax, tallage, aid or other like charge not set by common consent in Parliament."[15] It was this precedent that Americans referred to when they claimed that the Stamp Act and Townshend duties were unconstitutional. Britain required consent of its people or their representatives in order to levy taxes. Since Americans believed that they were not represented in Parliament, they believed that Parliament could not tax them legally. The doctrine of taxation by consent was so well established that a British author wrote, "[N]o writer of any credit had disputed [it] in this country since the [Glorious] Revolution." The major difference between the American and British side of the argument was that the British believed Americans were represented indirectly, and the Americans believed they were not.[16]

The Stamp Act challenged the American perception of taxation by consent. It required all legal documents, clearance papers, college diplomas, printed publications, and other documents to be printed on paper affixed with stamps of various, specified denominations. Sellers of the official paper sent part of their proceeds to Great Britain, which Americans viewed as a form of direct taxation.[17]

To voice their grievances, delegates from nine of the thirteen colonies met in the Stamp Act Congress, October 7, 1765. There the ideal of provincial sovereignty gained great strength. After lengthy debates,

---

[13] See Morgan, *Inventing the People*, for more on virtual representation and its impact on the Anglo-American debate.

[14] Holt, *Magna Carta*, 455. In feudal law, scutage was a tax paid by the lord of knight, usually in lieu of the knight's military service.

[15] Session of March 26, 1628, *Commons Debates*, 1628: 2: 125, quoted in Reid, *Constitutional History: The Authority to Tax*, 140.

[16] "American Controversy," February 1776, *Monthly Review*, 54: 146.

[17] Weslager, *Stamp Act Congress*.

delegates to the Stamp Act Congress declared that colonial legislatures had the sole authority to tax the American people. "The only Representatives of the People of these Colonies are persons chosen therein, by themselves & that no Taxes ever have been or can be constitutionally imposed on them but by their respective legislatures."[18] State legislatures bolstered the Stamp Act decree by passing resolutions of their own. South Carolina's Common House of Assembly declared that "the only Representatives of the People of this Province are Persons chosen therein by themselves; and that no Taxes ever have been, or can be, constitutionally imposed on them, but by the Legislature of this Province." Legislature after legislature passed similar resolves in formal opposition to the Stamp Act.[19]

These declarations were a tool to force the repeal of the Stamp Act, but they also became part of colonial law. The precedents applied not only to Parliament, but to all legislative bodies. If Congress wanted the power to tax ten years later, it would have to overturn these colonial declarations.[20]

On October 4, 1774, nine years after the Stamp Act Congress, the first Continental Congress met and backed colonial precedents of reserving powers of taxation to the provinces. A resolution first written by Richard Henry Lee declared that "parliamentary taxes on America have been laid, on pretense of defraying the expenses of government . . . in

---

[18] "Resolutions of the Stamp Act Congress," ibid., 201.

[19] For example, the Pennsylvanian Assembly resolved "that the only legal Representatives of the Inhabitants of this Province are the Persons they annually elect to serve as Members of Assembly." South Carolina Resolves, November 29, 1765; Pennsylvania Resolves, September 21, 1765, in Morgan, *Prologue*, 58 and 51, respectively.

[20] Earlier colonial laws further buttressed the principle of taxation by consent. Two years after the colonization of Massachusetts Bay, Massachusetts towns rejected the taxes laid by colonial magistrates. They demanded that all taxes come from a representative body and that their colony create a representative body for such purposes. As a result, they successfully created a legislature. Virginians later incorporated taxation by consent into their charter by declaring, "That Virginia shall be free from all taxes, customs and impositions whatsoever, and none to be imposed on them without consent of the Grand Assembly." During the reign of Queen Anne in the eighteenth century, New York passed a similar resolve. It declared, "that the imposing and levying of any monies upon her Majesty's subjects of this colony, under any pretence or colour whatever, without consent in General Assembly, is a grievance and violation of the people's property." Although each resolution approached the problem from a slightly different angle – consent of local assemblies versus an individual's right to property – they all established a legal precedent that required taxation by popular consent. In Virginia and New York this right was assigned to the colonial legislatures (Law of March 5, 1623/24, *Foundations of Colonial America*, 3: 2132, quoted in Reid, *Constitutional History: The Authority to Tax*, 141; *Boston Post-Boy*, September 9, 1765, p. 2, col. 1, quoted in ibid., 144–145. Also see 141–146).

case of war, the *colonies* are ready to grant supplies for raising any further forces that may be necessary."[21] Members of the Continental Congress were not legally bound to declarations made by the Stamp Act Congress, but they did not want to violate colonial law either. Issuing taxes without popular consent would only threaten the legitimacy of Congress.

In addition, the framers wanted a central government that served the biddings of the states and played a small role in national affairs. A strong central government might enact arbitrary legislation or subvert the democracy growing within the states as the British government had done before. America was too large with too many diverse interests to create a consolidated republic. It would be a better idea to allow the states to carry out republican principles of government and let the central government represent the states. The Articles of Confederation outlined these principles in a manner that was consistent with colonial law.[22]

Even more interesting is the fact that Parliament eventually proposed the American system of requisitions. Shortly after the Stamp Act crises, Parliament surrendered the idea of taxing the Americans directly and debated the possibility of allowing the crown to requisition the colonies for British revenues. The provincial assemblies would then tax the people in line with the needs of the empire. This proposal allowed the Americans to preserve their authority to tax while still providing sufficient revenue for Great Britain. As long as constitutional law did not oblige the provinces to adhere to this scheme, Parliament was sure that the Americans would accept it. After all, the Pennsylvania legislature had already resolved that

whenever his Majesty's Service shall, for the future, require the Aids of the Inhabitants of this Province . . . it will be their indispensable Duty most cheerfully and liberally to grant to his Majesty their Proportion of Men and Money for the Defence, Security and other public Services of the *British American* Colonies.[23]

Republican government could be maintained in the colonial assemblies which, in turn, could freely support the needs of the empire. Pennsylvania adopted this clause to soften its stance against the Stamp Act. Some Parliamentarians believed that other colonies would relinquish the same

---

[21] *JCC*, 1: 54, emphasis added.
[22] As presented in Chapter 4, early Americans adopted the union for pragmatic reasons as well. Since this chapter focuses on the legal and philosophical principles underlying the union, pragmatic explanations are not elaborated on here. See Rakove, "Collapse of the Articles," for the practical reasons to adopt the Articles of Confederation.
[23] Pennsylvania Resolves, September 21, 1765, Morgan, *Prologue*, 51, emphasis in original. For the same in Connecticut, see Connecticut Resolves, October 26, 1765, ibid., 55–56.

powers. If the new system worked, Britain could raise the revenue it needed to pay off debts from the French and Indian war without violating the doctrine of taxation by consent.

After the Townshend acts in 1767, Parliamentarians believed that the provincial assemblies wanted to control the mode and size of requisitions as well. Colonial legislatures would not take cues from Great Britain about how much to tax their people, and Parliamentarians amended their plan to allow the colonies to determine the size of requisitions. But if Parliament did not set the proportions of the requisitions, colonial legislatures might pay uneven amounts. Some states would enact lighter taxes than others, resulting in insufficient funds for Parliament. To address this problem, William Pitt and other members of Parliament agreed that a Congress of states should set the size of requisitions and their apportionment. They proposed a bill in 1772 that would authorize Congress to vote a "free grant to the king, his heirs, and successors, of a *certain perpetual revenue*, subject to the disposition of the British parliament." Representatives from the colonies would then apportion requisitions according to the general needs of the British empire and the abilities of the thirteen colonies.[24] This would allow for fluctuations in ability to pay and bring imperial institutions in line with American demands.

Although the bill created a solution to the constitutional impasse between Britain and North America, Parliament had no intention of allowing the Americans to determine the merits of British expenditures nor to determine the total amount states needed to pay in requisitions. The arrangement included a tacit understanding that the colonies would pay part of Britain's expenditures despite local sovereignty over taxation. Moreover, there was no way of assuring that Pitt's bill would become part of British constitutional law and no way of ensuring that future Parliaments would acknowledge it as precedent. If Americans conceded to the plan, they would subject themselves to Parliament's rule and risk losing their authority to tax. This would undermine the whole constitutional stance they had developed over the last ten years. When the fighting broke out at Lexington and Concord three years later, the risks were too high and the constitutional issues too important for Americans to accept the proposal. The bill passed Parliament, but the Americans did not accept it.

Ironically, this system later became the official source of revenue for the confederation Congress – without the British, of course. State legislatures maintained the authority to tax while delegates to Congress

---

[24] Lord Chatham's proposed Bill . . . , *London Magazine*, 44 (1772): 72, quoted in Reid, *Constitutional History: The Authority to Tax*, 245.

decided the size and frequency of requisitions. Like the British proposal, the American system gave Congress the authority to determine the size of requisitions without the authority to enforce its edicts. Congress determined common demands, but it could not infringe upon state rights.

Unlike the British proposal, however, the American version established the apportionment of requisitions constitutionally rather than allow Congress to alter the distribution according to changing circumstances. To complete the design, distinctions between taxation and legislation increasingly blurred. State legislatures became the only bodies capable of representing the people in taxation or in legislation. This made them the heart of democratic government in North America and kept Congress out of the affairs of the people. Congress had the same amount of authority that the British had proposed, but when the ideas were written in the first drafts of the Articles of Confederation, many worried that the central government still had too much power.

GOALS OF THE CONFEDERATION

The institutions created by the early Americans were consistent with the constitutional debates between British Parliamentarians and American political leaders. Nevertheless, the framers wanted more than a system founded in constitutional law. They wanted a system that functioned as well. In particular, they wanted a confederative government that met two goals: providing for common state interests and protecting state sovereignty. The Articles of Confederation enumerated these goals in 1781.

Providing Common State Interests

To provide for common state interests – public goods in modern parlance – framers of the American republic created a confederation based on the sovereignty of thirteen separate states. Representatives from each state met in a common assembly called Congress to discuss and promote matters of common concern. Congress acted as the legislative, judicial, and executive body of the federal government and was charged with the specific tasks of providing for common defense and mutual welfare. Common defense and mutual welfare did not refer to the American people. In the Articles of Confederation, they referred to the states.

Of the two categories of positive powers – providing common defense and promoting mutual welfare – common defense was clearly the more important. More than half of the positive powers assigned to Congress dealt with defense, and Congress spent almost all of its energies on this single task from 1775 to 1783. In simplest terms Congress could be considered the decision-making body at the center of a national war machine. According to the Articles, Congress had the sole power of declaring war, determining the conditions for peace, maintaining a navy, and writing letters of marque, while the states maintained well-regulated militias including all officers of or under the rank of colonel.[25] When Congress needed troops, it requisitioned the states by first determining the number of soldiers needed and calling on the states to raise men according to a set apportionment. Troops were then instructed to rendezvous at a designated location where senior officers, commissioned by Congress, would take command. To guarantee that states shared the expense, Congress paid all costs out of the federal treasury, including the cost of clothing, equipping, and supplying the army. The treasury was then resupplied through requisitions in money.

The system of requisitions gave the union a specific procedure for raising the army, provided the nation with a unified command, and facilitated the sharing of national costs. Issuing federal expenditures out of a common treasury distributed costs more evenly than independent donations and was supposed to encourage payments from the states.

Secondary powers assigned by the Articles came under the heading of mutual and general welfare. These included the power to negotiate treaties, manage Indian affairs, coin money, maintain an efficient postal service, and act as a judicial authority in specific areas of interstate dispute.[26] These services affected the nation in general and were best provided at the federal level. Indian affairs and trade regulation required uniform application across the states in order to be effective. The nation

---

[25] According to the Articles, "no state shall engage in any war without the consent of the United States assembled unless such state shall be actually invaded" (Article VI). Congress "shall have the sole and exclusive right and power of determining on peace and war" and "of granting letters of marque and reprisal in time of peace" (Article IX). In contrast, the states "shall always keep up a well regulated and disciplined militia . . . and shall provide and constantly have ready for use in public stores, a due number of field pieces and tents, and a proper quantity of arms, ammunition, and camp equipage" (Article VI). "When land forces are raised by any state for the common defence," state legislatures also have the responsibility to appoint "all officers of or under the rank of colonel" (Article VII). Congressional powers over the navy are scattered throughout Article VI.

[26] According to the Articles, no state shall enter into any treaty without the consent of Congress (Article VI). Congress had "the sole and exclusive right and power of regulating the value of alloy and coin . . . regulating the trade and managing all affairs with the Indians . . . [and] establishing or regulating post-offices from one state to another" (Article IX). Congress also had the sole power to decide "in all cases what captures on land or water shall be legal," to appoint "courts for the trial of pirates and felonies committed on the high seas," and to establish "courts for receiving and determining final appeals in all cases of captures" (Article IX). Congress "shall also be the last resort on appeal of all disputes and differences now subsisting or that hereafter may arise between two or more states" (Article IX).

could not resolve disputes between Indians and settlers nor enact uniform trade barriers unless the preponderance of states carried out such policies. Coining money and maintaining an efficient postal service facilitated interstate commerce and required uniform provision in order to be maintained. Finally, Congress held the authority to try pirates and high seas felons, to determine appeals in the case of captures, and to act as the court of last resort in disputes between states. Arbitration of disputes required a higher, more neutral body than any two states could provide by themselves, hence the power was naturally assigned to Congress. The federal government was in a better position to carry out these functions than the states because it represented the union as a whole.

To help promote national defense and general welfare, Congress was also given significant financial powers. It maintained the authority to determine and defray all expenses "that shall be incurred for the common defence or general welfare," to regulate the value of both national and state coinage, and "to borrow money or emit bills on the credit of the United States."[27] These powers gave Congress the ability to make financial decisions, but it did not give it a mechanism of enforcing its decisions nor a permanent source of revenue. Instead, permanent revenue was left to the requisition system laid out in Article VIII.

To facilitate the implementation of its powers, the framers allowed Congress to appoint a President who would preside over meetings and civil officers deemed "necessary for managing the affairs of the United States" (Article IX). The President of Congress supervised meetings but maintained less power than influential members on the floor. He had no control over the agenda, he could not engage in debate, and he did not vote. The President only facilitated discussion and tabulated the votes of the other members, similar to the President Pro Tempore in the modern U.S. Congress. A weak presiding officer helped decentralize Congress and prevented any one individual from ruling by law.

Civil officers included a Superintendent of Finance, a Secretary at War, and a Secretary of Foreign Affairs, who oversaw the confederation's finances, the management of federal troops, and the administration of foreign policy, respectively. These officers helped administer congressional affairs year-round and to carry out congressional edicts when Congress was not in session. Although men such as Robert Morris, Superintendent of Finance from 1781 to 1784, became very influential, civil officers were agents of Congress and could not act independent of its body. The Articles of Confederation would not allow nonelected officials to maintain control, even though they were essential for continuity and the administration of business.

[27] Article VII, Article IX; *JCC*, 9: 913, 919–920.

In general, Congress maintained the responsibility to make and implement decisions common to the states. The states maintained the authority to enforce these edicts and were constitutionally obliged to do so. Congress was little more than an assembly of states. Even though the assembly represented the union, it maintained no authority to act independent of the states and would be considered a lesser body than the thirteen states as a whole. To guarantee this, the Articles established several mechanisms that prevented Congress from infringing on state rights.

Protecting State Sovereignty

In light of their experiences with Great Britain, state leaders tried to protect local governments from the tyranny of centralized rule, and they instructed their delegates to write specific institutions into the Articles of Confederation that would severely limit congressional authority. To preserve the authority of the states, the Articles created three institutional mechanisms: contractual agreement, super-majority voting procedures, and financial dependence on the states. These controls kept Congress in line with state interests and prevented it from usurping state authority.

The first way that the Articles protected state sovereignty was through contractual agreements among individual states and between Congress and the states. With regard to the former, the Articles bound all states into a "firm league of friendship" and obliged them to "assist each other, against all force offered to, or attacks made upon them, or any of them" by an aggressor (Article III). Each state that signed the Articles agreed to defend other states. Such a commitment not only provided legal assurances that some states would not sacrifice other states to foreign aggressors but also assured that Congress would not transcend the alliance. If Congress acted against a state, the states could legally intervene on the state's behalf. This was the first step toward protecting states from the tyranny of central government.

The latter type of contractual agreement was between Congress and the states. Congress had the power to promote national defense and explicit aspects of the general welfare. However, the thirteen states reserved all the powers not explicitly assigned to Congress within the Articles of Confederation. As directed by Article II, "each state retains its sovereignty, freedom and independence, and every power, jurisdiction, and right which is not by this Confederation expressly delegated to the United States in Congress assembled." States had the authority to manage their own affairs, enforce federal treaties, raise men for the federal army, and levy taxes for both state and federal purposes. They had considerable authority over areas affecting national policy and could exercise their powers in the event that Congress went out of control. Article II made the line between Congress and state explicit.[28] This minimized discrepancies between the two levels of government and ensured that Congress could not legally infringe on state authority. It also prevented future Congresses from increasing their power with respect to the states.

The authors of the Articles of Confederation further protected state sovereignty by requiring members to vote in state delegations rather than allowing them to vote as individuals. This brought the unit of voting in line with the ideals of the confederation and made vote trading among individuals difficult.[29] Congress's unicameral assembly was composed of thirteen state delegations with two to seven members from each state. The votes of a majority of delegates from each state acted as the state's vote. If a state did not obtain a majority among its delegates, the state's vote was counted as an abstention. This practice of voting in state blocks treated all states as equals. John Witherspoon, a minister and delegate from New Jersey, argued the reason for this procedure quite eloquently. From his speech on August 1, 1776, Thomas Jefferson records:

[T]he colonies should in fact be considered as individuals; and that as such in all disputes they should have an equal vote. [T]hey are now collected as individuals making a bargain with each other, and of course [have] a right to vote as individuals. . . . he admitted that equality of representation was an excellent principle; but it must be of things which are co-ordinate; that is of things similar, and of the same nature.[30]

For Witherspoon, the national government was a compact between individual, self-sufficient communities. Since Congress dealt with relations between whole states, Witherspoon reasoned that a state entity should be the unit of representation and treated like any other state in Congress. Apportioning representation according to the size of each state required an examination of each state's constituent parts and violated the ideal of state equality. Although many disagreed with Witherspoon's position, the fact that Congress did not act on individuals bolstered the idea of treating states as equal entities. These entities were best represented by state delegations voting in equal blocks.

---

[28] Contrast the state sovereignty clause of Article II with the national supremacy clause of Article XIII. The wording and early location of Article II suggests that it took precedent over Article XIII. The national supremacy clause gave Congress authority over its delegated powers only, while the state sovereignty clause reserved undelegated power to the states.

[29] On the latter point, see Jillson and Wilson, *Congressional Dynamics*.

[30] *JCC*, 6: 1103.

The real control over state delegations, however, came from the states themselves. States with bicameral legislatures elected delegates by a joint ballot of both houses, while states with unicameral assemblies elected delegates from meetings of the whole. In public choice jargon, joint ballots may have kept delegates in roughly the median of their legislatures – when stable medians existed. In other words, delegates would be representative of their assemblies. Since congressional delegates were elected annually and all state legislators were elected for equally long or longer terms,[31] no delegate could hold office without approval of his assembly. Each change in state personnel corresponded with a new election of congressional personnel. This made delegates responsive not only to their state assemblies but to current interests within their assemblies.

Since delegates were almost exclusively members of their state legislatures, they had additional reason to represent their states. Political experience helped delegates know the differences between state policies and state rhetoric and to exchange information back and forth between Congress and state officials. In fact, delegates frequently consulted their legislatures before making controversial decisions. If delegates acted against their state's interest, state legislators would have them removed.[32] State legislators frequently replaced delegates that acted against their interests and reelected delegates that advanced their desires. These institutions gave delegates additional reasons to adhere to state wishes. As John Jay reminded state lawmakers, "it is certainly not necessary to remind you that your representatives here are chosen from among yourselves; that you are or ought to be acquainted with their several characters; that they are sent here to speak your sentiments, and that it is constantly in your power to remove such as do not."[33]

Tight relations between delegates and legislatures are important because they suggest that Congress did a fairly good job of representing state governments when it passed bills or requested funds. Delegates voted for proposals that their assemblies wanted and Congress proposed bills demanded by the states. Close ties between Congress and state were one of the strongest parts of the confederative design. Delegates had incentives to act as desired by their state legislatures and to pass measures acceptable to most of the states. If the states did not support

---

[31] Thorpe, *Federal and State Constitutions*.

[32] The power to recall delegates at any time was further codified by Article V of the Articles of Confederation.

[33] Circular letter from the President of Congress to the States, September 13, 1779, *JCC*, 15: 1060.

requisitions, it was not because they opposed the measures passed by Congress, it was because of something else.[34]

To further protect state sovereignty, the Articles required that all the major decisions of Congress – such as issuing currency, borrowing money, raising military forces, and requisitioning the states – pass by a favorable vote of nine of the thirteen state delegations. This limited the power of Congress and assured that a small majority could not impose its will upon other states.[35] Adoption of a nine-state majority for "important" issues gave the states power to vote against issues that violated state interests in favor of the status quo. This made it difficult for Congress to pass legislation without going so far as to require unanimity on every issue.[36] As congressional attendance tapered off in later years of the confederation, delegates found it difficult to obtain a nine-state quorum and passed only those measures that tightly conformed with state interests. This made it difficult for Congress to promote common state interests, but it protected the states from the possibility of oppressive government. As time progressed, Congress was able to pass only those measures that were in virtually every state's interest.

Finally, the Articles of Confederation protected state sovereignty by making Congress financially dependent on the states. This dependence was designed to bring congressional actions closer to state interests and to prevent Congress from using its army tyrannically. Nothing was more central to the early understandings of government control. "The power of the purse was to them the determinant of sovereignty, and upon its

---

[34] Jillson and Wilson present empirical evidence which suggests that delegates from the same state did not vote consistently with each other. They also suggest, however, that state interests were a better determinant of coalition structure than regional interests, occupational backgrounds, or other determinants (see *Congressional Dynamics*, 167–286).

[35] There was one exception to the rule of nine states for major decisions. Congress had the authority to appoint a "Committee of States," composed of one delegate from each state, "to sit in the recess of Congress" in order to determine major decisions (Article IX). Congress never requisitioned the states using this power; instead, it passed all pecuniary requisitions from the floor.

[36] Why the framers chose the exact ratio of nine thirteenths is unclear. Certainly Congress wanted a super-majority to decide important issues but could have adopted several ratios. Donald Lutz argues that this procedure was consistent with precedents established by the Albany Plan in 1754, which required major decisions to obtain support from two out of the three major geographic regions – New England, the Mid-Atlantic and the South. Lutz argues that the nine-thirteenths rule was consistent with a 4-5-4 parity that existed between these regions. At least two of the three regions would have to support a bill in order for it to pass. This allowed issues salient to the states in two of the regions to carry, but prevent measures from passing when they maintained less support.

location and extent depended the power of government, the existence of civil rights, and the integrity of representative institutions."[37] If Congress passed measures against the states, state legislatures had the ability to withhold congressional funds and to prevent Congress from enacting harmful legislation. The founders viewed the ability to withhold requisitions as somewhat of an additional veto power that could protect the states. As long as Congress depended on the states for its income, it would have to pass measures that the states wanted to fund. Making the federal government financially dependent on the states was an important method of controlling the central government, which the founders intentionally employed.

For states to truly maintain the power of the purse consistent with Whig theory, contributions had to be voluntary. If Congress could force states to pay their requisitions, it could act like a separate body and subvert the proper domain of the states. Coerced compliance would give Congress the power to tax the people indirectly, against their consent. "Let these truths be indelibly impressed on our minds," wrote John Dickinson, "that we cannot be happy, without being free – that we cannot be free without being secure in our property – that we cannot be secure in our property, if without our consent."[38] If state legislatures were to maintain the principle of taxation by consent, authority would have to come from the bottom up and requisitions would have to remain unenforced. Although this institution proved ineffective, it clearly reflected the Whig ideal of how to confederate republican governments.

The Articles of Confederation embodied a social contract between states. On the one hand, it provided for common state interests by assigning the nation's defense and explicit facets of the general welfare to a central body. On the other hand, it protected state sovereignty by reserving particular powers for the states. To guarantee that Congress would respect state interests, the Articles instituted contractual agreements, established super-majority voting procedures, and adopted a system of requisitions that made Congress financially dependent on the states. These institutions guaranteed that Congress would administer its policies in accordance with state interests and the principles underlying republican government.

CONCLUSION

The framers established a union to promote common state interests and to protect state sovereignty. But they found it difficult to promote both goals. Fearing a powerful central government, the authors of the

---

[37] Ferguson, *Power of the Purse*, xiv.   [38] Letter XII, Dickinson, *Political Writings*, 1: 275.

Articles of Confederation did not give Congress the means of enforcing its own edicts nor the authority to act independent of the states. Instead, they created institutions that protected state sovereignty and kept Congress financially dependent on the states. This left the nation's revenue system open to problems of collective action. States withheld their resources and Congress became underfunded.

Deficiencies within the design became apparent shortly before the Articles of Confederation took effect. Without an enforcement mechanism, Congress could not raise the monies needed to pay its Continental soldiers nor forward all the supplies needed to feed, clothe, and equip them. States consistently returned fewer men and money than Congress requested and scolded other states for their inadequate support. Under such circumstances, it is not surprising that the nation had problems raising an army and paying for its supply.

The next chapter shows why. Without an enforcement mechanism, the Articles of Confederation did not solve a natural collective action problem among the states. States paid requisitions as if they were not confederated and did not have the incentive to contribute toward goods commonly demanded. They wanted public goods but were unwilling to pay for them.

3

Collective Action and the Provision of Public Goods

> Not a shilling has been put into the Continental Treasury,
> but by the utmost reluctance. The probable delinquency of
> other States has been the pretext for non-compliance with
> every State.
>
> – Edmund Randolph[1]

The framers of the Articles of Confederation adopted the system of
requisitions to divide the cost of common state interests and to facilitate
the production of collective goods. They believed centralized purchasing
agents could acquire supplies more effectively than thirteen separate
state agencies and requested states to pool their monies in order to facilitate national purchasing. Centralized purchasing helped the nation co-
ordinate its military policy, improved accountability, and strengthened
the nation's bargaining position with suppliers. It was more effective
than supplying thirteen armies separately. Even though the system of
requisitions may have provided effective purchasing and enabled a
unified command, it did not give the states any reason to contribute to
the national treasury. Instead, Congress depended on legal obligations
and external incentives to obtain contributions from the states. This left
the states purchasing public goods as if they were in an institution-free
setting.

This chapter analyzes the collective action problem under the Articles
of Confederation and the amount of contribution we should expect from
the states. It does this by first developing a theory of pure public goods
based on Mancur Olson's *Logic of Collective Action*. It is shown that
typically one, or no, state should contribute to the provision of a public
good as opposed to the privileged group that Olson described. The

---

[1] Edmund Randolph, Convention Debates, June 7, 1788, Jensen, ed., *Documentary History*, 9: 1017.

second section compares the contribution predicted by the theory of public goods to the contribution actually paid by the states. The comparison shows that states contributed more money to the national treasury than predicted by the theory of pure public goods. This presents a bit of a mystery. If states paid more than predicted by the pure theory of public goods, then why did they pay so much? The third section offers an answer. It develops the theory of joint products and suggests that the private benefits from congressional goods and services encouraged state payments. Material incentives, not institutions, bond the union together and they explain the moderate level of state contributions made throughout confederation.

THE VOLUNTARY PROVISION OF PURE PUBLIC GOODS

As previously stated, 95 percent of congressional expenditures during the war were spent on the nation's defense and 88 percent of its budget after the war was spent on the war debt. Since both goods were public goods, the theory of public goods should apply. The Continental army created public benefits for the states when it expelled the British from American soil or deterred international threats, such as the Spanish. After the war, Congress created public benefits when it reduced debts commonly owed by the states. These benefits were nonexcludable and nonrival, giving the states few reasons to contribute to their production. According to the theory of public goods, states should have withheld the money and men needed to provide the confederation's defense and to reduce common debts, even when both goods were demanded. To show this, we must first develop the theory of public goods and determine the precise level of contribution it predicts. The level of contribution is then compared with actual state behavior to show that the theory of pure public goods is not consistent with state behavior.

The problem of producing public goods stems from a paradox in the behavior of groups. It often has been taken for granted that everyone with a common interest has a tendency to further that interest. Citizens with a common political interest will lobby their legislatures to get their voices heard, workers will organize unions to obtain higher wages, and those who benefit from clean air will clean up the environment. If actors in a common class all agreed on some common interest, they must advance that common interest.

But the logic of this assertion is faulty. The successful lobbying effort, strike, and pollution abatement produces a louder voice, higher wage, or environmental cleanup that everyone in the group obtains. Since these benefits go to everyone in the group, those that contribute nothing will obtain just as much as those who make a contribution. If the political citizen contributes only a few hours to lobbying, the individual worker strikes on her own, or the environmentalist stops driving his car to obtain clean air, what will the sacrifice obtain? At best it will succeed in advancing the cause of each group to an imperceptible degree and produce only a minuscule share of the collective benefit that each individual wanted. They would not reach the outcome demanded unless others contributed as well. In such cases, it pays to let others contribute to the common cause and to free-ride on their contributions. Of course, others face the same incentive problem and should not be expected to contribute either. In the absence of selective incentives, political entrepreneurs, or other external forces, little if any group action should be expected in these groups. The paradox is that whenever rational actors obtain nonexcludable benefits they do not have incentive to act in the interest of their groups.[2]

The same paradox applied to the American confederation.[3] The thirteen states had a common interest in defending themselves from the British and in paying confederation debts. Defeating the British produced national independence and paying common debts helped the confederation obtain further loans. The states even organized a Congress of states to determine their common interests and the quantity of resources needed to supply these interests. But expelling, or deterring, the British and paying off common debts produced benefits for all the states that could not be excluded from those states that did not contribute to their provision. In such a case, it was not in an individual state's interest to contribute to confederation concerns – not because confederation and state interests were somehow inconsistent, but because there is a problem with providing pure public goods. Even when all states wanted these goods, no state has incentive to comply with the requisitions needed to produce them.

Take national defense as an example. Clearly, all of the states gained from the nation's defense, particularly during the Revolutionary War. But since one requisition payment in one year could be withheld from the

---

[2] Olson, *Rise and Decline of Nations*, 17–19.

[3] The collective action argument is quite distinct from the standard historical argument that national politicians pursued national interests while state politicians pursued local interests (see, e.g., Jensen, *New Nation*; Brown, *Redeeming*; and, to a lesser extent, Ferguson, *Power of the Purse*). In the collective action framework, national interests are nothing more than the interests that states have in common. Locally minded politicians may gain from mutual contributions but have no unilateral incentive to contribute to their common concerns. For the scholar unfamiliar with this idea it may be useful to think of every actor as locally minded, rather than some locally minded and others nationally minded. The collective action framework might help clear up the tension between state and national interests in Davis, *Sectionalism in American Politics*, and Marks, *Independence on Trial*, for example.

confederation without affecting the outcome of the war, a state could gain by withholding its contribution and watching other states pay for their mutual defense. This was particularly true when a state expected other states to defeat the British with or without its contribution. Under such circumstances, a state would gain from contributing toward the nation's independence, but gain even more if it withheld its contribution and allowed other states to carry out the war without its support. If all states approached the problem this way, public goods would be under-supplied. Similarly, if the ravages of war prevented several states from paying their shares, more diligent states might react adversely and with-hold their payments in response. They would not want to contribute alone, particularly if their contribution had an unnoticeable effect on the outcome. In either case, states would withhold their contributions and public goods would be undersupplied. This is the fundamental prob-lem of unenforced taxation, and it was the fundamental problem of the Articles of Confederation.

Now it is important to note that states can withhold resources in several different ways. They can raise the revenue (or men) needed to comply with a requisition, then declare their intention of keeping these resources from the federal government. They can combine revenues raised for confederation and state expenses, then apply both funds toward state expenses to conceal their aversion toward contributing to the common welfare. In this case, the treasury of noncomplying states would appear just as bare as the treasury of complying states, and the conscious retention of resources could be confused for inability to con-tribute. Finally, states can withhold resources by failing to raise the taxes (or men) needed to fulfill their quotas even when their citizens are fully capable of paying. In this case, a state government can choose to not issue a tax or to not enforce a tax that it issues – the latter would produce few objections without overtly disturbing tax payers. All three forms of noncompliance would be a means of withholding resources that a state is fully capable of paying. When states withhold resources in one of these forms, the federal government will receive fewer resources than it requested.

The Appearance of Large Marginal Costs

The best way of viewing the collective action problem is from a state's point of view. If some of the states contributed while others did not, mar-ginal costs would appear to be greater than their market value. The appearance of large national costs would give states additional justi-fication to withhold their requisition payments against the dictates of the union.

Table 3.1. The Requisition to Suppress Shays' Rebellion

State	Requisition	Number of soldiers paid for	Percent of total cost
VA	$90,630	349	17.1
MA	79,288	305	15.0
PA	72,504	279	13.7
MD	49,979	192	9.4
CT	46,746	180	8.8
NY	45,368	175	8.6
NC	38,474	148	7.3
SC	33,973	131	6.4
NJ	29,415	113	5.6
NH	18,603	72	3.5
RI	11,395	44	2.2
DE	7,950	31	1.5
GA	5,671	22	1.1
Total	$530,000	2,040	100.0

Source: JCC, 31: 894.

Note: Figures in the first column are listed as they appear in the source, but do not sum to $530,000, apparently due to rounding. The second and third columns are calculated from the first using the 2,040 soldiers proposed for the expedition at a constant marginal cost of $260 per soldier.

States faced costs consistent with their constitutionally defined shares only when all the other states combined paid n − 1 shares of the requisition. When other states paid too little or too much, costs would not be divided as intended. This misallocation stemmed from the fact that the proportion of costs a state paid depended on the amount donated by the other states, not the amount requisitioned.

When a state paid its quota while other states did not, it would usually pay a higher unit cost than it was assigned. An example illustrates the point. On October 21, 1786, Congress requested $530,000 from the states in a special requisition to suppress Shays' Rebellion. The $530,000 requested was then divided among the states according to each state's constitutionally defined share (see Table 3.1). Massachusetts, for example, was assigned 15 percent, or $79,288. Massachusetts was supposed to receive 2,040 soldiers when it paid this amount. Like any public good, however, the amount supplied depended on the amount contributed by other states as well as the amount donated by Massachusetts. Congress would raise enough money to provide 2,040 soldiers, only if the other states paid the difference, in which case Massachusetts would pay its share and national costs would be divided as planned.

But if Massachusetts paid the full amount of its requisition while the other states paid nothing, Congress would raise a smaller force than originally intended and Massachusetts would pay more than it was proportionally assigned. As history revealed, Virginia was the only state to pay any portion of its requisition, donating roughly $40,000.

Massachusetts did not pay its quota, but consider a hypothetical example where it did. Suppose Massachusetts paid its full share of $79,288 while Virginia provided $40,000. Congress would receive a total of $119,288 from the states and raise a force of roughly 460 soldiers in return. In this example, Massachusetts's actual share of the total costs then would be 79,288 divided by 119,288, or roughly 66 percent. This is a much larger percentage than the 15 percent Massachusetts was assigned. Assuming that marginal costs were constant, this would imply that soldiers cost $172.37 per soldier for 460 soldiers, instead of the $38.87 per soldier for the 2,040 soldiers intended. Such a large amount may have been more than Massachusetts was willing to pay. If Massachusetts valued a second-best alternative more than that amount, it would not contribute to the federal requisition. It would either create a state force of its own or use the money elsewhere. As we shall see in Chapter 6, this is exactly what Massachusetts did. Without contributions from other states, Massachusetts raised a state force of its own. The force may have cost the same as a federal force based almost entirely on Massachusetts soldiers, but the state force was under state command, more capable of carrying out state interests, and was likely to produce more benefits for Massachusetts than the federal army. This gave Massachusetts reason to provide a state militia. Raising a federal army *was* in the state's interest. Contributing to it was not. Similar considerations would encourage states to withhold their contributions from requisitions.

Though Congress divided costs among the states under the assumption of full compliance, the amount of goods supplied, and the marginal costs incurred by a state, depended on how much was donated by the states as a whole. If some states failed to pay their portion of a requisition, unit costs would increase from a paying state's point of view. States that paid their requisitions would carry a greater portion of the national burden and pay a higher price than if all states contributed. This gave states reason to ignore the costs assigned to them in a requisition and to use more autonomous criteria in determining the optimal amount to donate. The seemingly high price of a requisition resulted from the incentive to withhold contributions. Unless states had reason to contribute the shares assigned by Congress, they would not pay the proportions intended. The act of contributing would become very expensive and states like Massachusetts might withhold their requisitions when they wanted to raise an army. Clearly, the authors of the American confederation wanted something more.

Expected Behavior

If we follow the framework established by Mancur Olson, we can derive a specific prediction about the amount each state will contribute to a pure public good.[4] To do so, consider the general decision facing any state which acts independently. In simplest terms, a state wants to maximize the benefits it receives from a public good over its costs. This can be written as

$$V_i = B_i - C,$$

where V_i is the net value a state receives from a public good, B_i are the nonexcludable benefits it gains, and C is the cost of producing the good. Without a budget constraint, each state chooses the action that gives it the most benefit for the buck. In other words, each state contributes the amount that maximizes V_i. If no state contributes, each state receives nothing.

In the example of confederation defense, the benefits of deterring additional British forces were obtained at a specific cost. A national army capable of expelling the British required soldiers, munitions, and supplies. It also required men to serve in the army who would risk their lives in battle. These were the costs of defense. A state received positive net benefits from deterring British forces when the benefits it received exceeded these costs. They received a negative valuation when benefits were less than costs.

Consider two interesting cases. First, it is possible that every state benefited from national defense but no state gained enough benefits to pay the costs of a single unit by itself. In other words, B_i was positive but $C > B_i$ for each state. If we added together the benefits from each state, we might find that the total benefits actually exceeded the costs. In other words, we might find that the states as a whole received net gains from providing the good and concluded that the good ought to have been produced. When the unit costs were divided, V_i would be positive for every

---

[4] Cornes and Sandler, *Theory of Externalities*, develop a more general theory of pure public goods based on utility. Although their model does not always predict the zero or near-zero levels of provision derived here, most of its implications are the same. Actors are expected to supply suboptimal amounts of pure public goods, and this suboptimality is greater for more valuable public goods. The advantage of Olson's expected value framework is its simplicity and ability to restrict the number of equilibria through convincing assumptions. Olson introduced the framework in *The Logic*, which Olson and Zeckhauser tried to work out in "An Economic Theory of Alliances." The correct derivation of equilibria is laid out in the Appendix. See Luenberger, *Microeconomic Theory*, 290–94, for a utility model that predicts the same zero levels of provision.

state. Each state would then obtain a positive valuation from mutually contributing to the good.

The problem is that when states act individually, the costs exceed the benefits and V_i is negative. Each state prefers to withhold its resources and to obtain a net value of zero rather than pay the entire unit cost on its own and take a net loss. In other words, the states had a free-rider problem. Despite the fact that mutual gains can be made when every state contributes, no state would contribute to the common good. Unilateral and multilateral interests would conflict and the good would not be provided. No state would have contributed even when they can mutually gain from contributing.

In the second interesting case, consider what happens when some state benefits exceed the costs, while other state benefits are still less. In other words, $B_i > C$ for some states while $C > B_i$ for others. What happens in this case? We might expect that all the states with positive net benefits would contribute and all those with negative net benefits would not, but this is not what occurs. If states wanted to maximize their net returns, the states which gained positive net benefits would gain even more by letting the "largest" state produce the public good on the confederation's behalf while they took a free ride. The "largest" state would produce the good, or some portion of it, for all states, and the other states would receive the good without paying its costs. In this context, "largest" does not mean the most populous or the one with the biggest economy. "Largest" means the state that benefits the most from the public good. This leads to our second prediction from the pure theory of public goods. If some, or all, states received positive net benefits from a public good, the state which benefited the most would contribute to the public good while the other states would contribute nothing.

These are the equilibria associated with Olson's framework. Either no state contributes to the union or the state that benefits the most contributes while all other states contribute nothing.[5] The Appendix describes these predictions more precisely. It illustrates the equilibria associated with Olson's collective action game and shows that the requisition system does not affect the rational decision to contribute to public goods. States have the same incentive to contribute under the Articles of Confederation as they would in an institution-free setting. Including states that receive net loss from a public good does not change the result. If a state received negative benefits, it simply does not contribute as well. The only difference is that providing the public good is no longer in every state's interest, though it may still be in the confederation's interest as a whole. Similar predictions can be made

[5] A third equilibrium exists as described in the Appendix.

for contributions after the war, when Congress attempted to pay the nation's debt.

ACTUAL STATE PAYMENTS

To determine whether the theory of pure public goods accurately describes state behavior we can compare these predictions to state contributions. Data to make this comparison can be obtained from several sources, but the most complete are the treasury waste books, blotters, and ledgers of the Bureau of Accounts.[6] These statements record quarterly receipts from the thirteen states from June 1782 to March 1789. Although they are the most complete records to survive, they do not contain receipts from requisitions made prior to October 1781, the requisition of December 31, 1782, nor any special requisitions. Earlier records were destroyed by fire during the War of 1812, and receipts from special requisitions were kept in separate ledgers.

The payment of monetary requisitions after the war is summarized in Figure 3.1. The top graph displays the aggregate nominal returns from congressional requisitions each quarter, while the bottom tracks the percent of money requested that was actually received.[7] I refer to the latter as the compliance level. Although requisition payments were less than desired, they were far from zero. States continued to comply throughout the confederation despite limited budgets and changes in legislative personnel. The peaks and valleys of this figure probably reflect interesting stories about state taxes, local elections, economic conditions, and other factors affecting state compliance, but they are not central to the current study of why states paid.[8]

---

[6] See *Statement of the Accounts*. These records are corroborated by the less complete Account of Taxes, United States, *Papers of the Continental Congress* (hereafter cited as PCC), RG 360, M247, r151, i138, 1: 191; r154, i141, 1: 113, 191, 229, 277; 2: 51, 63, 125, 203, 237, 291, 399, 429, 491; and *Statement of the Financial Affairs of the Late Confederated Government*, Peter Force Papers.

[7] The data can be corrected for inflation using a relative price index compiled by Bezanson, *Prices and Inflation*. Since prices were mildly deflating during the first years and mildly inflating in later years, correcting for inflation has little effect on the trends suggested in Figure 3.1 and little effect on the empirical results presented in Chapter 5.

[8] Fitting a line to the data in Figure 3.1a and b indicates a slight increase in payment and a slight decrease in compliance over time, primarily due to indents. Both slopes are statistically insignificant and less positive when corrected for inflation. The lack of slope contradicts Brown's claim that receipts "declined substantially" over time (*Redeeming*, 25). Brown uses "Schedules of Requisitions on the Several States," PCC, March 31, 1787, as evidence in support of his claim that states fulfilled their quotas early but later lost enthusiasm when tax relievers took majorities in state legislatures. In "Schedules of Requisitions," later receipts were frequently credited toward earlier requisitions. Such crediting overstates the returns made in earlier years and gives an inaccurate picture of the overall trend in payment. The receipts reported here do not face the same problem. They were compiled as a running total of money received and requested each quarter.

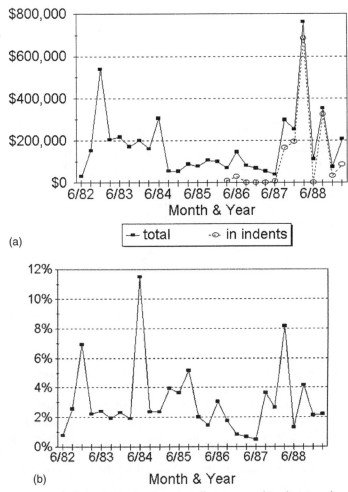

(a)

(b)

Figure 3.1. Quarterly requistion payments (all states combined) (*a*) and quarterly compliance with requisitions (all states combined) (*b*). Compliance is the amount paid in period *t* divided by (the total amount requested up to and including *t*, minus the amount paid prior to *t*). This makes it an accurate description of the running total, but not directly comparable to the figures in Table 5.3. The sharp peak in June 1784 (*b*) is partially due to the downward adjustment of state quotas in the requisition of 1784. As a consequence, the running total was restarted on that date. *Sources:* Quarterly payments come from *Statement of the Accounts*, RG 39, M-1014, roll 23. Quotas come from Table 4.2 and *American State Papers*, 1 (finance): 56–57.

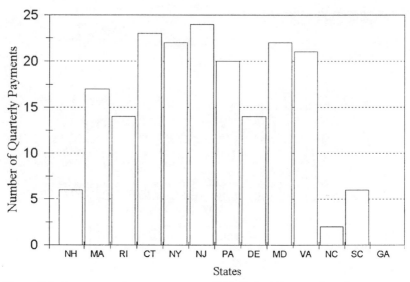

Figure 3.2. Frequency of state payments, 1782–1789. The sample is from twenty-eight possible quarters. *Sources*: Requisition payments were found in *Statement of the Accounts*, RG 39, M-1014, roll 23. Quotas came from *American State Papers*, 1 (finance): 56–57.

What is more interesting to note is that twelve of the thirteen states made at least one payment during the latter half of the confederation. This can be seen in the frequency table depicted in Figure 3.2. With the exception of Georgia, all states contributed part of the money requested by Congress. Although these contributions were sporadic and almost always less than requested, they certainly represent more frequent payments than the amount predicted by the theory of pure public goods.

The theory of pure public goods predicts that either the state which gains the most benefit from a public good would be the lone contributor or no state would contribute at all – barring ties for the "largest" state, of course (see the Appendix). Since Congress spent its money on slightly different goods each year, state benefits would have varied annually and the "largest" state could have changed with it. If this were the case, there could be a different donator and twelve different holdouts each year – or something close to it. Changing benefits could explain why twelve of the thirteen states complied during the period.

However, this simply did not happen. Between 1782 and 1789 an average of nine states paid part of their requisition each year, with no fewer than eight states complying in any given year. To claim that the pure public goods model tells the whole story, an average of nine states would have to misjudge themselves as the "largest" state. Since this seems highly unlikely, even with incomplete information, state compliance levels are simply too large and too frequent for the pure public goods model to accurately describe state behavior.[9]

Clearly, Congress purchased public goods for the states and public goods analysis should apply. But if states contributed more than predicted by the theory of public goods, what explains their additional contributions? The authors of the confederation may have thought that the Articles of Confederation encouraged state payment. However, as shown in the second part of the Appendix, the Articles had no effect on the rational decision to contribute to public goods. Its institutions did not explain the moderate level of state contribution made during the confederation. State behavior had to be explained by something else.

JOINT PRODUCTS

Perhaps Joseph Galloway solved the mystery of state contributions when he reflected on an earlier requisition system. As a member of the first Continental Congress, Galloway was keenly aware of the problem with state cooperation under British rule. In his *Historical and Political Reflections on the Rise and Progress of the American Rebellion*, Galloway brashly pointed to the pursuit of local interests as the motivation for state payments. Referring to the French and Indian War, Galloway declared:

You all know [that] there were Colonies which at some times granted liberal aids, and at others nothing; other Colonies gave nothing during the war; none gave equitably in proportion to their wealth, and all that did give were actuated by partial and self-interested motives, and gave only in proportion to the approach or remoteness of the danger. These delinquencies were occasioned by

---

[9] One could argue that actors typically contribute more than the model predicts. People clean up the environment, contribute to charities, and form labor unions at greater rates than the theory of pure public goods predicts. Even in the highly controlled settings of experimental prisoners' dilemmas, roughly 55 to 65 percent of individuals contribute nonzero amounts over several periods. If this evidence is applicable to the thirteen states, higher levels of cooperation should be expected under the Articles as well. However, comparing the contributions made in experimental settings with those made under the Articles suggests that states contributed more than subjects in experiments. More than 90 percent of the states contributed some money during the confederation. This is more than the 55 to 65 percent found in experimental settings. If experimental evidence is applicable to the thirteen states, then again it appears that the states contributed more diligently than predicted. The question for the Articles, and for other public goods settings, is, Why? (See Ledyard, "Public Goods," and Isaac, McCue, and Plott, "Public Good Provision," for a sample of the experimental literature on public goods).

the want of the exercise of some supreme power to ascertain, with equity, their proportions of aids, and to over-rule the particular passions, prejudices, and interests, of the several Colonies.[10]

Shared responsibilities were ill attended during both the French and Indian War and the American Revolution. States contributed according to the remoteness of the danger, and the states which were most remote typically contributed nothing at all. Galloway further observed that Parliament had to "reimburse" the colonies for monies raised to protect "their own safety" during the French and Indian War. Without such side payments, states would not contribute to their own common interests. This must have been difficult to reconcile without some conception of a collective action framework. And it would have been equally hard to understand during the Revolution. Collective aspects of both wars held state contributions to a minimum, but private aspects, such as the danger from an approaching enemy or the subsidies of the British Parliament, may have induced states to comply in both cases.

Referring specifically to the confederation, Madison made a similar observation. He believed that differences in compliance resulted more from differences in the vulnerabilities of the states than from differences in civic virtue:

Some parts of the United States are more exposed than others. Will the least exposed states exert themselves equally? We know that the most exposed will be more immediately interested, and will make less sacrifices in making exertions.[11]

According to Madison, states with exclusive interests at stake sacrificed "less" of their own interests by contributing to a common force than states which did not have such interests at stake. States that were more exposed to the enemy were more likely to lose local lands or to have their residents killed than states farther away. They also had greater incentive to contribute to Congress. Perhaps the promise of protecting state resources and saving the lives of state citizens encouraged them to comply. In the economic parlance, private benefits encouraged state contributions.

During the war, the confederal government created private benefits when the Continental army defended a state exclusively. Regiments within the state of New York, for example, could limit the damage that

---

[10] *JCC*, 1: 45.
[11] James Madison, Virginia Convention Debates, June 11, 1788, Jensen, ed., *Documentary History*, 9: 1145. For similar quotations, see "A Native of Virginia: Observations upon the Proposed Plan of Federal Government," April 2, 1788, Jensen, ed., *Documentary History*, 9: 656; and North Carolina Delegates to Alexander Martin, March 24, 1783, Smith, ed., *Letters of Delegates*, 20: 91–93.

British troops would inflict on New Yorkers, they could defeat local Tories, they could prevent the British from quartering in New York homes, and they could trade with local citizens. But the same regiments could not provide these benefits to the citizens of Georgia. Regiments in New York could help deter foreign aggressors and provide excludable benefits, but they could not provide private benefits such as protecting local property and saving lives. States that wanted private benefits from local regiments had to contribute to the army in order to guarantee their provision – otherwise Continental regiments assigned to a local region might not be raised or adequately supplied.

After the war, the national government produced private benefits when it reduced domestic debts. All states gained nonexcludable benefits from the reduction of common debts, but only states with federal debt holders gained the additional private benefit of paying creditors within their state. The domestic debt included public bonds, debts owed to Continental soldiers, and notes issued to state citizens for conscripted belongings. When states paid their requisitions after the war, part of their money was given to these creditors. Receiving a debt payment from the federal government returned principal, and sometimes interest, to debt holders and stimulated the state economies where debt holders lived. Paying political constituents provided *excludable* benefits because each dollar paid to a debt holder in one state would not be paid to a debt holder in another state. Only states with debt holders gained the private benefits of a satisfied political constituent or a stimulated state economy. Those without debt holders would not receive such benefits.

In other words, Congress did not produce pure public goods at all. It produced joint products. Joint products are goods that produce both private and public benefits. For example, a state may have benefited from the Continental army in two ways. It may have received the public, nonexcludable, benefits of deterring foreign aggressors and the private, excludable, benefits of limiting damage to itself. If national defense produced both types of benefits, states would have incentive to contribute to the private aspects even though they would not have incentive to contribute to the public aspects. After the war, states would receive the public, nonexcludable, benefits of paying common debts and the private, excludable, benefits of paying bond holders, soldiers, and citizens who had their wares conscripted. They would benefit from both, but only the private benefits would encourage them to pay. States were faced with mixed motives during both periods and contributed at a level that reflected both public and private forces.

The reason for this is clear. Private goods are those goods that a state can consume without providing benefits for others. States that want to consume private goods usually have to pay for them. In our case, this requires that a state contribute to the federal treasury in order to obtain the private benefits of the Continental army or to reduce federal debts owed to its citizens. If goods provided by the confederation were both private and public, states would have an incentive to contribute to the union in order to receive private goods. At the same time, they would have incentive to free-ride via the public benefits. These two countervailing forces could explain the modest levels of state compliance throughout the Confederation.

Adding private benefits to the model alters the payoff function and changes the game from a pure public goods game to a joint products game. In addition to obtaining nonexcludable benefits from the good, a state now gains private benefits from the good's provision. These outputs vary by state and good, and produce a payoff function that looks like

$$V_i = B_i - C + R_i$$

where B_i are the public benefits a state obtains from the good, R_i are the private benefits it obtains, and C is the cost of those units.[12] Now it is possible that a state can receive private benefits from the contributions of other states, as well as its own contribution. The side effects from the contributions of other states is important because a state has reason to free-ride when it expects private goods to spill in from the contributions of others. These private spill-ins prevent states from reacting exactly as predicted by the theory of joint products. When a state expects private spill-ins, its contributions will be less responsive to the presence of private benefits. But states usually cannot rely on other states to inadvertently purchase private benefits on their behalf. They usually have to make their own contributions to obtain them. States that could gain few private benefits will withhold their resources, while those that could gain many private benefits will contribute to obtain them.

The effect of private benefits can be seen without additional formalism.[13] When private benefits were not available, one, or no, state would contribute according to the theory of pure public goods. When nothing but private benefits were available, and valued more at the margin than a second-best alternative, the state (or states) which received private benefits would contribute as the theory of pure private goods would predict.

---

[12] In the continuous function form of the Appendix the equation would be written $V_i(x) = B_i(x) - C(x) + R_i(x)$, where x is the amount of the good and each term is a function of x.

[13] Joint products models and their applications to alliances have been developed by Sandler, "Economic Theory of Alliances"; Murdoch and Sandler, "Complementarity"; Hansen, Murdoch, and Sandler, "On Distinguishing the Behavior"; and Gonzales and Mehay, "Burden Sharing."

They would contribute to the point where their marginal value for the good was equal to their marginal value of the second-best alternative. If the theory of joint products applies to the confederation, each state's contribution would lie within these two extremes and vary according to the private benefits a state expected from contributing. At the one extreme, a state would contribute nothing. At the other, it would contribute enough resources to provide the entire public good by itself.[14]

Unfortunately, the joint products model does not create a nice point prediction as does the pure public goods model. But it does generate a relationship that we can evaluate. If the theory of joint products applies to the confederation, states should contribute from zero to the full cost of the good depending on the amount of private benefits they expected from contributing. States which gain more private benefits should contribute more than states which gained fewer private benefits. This relationship can be expressed as a hypothesis:

The Private Benefits Hypothesis: States that gain more private benefits from paying congressional requisitions will contribute more than states that gain fewer private benefits.

Evidence in favor of the private benefits hypothesis supports the joint products argument. Evidence against it suggests that joint products do not explain the unusually high levels of state payments made during the confederation. Corroborating this hypothesis is the primary task of the next three chapters.

CONCLUSION

The theory of joint products does not deny the existence of public goods nor the collective action framework. It merely extends the collective action framework to impure public goods. If states responded to the private aspects of joint products, their contributions should fluctuate with the level of private benefits obtained. Chapter 5 tests this hypothesis empirically. For now it is important to note that states behaved in a way that was not fully consistent with the model of pure public goods and that state contributions *could* be explained by the presence of joint products.

---

[14] Other factors affect state contributions as well. These include the cost of congressional goods, $C(x)$ in the appendix; budget constraints; opportunity costs, such as state purchases (not modeled); the amount of spill-ins expected from other states; and whether a state believes it is the "largest" in terms of nonexcludable benefits. Although these factors increase the statistical error discussed in Chapter 5, they should not reduce its ability to corroborate the private benefits hypothesis.

Although the framers of the Articles of Confederation hoped to design institutions that facilitated the production of public goods, the institutions they created did not give the states incentive to contribute. This affirms many of the Federalist's fears about the inadequacy of the union. The Articles of Confederation did not encourage state contributions, as the authors of the confederation had hoped.

The fact that states maintained limited economic resources exacerbated the problem. Without a sound currency, specie, or marketable wares within a state, a state could not obtain the taxes needed to fully pay its obligations to Congress. Lack of resources prevented states from paying their quotas and lowered contribution levels beyond the low levels described here. Combined, problems of collective action and limited state resources would predict an extremely low level of compliance from the states.

But expanding state resources would do little to solve the problem. As this chapter has shown, one or no state would contribute to a pure public good even when all the states have unlimited resources. Increasing resources does not alleviate the collective action problem. It can only improve state responsiveness to the private aspects of joint products. In other words, more favorable circumstances would not create dramatic improvements in state contributions, as the Anti-Federalists had claimed. States would still be tempted to free-ride during better times. If the theories developed here correctly describe the American confederation, more optimistic contributions should not be expected.

The next three chapters evaluate the applicability of joint products to the American confederation. Chapter 4 investigates the confederation more generally and shows that states frequently pursued local interests in lieu of their common concerns. It focuses on the public aspects of joint products and shows how the pursuit of local interests unraveled the confederation. Chapter 5 tests the private benefits hypothesis more systematically. It compares state compliance to the proximity of the Continental army and to the ownership of the public debt. It shows that states contributed to the confederation as if they were pursuing joint products. Finally, Chapter 6 examines state compliance in a case study. It shows that states reacted to the special requisition for suppressing Shays' Rebellion in a way that was consistent with their local interests. Each piece of evidence supports the private benefits hypothesis and suggests that local, not collective, interests bound the union together.

4

The History of State Compliance

> Since the close of the war, some of the states have done
> nothing towards complying with the requisitions of Con-
> gress; others, who did something at first, seeing that they
> were left to bear the whole burden, have become equally
> remiss.
>
> – Oliver Ellsworth[1]

The Continental Congress convened in 1774 to reconcile differences
between colony and crown. At this early date, members did not consider
an independent federal government nor a means of providing national
public goods. It was not until after the Battle of Lexington and Concord,
in April 1775, that the second Continental Congress met to consider
raising a national army. Without the authority to tax, Congress issued
currency to finance the Revolution and backed it with requisitions on
the states. But the costs of the war were high and states could not keep
up with congressional requests. Even though members of Congress, like
Robert Morris, tried, they could never get the system of requisitions to
fully work. Members of Congress requisitioned the states in men, currency, specie, and specific supplies. They even created a paper tender
receivable for interest due on federal bonds. Returns were always less
than they desired. States were more capable of raising money at the war's
end, but less willing to comply with requisitions. As a result, Congress
could not muster the resources needed to provide even the most basic
public goods.

This chapter tells the story of national finance during the Confederation and of congressional attempts to make the system of requisitions
work. It is divided into three chronological periods marking three sepa-

---

[1] Oliver Ellsworth, Connecticut Convention Debates, January 4, 1788, Jensen, ed.,
Documentary History, 3: 544.

rate eras of finance: the Revolutionary years, the Morris years, and the waning years of the Confederation. During the Revolutionary years, Congress relied heavily upon the emission of currency to finance the expense of its army; during the Morris years Congress attempted to strengthen the national government and provide a permanent means of financing its debts; while during the waning years Congress defaulted on many of its obligations and failed to slow decentralizing trends. Understanding the complexities of these three periods puts the system of requisitions in context and shows that Congress attempted to provide the goods demanded by the states. Although Congress requested large sums from the states, these monies were needed to carry out the war. After the war, Congress reduced its expenditures and decreased its requisitions accordingly, but states contributed even less.

Intertwined in this story are the priorities of the states and the jealousies between them. These events suggest that states were aware of their neighbors' behavior and likely to advance local interests at the expense of the union. States assumed debts owed to soldiers in the Continental army "as if" they wanted to avoid the debts owed to citizens within other states; they resisted national taxation powers "as if" they wanted to free-ride on requisitions; and they diligently gathered records of their own contributions "as if" they wanted to pay smaller portions of the national burden. Such behavior is consistent with the pursuit of local interest and the collective action framework surrounding the theory of joint products.

THE REVOLUTIONARY YEARS, 1775–1780

In addition to the philosophical objections to national taxation described in Chapter 2, Congress was simply incapable of gathering its own taxes when the war began in 1775. The federal government did not have a national treasury, custom houses, or tax collectors needed for direct taxation. Congress was equally unable to obtain foreign and domestic loans since no investor wanted to lend money to a group of unconfederated states engaged in a seemingly hopeless war against Great Britain. As a result, Congress turned to the emission of currency as its first means of financing the war. On June 22, 1775, members of the second Continental Congress issued the first of eleven emissions of Continental currency. They authorized $2 million in bills of credit, affectionately known as "Continentals," followed by another $1 million one month later.[2]

To support the currency, Congress made each state responsible for taxing its part of the issue and required all states to provide the sum

---

[2] When the presses finally stopped in 1780, Congress had issued $241,550,000 in currency (Anderson, *Price of Liberty*, 3).

requested from any defaulting state. Members agreed to divide shares among the states according to a rough distribution of the population, though they noted that such an apportionment was only temporary.[3] They then instructed states to tax their part of the issue in "such a manner as would be most effectual and best adapted to the condition, circumstances and equal mode of levying taxes."[4] Congress did not care how the states removed the currency from the economy; it merely wanted the money raised quickly and fairly. Hence, the system of requisitions was born. States were directed to pay the unbacked funds in four annual payments beginning November 30, 1779, and return the sums in Continental currency, provincial bills, or gold and silver.

By June 10, 1776, it was clear that the $3 million previously emitted would be inadequate for the national expense, and Congress agreed to print an additional $3 million. As the costs of the war continued to rise, the size and frequency of emissions grew with them. Theoretically, the states could have preserved the value of the Continental currency by limiting the amount in circulation through taxation, but state governments were not firmly established and did not want to sacrifice popular support by overburdening their citizens. As Gouverneur Morris declared, taxing the people at that stage of the game would have been "madness." Hence the states laid no taxes in 1775 and 1776, and by the time they collected at least some taxes to back the Continental, its value had already declined. At the end of 1780 costs of the war had outstripped receipts from the states by nearly forty to one. The increasing size and frequency of the "old money" requisitions are shown in Table 4.1.[5]

Exactly how much the states paid is unclear. Poor record keeping did little justice to the costs incurred by the states on behalf of the union – such as recruiting soldiers and maintaining fortifications. By Hamilton's account, however, the official figure was roughly $10 million in Continental currency, one tenth of the amount requested before 1780.[6] Such returns were extremely low, even for the hard times of the Revolution.

---

[3] Congress agreed to apportion requisitions according to white population in 1775. When the Articles were adopted in the spring of 1781, the official mode of apportionment became land value. But the states did not supply Congress with adequate surveys and Congress continued to apportion requisitions according to its best approximation of white population. These apportionments were continually readjusted until April 1783 when they were fixed on a specific population estimate. In practice, Congress never apportioned requisitions according to land value. See Burnett, *Continental Congress*, and Jensen, *New Nation*, for the events surrounding early apportionments.

[4] JCC, 19: 408.   [5] JCC, 12: 1048–52; Ferguson, *Power of the Purse*, 28, 30–31, 43–44.

[6] Ibid., 35. The amount paid is the total amount collected in taxes or destroyed by the states prior to 1781 (*American State Papers*, 1 (finance): 59–62). Accounting for inflation would lower the rate of compliance, while adding direct payments to soldiers would raise the ratio.

Table 4.1. Old-Money Requisitions, 1775–1779

Date requested	Amount ($)	Mode of payment
July 29, 1775	3,000,000	
January 14, 1777	state discretion	
November 22, 1777	5,000,000	
January 3, 1779	6,000,000	annually[a]
January 4, 1779	15,000,000	
May 21, 1779	45,000,000	
October 7, 1779	15,000,000	monthly[a]
Total	98,000,000	

Source: *JCC*, 2: 200–224; 7: 36; 9: 948–958; 13: 26–29; 14: 619–626; 15: 1150–1151. These figures can be compared with Ferguson, *Power of the Purse*, 34.
[a] The requisition of March 18, 1780, superseded the annual requisitions of October 7 and January 3, 1779. By this time, none of the January 3 requisition was active, while only two of the October 7 requisitions were active (payments on the former were scheduled to start in 1780, while payments on the latter began February 1, 1780). Eliminating the former and doubling the latter gives the total of $98,000,000.

The reason was unclear, but Washington thought the problem lay with requisitions themselves. He wrote, "One state will comply with a requisition of Congress, another neglects to do it, a third executes it by halves, and all differ either in the manner, the matter, or so much in point of time, that we are always working up hill . . . unable to apply our strength or resources to any advantage." States were either unable to pay their requisitions or did not want to pay individually. With the increased volume of Continentals in circulation, suppliers began to raise their prices and the currency lost its value to inflation.[7]

When the war was well under way, a second source of revenue became the sale of loan office certificates. Loan office certificates were public bonds sold to individual investors. Congress established loan offices in each state to sell these certificates and to receive or distribute public monies. Loan officers administered the finances of Congress and were the administrative link between Congress and the states. Congress offered its first loan office certificates in October 1776, for a total of $5 million at 4 percent interest. Investors could purchase these certificates in denominations of $300 or more using coin, bills of exchange, or

[7] As one congressman noted, the "prospect of future taxes served only as a stimulus to urge those who had in their possession the supplies and necessaries wanted, to enhance the price." *JCC*, 19: 409.

Continental currency.[8] The initial response to the offer was poor. Four percent was a low return for a revolutionary government and less than expected from private loans. After initially poor subscriptions, Congress raised interest on its bonds to 6 percent in February of 1777 and promised to pay the interest in bills of exchange. Six percent interest paid in the equivalent of specie was a real inducement, particularly when the value of the Continental was starting to decline. By using paper money to purchase loan office certificates investors could expect a real return of 7.5 percent to 30 percent in specie.[9] When Congress realized its error and the corresponding drain on its foreign resources, it revoked its offer. On March 1, 1778, Congress stopped paying interest in bills of exchange.

In its place, Congress promised to pay interest in paper money. This gave investors a much lower return. Despite lower yields, however, Congress issued roughly $60 million in loan office certificates between 1778 and 1781. This combined with the roughly $7 million received from loan office certificates prior to March 1778 made up roughly 11 percent of Congress's income during the Revolution.[10] Most of these subscriptions did not come from sales to investors. They were simply exchanged for supplies. Despite the inappropriate use of loan office certificates, Congress treated them as a preferred security, which helped maintain their value: "when Continental money was about 75 to 1, loan certificates dated November 20, 1779, sold at 24 to 1."[11] Their transferability and relative strength against the Continental helped maintain their value and made them something of a preferred currency for the merchant class.

Continental currency emissions and loan office certificates filled the earliest demands of the confederation, but neither provided materials needed from abroad. European suppliers would not accept Continental currency or risky security. They wanted payment in specie; and without a domestic source of precious metal, Congress had to obtain specie from foreign loans.

But foreign loans did not start off with a bang. Foreign governments were reluctant to lend money to Congress in the early years of the war,

---

[8] Bills of exchange were drafts drawn on foreign loans. When France loaned money to the United States in specie, for example, the actual coin remained in France while American commissioners drew from it using bills of exchange. Bills of exchange usually maintained their stated face value in specie.

[9] Ferguson, *Power of the Purse*, 37.

[10] See Ferguson's table "Federal Income prior to 1780," ibid., 43–44, for the calculation of this figure.

[11] Ibid., 40.

and Congress had to wait for the victory at Saratoga in 1778 to obtain most of its foreign support. The French made twenty-two separate loans to Congress between 1778 and 1783 totaling $4.5 million in specie. Spanish and Dutch investors lent an additional $94,000. This gave Congress the supplies it needed from abroad and deferred a large portion of its current expenditures.[12] Nevertheless, it did not reduce domestic expenditures nor aid the bulk of Congress's financial woes. Congress had to rely on issues of currency and other sources of revenue to supply its army.

At the end of 1778, Congress had borrowed and emitted a total of $108 million in Continental currency. Anxious to stop its issues, Congress again called upon the states. On January 5, 1779, it requisitioned the states for $15 million to cover the next year's estimated expense and an additional $6 million annually, starting in 1780, to sink the currency in circulation. Congress quickly realized that the amount requested for its annual expense was insufficient to meet the demands of the union. By the following May, it increased its request by an additional $45 million. Rapid devaluation of the Continental currency and rising costs of the war made $45 million a small sum – just enough to cover the army at a minimal cost. Without additional revenues to pay for food and supplies, Washington was left with the sad alternative of either disbanding the army or collecting goods by military force. He chose the latter and the citizens in New Jersey and New York reluctantly succumbed.

As the Continental currency collapsed in 1779, impressment became a fourth method of financing the war. To obtain supplies through this method, the army simply appropriated the goods it needed from local towns, merchants, and farmers and gave the owner of the goods a certificate in return.[13] Certificates, not to be confused with loan office certificates, were promissary notes for conscripted belongings, similar to an I.O.U. They did not bear any interest and it was not clear that Congress would ever repay them. All military departments issued certificates, but the Quartermaster and Commissary departments issued the largest sums. Wherever the army moved, certificates followed. In 1779 and 1780 the middle states maintained most of the nation's certificates, while in 1781 certificates flowed heaviest in the South. Since they were frequently reexchanged for goods and services desired by the bearer, certificates became yet another form of currency. As historian Alan Nevins pointed out,

---

[12] *JCC*, 24: 57–63. Although this appears to be a large sum, Ferguson (*Power of the Purse*, 43–44) points out that loans received prior to 1780 made up less than 4 percent of Congress's income and were quite small in comparison to the total cost of the war.

[13] For a more precise description of the process of impressment, see Carp, *To Starve the Army*, 75–98.

"it was often difficult, in practice, to distinguish between the certificates and paper money, for they were passed from hand to hand like bills of credit."[14] The similar treatment of certificates and paper money made it even more difficult to sink the Continental currency. Citizens pressured state officials to accept their certificates as payment of confederation taxes, and eventually states succumbed.

To provide for the army while the national currency dwindled in value, Congress called for supplies in its next requisition.[15] In-kind requisitions, commonly called "supply requisitions," provided some support for the nation's army, but they did not allay the nation's burgeoning money supply. On March 18, 1780, Congress took the bold step of canceling its currency outright. This requisition superseded all previous requisitions directed toward currency reduction[16] and instructed the states to tax the Continental out of existence at a rate of $15 million a month. On that date Congress revalued its "Old money" bills at 40 to 1 in specie – a conservative rate – and asked the states to return the currency in order for it to be marked and destroyed. To replace the currency, Congress issued a new currency and exchanged it for the old at a rate of 20 to 1. This limited the economy to $10 million in new money. Since Congress intended to issue no more than this amount, the new currency was supposed to maintain its value.

Issuing the new bills could have provided up to $10 million in additional revenue for the confederation and its troubled states. If all went to plan, Congress would keep two fifths of each dollar issued and give three fifths of it to the state which collected the old currency. The intended effect of this resolution was to give the states a means of meeting future obligations and to give Congress a revenue for its next campaigns.[17] With this single resolution, Congress reduced the official value of the currency in circulation from a face value of $200 million to a legal value of $5 million in specie.

State actions foiled the plan. Victims of military impressment demanded that states accept quartermaster and commissary certificates as payment for taxes in addition to the old currency, and state politi-

---

[14] Nevins, *The American States*, 505; Anderson, *Price of Liberty*, 11.

[15] On January 12, 1780, Congress requisitioned the states for $60,128,073 in clothing, forage, soap, and other supplies needed to carry out its campaigns (*JCC*, 16: 33–38). For other supply requisitions, see *JCC*, 14: 725–733, 827–876; 15: 1371–1372; 16: 195–197; 18: 1010–1021; and Committee of Headquarters to Certain States, June 2, 1780, Smith, ed., *Letters of Delegates*, 15: 225–232.

[16] Superseding previous requisitions amounted to overriding the October 7, 1779, requisition for $15 million monthly and the January 3, 1779, requisition for $6 million annually.

[17] *JCC*, 19: 411.

cians eventually capitulated. Refusing certificates as a form of tax payment was politically impossible for state officials, particularly considering that the army continued to issue certificates for its supplies.[18] As a result, states acceded to political pressures and accepted certificates in violation of the procedures established on March 18. Since certificates were more worthless than the Continental currency, people paid the bulk of their taxes in certificates that year. By January 1781, only $2 million of the old money was withdrawn from circulation. With few Continentals coming in, the states gained little income from the exchange of old currency for new. In desperation, states simply issued the new bills without waiting for tax receipts in the old currency.[19] This gave them immediate revenues. But issuing the new bills contrary to plan tied the value of the new currency to the old, rather than maintaining its value in specie. The Continental remained the standard, and the new currency depreciated with the old, until it was virtually worthless. In December 1780, the market value of the old money in specie was 75 to 1. In the following April, it was worth 150 to 1, and the new currency devalued with it. Soon both passed out of circulation, leaving future thoughts of currency finance out of the question. In 1781, Congress realized that old money requisitions could not provide any additional revenue for the union. The states took their time removing the notes from circulation; by the confederation's end most of the old money had been returned.[20]

At the peak of the war, Congress had experimented with numerous forms of federal finance. Of the five principle modes of federal revenue used during the Revolution – currency emissions, requisitions upon the states, loan office certificates, foreign loans, and military certificates – currency emissions produced the greatest returns. But since the states did not pay the requisitions needed to back the currency and Congress printed its currency at ever-increasing rates, the Continental inevitably depreciated in value. Congress issued conscription certificates and federal bonds in its place, but without proper backing, they depreciated as well. The decision to abolish the Continental in March 1780, and the subse-

---

[18] Ferguson, *Power of the Purse*, 53. As Philip Marsteller, representative to the Pennsylvanian General Assembly, wrote two years later, "it is very Grievous to any Man to have his property Sold for Taxes when at the same time the Public is indebted to him a much larger sum, and [he] can obtain no part thereof . . ." (to George Bryan, March 23, 1782, *George Bryan Manuscripts*, quoted in Brunhouse, *Counter-Revolution*, 110).

[19] Some of the new bills were used by the states to pay state troops in the Continental army, and Charles Thompson, the Secretary of Congress, claimed that states actually used part of the two fifths reserved for Congress for this purpose (From the Secretary of Congress, June 29, 1781, Morris, *Papers*, 1: 198).

[20] Ferguson, *Power of the Purse*, 66; *American State Papers*, 1 (finance): 58–59.

quent state decision to emit new currency before receiving the old, left Congress without the use of paper money after the war. Creditors now demanded payment in specie, and Congress had few options but to turn toward requisitions to provide the overdue sums. Hard-money requisitions became the trademark of the next era in federal finance.

The fiscal policies of Congress reflected reasonable reactions to the immediacies of a war. However, without a solid source of revenue, the increasing expenditures of Congress produced an ominous debt that was difficult to reduce in the later years of the confederation. Even when current expenses dwindled to near nonexistence in 1783, Congress could not muster the funds needed to pay its debts, let alone the salaries of its administrators. What it required was a more permanent source of revenue. Creditors assumed that this revenue would inevitably follow the Revolution. But when the Articles of Confederation were enacted in 1781, the confederation contained no form of revenue other than requisitions. Congress tried to make the system work, but unenforced taxation did not, and could not, provide the income needed for national public goods.

THE MORRIS YEARS, 1781–1784

The Articles of Confederation went into effect on March 1, 1781, giving Congress the legal authority to requisition the states as it had previously done. Article VIII required that all national expenditures, including the national debt, come from a common treasury replenished by annual requisitions on the states. The Articles mentioned no other method of raising revenue, though various forms of federal finance were presumably legal. Without an additional source of federal revenue the Nationalists believed that Congress would fall far behind the needs of the union.

After the financial chaos of 1779 and 1780 the Nationalists rose to power. Men such as Alexander Hamilton, James Madison, and Samuel Johnston were elected to Congress in the early 1780s, while Nationalists took majorities in many state legislatures. Together these men supported the confederation when war was inevitable, promoted a strong central government, and argued that inflation was better handled through taxation than price controls.

The Nationalists were led by a wealthy Pennsylvanian named Robert Morris. Morris became Superintendent of Finance on February 18, 1781. From the start, Morris took control of congressional finances by mingling his reputation with Congress's bewildered credit. He used his personal credit to secure loans for Congress and bolstered the body's reputation by issuing congressional notes in his name. Morris put Congress back on track. In exchange for his services, Congress gave him exceptional autonomy.[21] He negotiated contracts on behalf of the army, sold its surpluses to private buyers, and personally received the proceeds of foreign loans.

To help raise revenues, Morris proposed the Bank of North America, which Congress approved in May 1781. Morris arranged for the bank to be incorporated and drew loans from it to pay off national debts. These loans were backed solely by the credibility of the bank's stockholders. As part-owner, Congress gave the bank legitimacy. When the directors of the bank decided that Congress had borrowed enough, Congress sold its stock back to the bank and kept the principal it had borrowed for national expenditures. Financial tricks like this worked and they generated over $1 million in revenue.[22] But they did not last forever. The nation still had a revenue problem that it needed to address. Morris, and many others, recognized the importance of a coercive system of national taxation.

The 1781 Impost Amendment

The crises in 1780 led members of Congress to seek another source of revenue. In November of that year, a committee heard several proposals for financing the war. These proposals included gathering all the gold, silver, and plate people could spare with a promise to pay back donators with interest; depositing the same in a bank and issuing yet another paper against its metal value; raising money from the sale of western lands; and asking the states for an amendment to the Articles that allowed Congress to tax imported goods.[23] Many believed that the sale of western lands would produce inadequate revenue and supported the impost amendment instead. In February 1781, Congress requested the power to raise a 5 percent import tax for the exclusive purpose of discharging the debt. To preserve state sovereignty, it also agreed to relinquish this power as soon as the debts were paid.

One by one the states ratified the impost amendment. By the middle of 1782, all of the states, except Rhode Island, supported Congress's request for an import tax. Rhode Island's House unanimously opposed the measures based on three stated reasons. First, a federal import tax would adversely affect the states engaged in international commerce. Second, it would allow federal administrators to enter Rhode Island against a broad interpretation of the state's Constitution. Finally, it

---

[21] For a summary of the powers granted to Morris, see "Abstract of Reports from the Journals of Congress," appendix A in *Statements of the Receipts*, 1–4.

[22] Hammond, *Banks and Politics*.

[23] Jensen, *New Nation*, 58. Other forms of federal taxation were proposed in 1783. See Madison's "Notes on Debates," appended to the *JCC*.

would allow Congress to become financially independent. But despite the rhetoric, Rhode Island's motivations were primarily to serve local interests. Rhode Island's merchants knew that a federal impost would assign a greater portion of the federal burden to commercial states than would unenforced requisitions and it would force Rhode Island to carry a greater share of the burden. Rather than support the impost amendment, Rhode Island merchants preferred that the state assembly collect duties of its own and pay federal debts owed to them directly. This gave Rhode Island a higher portion of the receipts collected from import duties and guaranteed that the debts Congress owed to Rhode Island merchants would be paid off earnestly. The objection protected the interests of Rhode Island but hurt the general well-being of the confederation.

To ensure that Rhode Island defeated the amendment, David Howell and other Rhode Island merchants blanketed local newspapers with anti-impost rhetoric and soon gained the support of rural interests. Small farmers and craftsmen recognized that the state assembly would shift its taxes from import taxes to head taxes if federal duties were allowed. Farmers and craftsmen used few imported goods, and would certainly pay more if a head tax were imposed. In a rare unification, both merchants and rural interests preferred that Rhode Island oppose the federal amendment and keep import revenue for themselves. As David Howell told Morris, "if any revenue can be raised from trade in the way proposed . . . the State is entitled to the exclusive benefit thereof." Rhode Island legislators saw no contradiction in their opposition to the amendment, and they did a surprisingly good job of paying their quotas throughout the confederation – always keeping some revenue from the state impost for themselves.[24]

Unwilling to accept the decision, Congress sent a special envoy to Rhode Island armed with concessions to help the Rhode Island Assembly change its mind. Not far into their journey one member of the envoy mentioned that he had received a letter from Virginia claiming that Virginia had repealed its grant of the impost amendment in the wake of Rhode Island's decision. Startled by the news, the envoy returned to Congress where they found other letters that verified the report. Without

---

[24] "Some objections against passing an Impost Law, in the State of Rhode Island and Providence Plantations, briefly stated at the request of the Superintendent of Finance, by his humble servant, D. Howell," Staples, ed., *Rhode Island in Congress*, 391–392. For propaganda both for and against the amendment, see From Thomas Paine, November 20, 1782, Morris, *Papers*, 7: 78–93, particularly the editor's head note. For official opposition to the federal impost, see Speaker of the House of Representatives of Rhode Island to the President of Congress, November 30, 1782, *Rhode Island in Congress*, 400; and Nevins, *The American States*, 632.

consent from the other twelve states, Congress abandoned its mission and accepted Rhode Island's decision as a defeat.[25]

National Finance

Even without impost duties, congressional finance was not entirely in disrepair. In a report issued July 29, 1782, Morris estimated that the public debt had reached more than $30 million.[26] But despite long-term problems associated with the debt, Morris believed that Congress could defer the principal for roughly a decade and pay the interest due on the debt alone. This amounted to a little more than $2 million a year. Current expenditures were further relieved by the reduced needs of the army. There were no major campaigns between late 1781 and the army's disbandment in November 1783, and military expenditures shrank dramatically as a result. Continental troops and attached militias declined from about 27,000 men in 1780 to 21,000 in 1781, 14,000 in 1782, and 13,000 in 1783. Figure 4.1 shows the corresponding decline in federal expenditures. The reduction in troops cut annual expenditures by more than three quarters, making Morris's job as Financier much easier. Morris did not have to react to the immediacies of the war as did his predecessors, and he did not have to finance large current expenditures that consumed previous Congresses. All Morris had to do was to figure out how to pay the interest due on the debt and to determine how to provide for a smaller, more manageable, army. Sinking the principal owed on the debt would be handled separately.[27]

After 1780, requisitions provided current income for Congress only when they were raised in kind or in specie. Requisitions paid in commissary certificates, quartermaster certificates, or outdated Continentals did not produce reusable income. They merely reduced federal debts. To give Congress current income, Morris insisted that Congress strip future requisitions of their requests for paper money and concentrate its requests on specie. This would give Congress a current income.

To encourage compliance with national requisitions, Morris wrote circulars to the states urging them to pay; he met with congressional dele-

---

[25] The Virginia legislature repealed its ratification of the impost amendment on December 7 after learning that the Rhode Island General Assembly opposed it (Ferguson, *Power of the Purse*, 153; James Madison to Edmund Randolph, December 30, 1782, Madison, *Papers*, 5: 472–75; Notes on Debates, December 6, 1782, ibid., 5: 371–377; and Hening, *Statutes at Large*, 10: 409–410).

[26] To the President of Congress (John Hanson), July 29, 1782, Morris, *Papers*, 6: 63–64. Using treasury figures, Pitkin estimated the debt at $42,000,375 in the following April (*A Statistical View*, 27).

[27] Ibid., 27; Report of the Secretary at War, *Statement of the Receipts*, 31–34; Ferguson, *Power of the Purse*, 126.

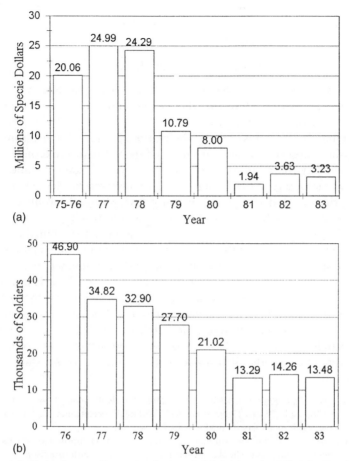

Figure 4.1. Federal expenditures (exclusive of debt) (*a*) and soldiers in Continental pay (*b*), 1775–1783. *Source*: Annual estimated expenditures come from Timothy Pitkin, *A Statistical View*, 26; soldiers in Continental pay, including regulars and attached militia, come from Henry Knox, "Report of the Secretary at War," May 10, 1790, *Statement of the Receipts*.

gates to promote laws that would help their states meet quotas; and he continually reminded each state about how much it owed.[28] Coaxing, prodding, and other social sanctions may have improved state compliance with requisitions, if only modestly. During Morris's four years as Superintendent of Finance, states contributed more specific supplies and paid more specie than they had in all the previous years. The federal

[28] Brown, *Redeeming*, 14–16.

treasury received $1,676,992 in specie and $539,233 in supplies from the states during Morris's administration. This was roughly 35 percent more than it received before 1781.[29]

Observations of the Receivers

To learn why requisitions went unpaid, Morris asked the Receivers of the Continental Tax to tell him why their states paid only part of the monies requested. Receivers from three states wrote back, offering valuable insight into the problems of the confederation. Joseph Whipple, from New Hampshire, argued that his state suffered from a destitute economy and could not pay the requisitions of Congress because state revenues were too low. He observed that refugees had immigrated to New Hampshire during the war and were incapable of growing enough produce to pay their taxes. Nearly four fifths of his state was in this condition, and the remaining one fifth depended on exports and imports to sustain their livelihoods. Threatening from the north, the British cut off New Hampshire's major port and prevented it from selling fish and lumber to the lower states. This, combined with unusually large salaries for New Hampshire's contingent of the Continental army, dampened the state's income and made it incapable of paying its federal quota.[30] Other states made similar but less convincing claims about their ability to pay.[31]

Alexander Hamilton, Receiver of the Continental Tax from New York, reported that the British had made it difficult for his state to pay

---

[29] See *American State Papers*, 1: 59–62; and *Statement of the Receipts*, 4, for receipts from 1777 to 1780 and 1781 to 1789, respectively. Although receipts increased, the amount received was still much less than Morris had hoped for.

[30] Undoubtedly, strains from the war made it difficult for New Hampshire to raise its taxes. But additional immigrants should not have decreased the wealth of existing residents. State revenues from those citizens should have rebounded shortly after export trade was reestablished in 1785. However, New Hampshire did not make a sizable requisition payment until 1789. This was well after fish and lumber exports to the lower states regained their prewar level and exports to England rose to one fifth of their 1775 volume. Perhaps factors other than poor economic conditions affected New Hampshire's low payments after 1783 (Joseph Whipple to Robert Morris, January 25, 1782, Morris, *Papers*, 7: 373–375; Robert Morris to Joseph Whipple, March 25, 1783, ibid., 7: 640; Value of Exports to and Imports from England, United States, *Historical Statistics*, series Z 213–226, 2: 1176–1178).

[31] The President of Pennsylvania claimed that Pennsylvania paid only part of its requisitions because the state revalued private property and this slowed its ability to collect taxes. In Virginia, Governor Jefferson complained that the large size of his state made it difficult for Virginia to collect taxes. This is why Virginia did not fully comply with its requisitions. Other problems were noted as well; see Statement of President Reed to Congress, July 30, 1780, *Pennsylvania Archives*, 8 (series 1): 458–468, and President Reed in Council to Congress, May 17, 1781, Reed, *Life and Correspondence*, 2: 300–306. See To Samuel Huntington, July 27, 1780, Jefferson, *Papers*, 3: 508–515.

requisitions as well. He estimated that the British occupation of New York City and four other major counties had reduced the state's revenue by two thirds. The loss of New York City disrupted the state's foreign trade and caused many citizens to flee the state, hurting its labor supply. Compliance with federal requisitions was extremely difficult under these circumstances and this explained part of New York's lack of payment.

But according to Hamilton, this was not the only source of New York's problems. Tax assessors required Tories to pay enormous portions of the state tax. The amount individuals should pay was determined more on "personal friendships or dislikes of the assessor" than on the individual's "proportion of property." This assigned a disproportionate share of the tax on a narrow segment of the population and limited state revenues. The fact that tax assessors and their supervisors were popularly elected and paid a flat rate for their services exacerbated the problem. State tax assessors had no incentive to collect large sums or to confront local residents. New York did not prosecute a single tax assessor for neglecting his duty and gave them no reason to collect taxes diligently.[32]

Hamilton believed that circumstances limited his state's ability to pay, but he also believed his state raised taxes poorly. This further limited New York's requisition payments. In addition, it was not beyond members of his legislature to accept congressional policies and to withhold requisition payments at the same time. Members of the New York legislature thought that Morris's funding program was "wise and indispensable but a majority thought it would be unwise in one state to contribute this way alone." New York legislators supported Congress's policies but they did not want to pay for them without guarantees that other states would pay as well. Although they recognized the union's interest, state legislators acted on the interests of their own constituents. They did not enact better mechanisms for raising Continental taxes and they withheld money to avoid being lone contributors. These were the behaviors expected by states attempting to free-ride.[33]

The receiver from New Jersey was much more blunt. He noted that his state passed acts to comply with the requisitions of Congress, but that poor compliance from the other states agitated New Jersey legislators. They "had often immediately and implicitly obeyed the recommendations of Congress and had suffered by so doing." After New Jersey contributed a larger portion of its quota than other states, Congress

---

[32] Alexander Hamilton to Robert Morris, August 13, 1782, Morris, *Papers*, 6: 186–198.
[33] Alexander Hamilton to Robert Morris, October 5, 1782, ibid., 6: 504–505. For a general observation, see James Madison to Thomas Jefferson, March 27, 1780, Burnett, ed., *Letters of Members*, 5: 96–97.

raised New Jersey's quota "in Comparison with many if not all of the other States." The more New Jersey paid, the more it got charged. Increasing their quotas agitated New Jersey legislators and discouraged them from paying.[34]

Many members of New Jersey's General Assembly believed that New York could raise more taxes than New Jersey and noted that New Jersey was assigned the higher quota of the two. They frequently compared their assiduous compliance with the negligent compliance of New York and the southern states. Although they contributed to the federal treasury in good faith in the early 1780s, they did not want to carry the federal burden alone. New Jersey assemblymen wanted contributions from all the states, and when other states fell behind, New Jersey's requisition payments sharply declined.

As states failed to pay their requisitions, the New Jersey Assembly, and other state legislatures, became increasingly reluctant to pay their shares. Such strategic interaction is typical of a pure public goods setting. States failed to pay their requisitions because they lacked resources. But they also failed to pay because they did not want to carry the nation's fiscal burden alone nor to allow their neighbors to pay less than their fair share. This strategic behavior demonstrated that states were unwilling to surrender local interests for the good of the whole. It demonstrated the first half of the joint products model. When states pursued public benefits, they eventually free-rode. But when the same states had private benefits to gain, the same local interests made them contribute to the union more diligently.

A Failed Campaign

After the British seized Charleston in May 1780, Americans turned their attention toward the southern campaign. At the same time, however, Washington prepared to launch a major attack on New York City. He worried that the British might take the highlands before he could attack and turned to Congress for additional troops. After debating the measure, Congress formally requested troops from the states. Each state reacted to Washington's proposal differently, depending on their distance from the campaign. Those that were closer had more excludable benefits to obtain and acted more diligently than those farther away.[35]

---

[34] William Houston to Robert Morris, July 6, 1782, Morris, *Papers*, 5: 540–542.

[35] Washington maintained more than three times as many troops in New Jersey and New York as he did in the South in preparation for the assault. Although history turns its attention toward the southern campaign around this time, the bulk of troops remained in the North (see Philip Schuyler to George Clinton, June 12, 1780, Smith, ed., *Letters of Delegates*, 15: 305; Lesser, 1976).

New York City was strategically important. It was the key to the Hudson River and British attempts to isolate New England from the rest of the states. But New Yorkers valued the liberation of New York City in an excludable way. New Yorkers wanted to free their family and friends from British occupation and to open their largest port. Not surprisingly, the New York General Assembly made great efforts to support Washington's attack on New York City. It purchased a surplus of wheat for the army and was prepared to use force if residents of New York failed to supply the army with adequate goods. Despite the hardships of the war, the state legislature attempted to raise its quotas in troops, money, and other supplies. In June, a member of New York's General Assembly wrote:

[T]he Insistence of the Enemy, ha[s] already had a very considerable Effect on the Legislature, as well as the Whiggs of this State. I am firmly perswaded that they are making great Exertions, that meat may be found here to feed the Army for five or six weeks and that afterwards the Eastern States will produce a competent Supply. . . . Men and Courage will not be wanting when the Danger or the prospect of Deliverance approach in fuller View.[36]

New York made every attempt to support the campaign despite its depleted condition and recalcitrant Tories.

Other states responded promptly as well. With the enemy at Elizabethtown, a two-day march from Philadelphia, members of the Pennsylvania legislature agreed to raise most of their quota in supplies. But they refused to pay Congress without some assurance that their contribution would benefit them directly. On June 1, the Pennsylvania General Assembly agreed to comply with the requisition of March 1780 only if a majority of other states did so as well. If Congress did not receive enough funds to launch its campaign on New York, Pennsylvania would withhold its resources and allocate its funds elsewhere. Pennsylvanian legislators feared that the taxes would not provide immediate subsistence for the army or any new benefits for their state. And they did not want to tax their citizens unless the money would be used to carry out Washington's campaign or benefit their state directly. Pennsylvanians wanted to remove the threat, but they were less committed than the people of New York.[37]

---

[36] James Duane to Philip Schuyler, June 6, 1780, ibid., 15: 263–264. Also see Robert Livingston to George Clinton, June 29, 1780, ibid., 15: 386–387. From Philip Schuyler, September 16, 1780, Hamilton, *Papers*, 2: 432–433.

[37] An Act for Funding and Redeeming the Bills of Credit . . . , Pennsylvania, *Session Laws*, 376–381. President Reed to Colonel A. Lochry, June 12, 1780, and Statement of President Reed to Congress, July 30, 1780, *Pennsylvania Archives*, 8 (series 1): 318–319 and 467, respectively.

Virginia was even further from the action and much less interested in the campaign. The Virginia legislature attempted to raise their state's quota for men, supplies, and money but found it difficult to ship the resources north. When the southern campaign got under way, they suddenly changed their mind and redirected money and materials southward.[38] On August 17, the Lieutenant Governor notified the Continental commissary that Virginia would no longer furnish funds for the northern army because the "Demands for the Southern Troops occur so frequently, as totally to exhaust our Treasury." The Articles of Confederation did not give Virginia the authority to decide where to send its requisitions, but Virginian officials chose to send them to the local campaign anyway.[39]

On that same day, Washington informed the Committee of Cooperation that he did not receive enough recruits from the states to undertake his attack on New York City. Returns were so poor that he would have to abandon the effort indefinitely. As he saw it, "the contest among the different States *now* is not which shall do most for the common cause, but which shall do least . . . one State waiting to see what another will or will not do through fear of doing too much." States did not raise the force Washington requested because they did not expect enough private benefits to make their contributions worthwhile. Without such incentives, the purely public benefits of Confederation defense could not encourage them to comply.[40]

Frustrated by the abandoned attempt, Governor George Clinton asked the New York General Assembly to propose an amendment to the Articles of Confederation that would give Congress the power to coerce the

---

[38] Governor Jefferson to the Committee of Congress at Headquarters, July 2, 1780, Virginia, *Official Letters*, 2: 137; To Samuel Huntington, July 27, 1780, Jefferson, *Papers*, 3: 508–513; and Governor Jefferson to John Mathews, September 2, 1780, Virginia, *Official Letters*, 2: 181–182.

[39] Lieutenant Governor Dudley Digges to Major Forsyth, August 17, 1780, Clinton, *Public Papers*, 6: 120–121. In the same vein Governor Jefferson of Virginia assured the French minister Luzerne that "[t]he interest of this State is intimately blended, so perfectly the same with that of the others of the confederacy that the most effectual aid it can at any time receive, is where the general cause most needs it." He then asked Luzerne to move the French fleet from the northern United States to the Chesapeake so that the French could open Virginia's commerce (To La Luzerne, August 31, 1780, Jefferson, *Papers*, 3: 577–578).

[40] To Fielding Lewis, July 6, 1780, Washington, *Writings*, 19: 132, emphasis in original. Oliver Ellsworth and James Madison made similar observations when reflecting on the union. See Connecticut Convention, January 4, 1788, Jensen, ed., *Documentary History*, 3: 544; and Virginia Convention, June 11, 1788, ibid., 9: 1144–1145. For Washington's decision to abandon the offensive, see To the Committee of Cooperation, August 17, 1780, Washington, *Writings*, 19: 391–394.

states into full compliance. On October 10 the Assembly unanimously
resolved that

> whenever it shall appear to [Congress], that any state is deficient in furnishing
> the Quota of Men, Money, Provisions or other Supplies, required of such State,
> that Congress direct the Commander in Chief, without Delay, to march the Army
> or such part of it as may be requisite into such State, and by a Military Force,
> compel it to furnish its deficiency.[41]

New Yorkers had much to gain from dislodging the British in New York
City and much to lose from surrendering the highlands. They wanted
other states to contribute to Washington's campaign and were willing to
sacrifice their own sovereignty to assure such contributions. This was
true when New York stood to gain some of the exclusive benefits of an
expanded Continental army in 1780. But their zeal was short-lived.
When the threat of the British faded, so did New York's enthusiasm for
paying requisitions and coercing compliance. As Washington wrote four
years after the war, "it is somewhat singular that a State (New York)
which used to be foremost in federal measures, should now turn against
them in almost every instance."[42]

When the British finally left New York City, the leaders of New York
had no reason to push for congressional authority over the states and
refused to authorize any source of national revenue other than requisitions. They supported coercive powers when it benefited their state, then
opposed them when national goods were no longer in their unique interests. They defended the system of requisitions because it allowed their state
to free-ride on national war debts and to avoid a national impost amendment which promised to crowd out state import taxes. New York,
Pennsylvania, and Virginia paid their requisitions when it helped
maintain a local campaign, but they waited for other states to pay when
the campaign subsided. This type of behavior was expected from
states pursuing goods that were jointly private and public. It was the
pattern of contribution that typified the confederation.[43]

---

[41] Resolutions of the New York Assembly, October 10, 1780, New York, *Journal of the Assembly, 1780*, 43. The amendment was presented before Congress but never passed (*JCC*, 18: 1032). For inclinations toward coercive powers in the state of New York, see John Hanson to Philip Thomas, September 19, 1780, Smith, ed., *Letters of Delegates*, 16: 91–93; To James Duane, September 3, 1780, Hamilton, *Papers*, 11: 400–418.

[42] From George Washington, March 31, 1787, Madison, *Papers*, 9: 343. Parentheses in original.

[43] Far from the danger, New Hampshire did not pass any laws to raise its quotas in money, men, or supplies (see Committee at Headquarters to Certain States, July 13, 1780, Smith, ed., *Letters of Delegates*, 15: 441–442).

The 1783 Impost Amendment

Two years after Congress proposed the 1781 impost amendment, it again sought a more permanent source of revenue. Poll taxes, land taxes, and excise taxes were all considered, but different coalitions of states strongly opposed each. Almost every tax produced an uneven distribution of the federal burden. A poll tax contradicted the constitution of Maryland and was summarily rejected; a land tax put greater burdens on the South, which it vehemently opposed; and most of the products considered for an excise tax burdened New England. Taxes on salt were onerous to fishing states, while the anticipated revenue from taxes on coffee and spirits were inadequate to cover the nation's expense.[44] After considerable debate, Congress again turned to duties on imports. In March 1783 members of Congress requested the power to lay a 5 percent import tax for the express purpose of funding the federal debt. To address objections raised in the 1781 impost amendment, the new proposal gave the states power to appoint federal tax collectors but reserved the power to remove tax collectors for Congress; it mandated that the power of impost cease after twenty-five years; and it urged states owning western lands to cede their claims to the union. The latter helped to appease states that would be asked to surrender duties of their own.

But the revenue anticipated from the impost was inadequate to pay federal debts. As a result, Congress attached several riders to the 1783 version. In addition to requesting the power of impost, the amendment requested a permanent tax of $1.5 million annually from the states and a reapportionment based on white population. The tax would be collected through the usual system of requisitions and allow Congress to fully fund the interest on its debts. Regretfully, however, the impost amendment of 1783 was not ratified. The requisition and proposal for reapportionment died with it.[45]

---

[44] *JCC*, 25: 878–885.

[45] Since requisitions were to continue, their exact apportionment had to be settled. Congress had problems developing a policy for uniformly surveying lands and could not get the states to forward even the roughest surveys. Since Congress had always apportioned requisitions according to white population estimates, the amendment included a request to reapportion requisitions according to the number of white inhabitants and three fifths of all other persons not including Indians. Although some members of Congress argued that apportioning the nation's burden according to white population was more fair, the real reason that Congress pushed for this provision was that it had better estimates of state population than it had of land values. It also needed the support of northern states that stood to lose from passage of the impost amendment. Without the amendment or suitable land surveys, Congress maintained the practice of apportioning national burdens according to its best guesses of the nation's white population. The exact apportionment was finally set on April 18, 1783, but it was never approved by the states. See Table 3.1 for this distribution. *JCC*, 24: 188–192, 256–262.

Despite attempts to address objections posed against the 1781 impost, the 1783 version again failed ratification by a single state vote. This time it was New York, not Rhode Island, that resisted.[46] Like Rhode Island, New York took advantage of its port to do a thriving impost business of its own. It did not want national duties to interfere with state commerce nor for the new tax to force the state to tax by other means.[47]

When the other states conceded to the impost amendment in the spring of 1786, proponents of the amendment brought it before the New York legislature in one final attempt to push it through. The New York legislature agreed to a modified version of the impost amendment, but the version passed on May 4 did not match the federal proposal in two key respects. John Lansing and other localists succeeded in substituting state tax collectors for federal collectors by a narrow vote of 33 to 22 in the assembly. The act also stipulated that Congress receive New York's currency on par with specie. Both revisions held in the senate, but they violated the whole system.[48] Unless collectors were responsible to Congress, there was no reason to believe that they would collect money from import duties any more diligently than they had collected taxes for requisitions. More important, Congress could not accept New York's paper because it could not use state paper to pay its foreign obligations. Other states were likely to withdraw their consent if New York gained such special privileges, and Congress needed hard currency to address its revenue problems. Finally, the act said nothing about supplementary taxes nor any of the other provisions outlined by the amendment.[49]

Despite the setback, Congress attempted to reconcile New York's differences with other states. Pennsylvania was one of the few states that agreed to both the impost and the supplementary taxes but accepted the amendment conditioned upon all other states granting both measures. The Pennsylvania legislature worried that the 1783 amendment would affect its own income and wanted assurances that states would raise sufficient income to pay federal creditors, since a large number of creditors

---

[46] Rhode Island merchants changed their position on the 1783 impost because their legislature was about to pay off federal debts with state currency. This currency was less valued than the medium in which Congress promised to pay its debts; hence, merchants preferred that Congress receive the power of impost to increase their returns. See John Brown to David Howell, October 23, 1783, *Rhode Island Historical Society*, 14(27); Jabez Bowen to James Warren, November 26, 1783, Lodge, ed., *Warren-Adams Letters*, 2: 234–235; and Main, *The Antifederalists*. Also interesting are the objections from the town of Smithfield, which opposed payment of creditors in specie (Staples, *Rhode Island*, 558–60).

[47] John Williams to His Constituents, February 25, 1788, Bailyn, *The Debate*, 119–120.

[48] Spaulding, *New York*, 176–177; Cochran, *New York in Confederation*, 172–173.

[49] For a summary of New York's resolution, see Pierse Long to the President of New Hampshire, June 1, 1786, Burnett, ed., *Letters of Members*, 8: 378–379.

resided in their state. In the summer of 1786 James Monroe and Rufus King went to Pennsylvania and asked the legislature to grant Congress the power to tax imports whether or not other states authorized the supplementary taxes. Pennsylvanian legislators fully appreciated the consequences of Congress's position but felt more obligated to Pennsylvanians than to the confederation. As a result, they rejected the envoy's proposal and continued their policy of conditional compliance.[50]

New Jersey reacted to New York's position on the federal impost with greater fervor. Many goods consumed by its citizens came through New York ports and were subject to New York duties.[51] In February 1786, the New Jersey legislature resolved to withhold requisition payments until all other states accepted the impost plan. "In a moody fit," as William Grayson put it, the lower house of the New Jersey legislature adopted a resolution declaring that New Jersey would not comply with the requisition of 1785 nor any future requisition until "sundry grievances" had been righted. Among these grievances was a demand for New York to accede to the federal impost.[52] New Jersey was unwilling to support a Congress that refused to remedy its commercial grievances with New York and believed that defying requisitions would bring the weight of the union against its neighbor. But the New Jersey policy hurt the confederation more than it hurt New York. Charles Pinckney, head of the congressional envoy sent to Trenton, pointed out that the policy would only turn the animosity of the states away from New York toward New Jersey. If New Jersey thought the powers of Congress were inadequate to prevent New York from taking advantage of the system, then New Jersey "ought immediately to instruct her delegates in congress, to urge the calling of a general convention of the states, for the purpose of revising and amending the federal system." New Jersey's assemblymen liked the idea, instructed their delegates to the Annapolis convention to

---

[50] JCC, 30: 70–76. For letters related to the Pennsylvania episode, see James Monroe to Thomas Jefferson, May 11, 1786; James Monroe to James Madison, August 10, 1786; Rufus King to Nathan Dane, August 17, 1786; James Monroe to Thomas Jefferson, August 19, 1786; James Monroe to James Madison, September 12, 1786; and Samuel Meredith to Thomas FitzSimons, November 1786, Burnett, ed., *Letters of Members*, 8: 359–360, 419, 437, 443–446, 464–465, 513, respectively. Also see Ferguson, *Power of the Purse*, 240–241.

[51] New York enacted the first of its state imposts in 1781. The impost distributed a large portion of state taxes on consumers in Connecticut, New Jersey, and Vermont. Some estimate that as much as 50 percent of the goods consumed in New Jersey and Connecticut came through New York's ports and were subject to New York duties (Spaulding, *New York*, 156–157). Like Rhode Island previously, New York stood to gain from this arrangement. See New Brunswick, November 15, 1786, *Pennsylvania Gazette*, no. 2946, p. 2.

[52] Burdett, ed., *Letters of Members*, 8: xxi.

consider general defects of the federal system, and generally supported the Constitution when it was proposed. The conflict with New York partially explains why New Jersey pushed for reform.[53]

New Jersey's failure to comply with the requisition did not alarm members of Congress. Noncompliance had become commonplace in the union. What alarmed Congress was that the New Jersey Assembly had openly defied the Articles of Confederation rather than simply let the requisition payment slip by as other states had done in the past. New Jersey legally opposed its obligation to Congress in an attempt to alter the behavior of New York, and in the process threatened the idea of a confederation based on civic duty. Fortunately, the situation did not degenerate into a tit-for-tat exchange over requisitions. The New Jersey Assembly rescinded its measure four days after hearing Pinckney's speech.[54]

Rhode Island's refusal to accede to the first federal impost and New York's refusal to accede to the second created resentment among the states. These were selfish acts designed to protect state revenues, and they saddled the rest of the union with the nation's financial burden. Despite condemnations from other states, both holdouts single-handedly defeated the impost amendment and its promise of a more stable source of federal revenue. This left Congress with nothing more than the power to request money from the states. As Morris observed, "while [the confederation] confers on Congress the Privilege of asking every Thing, it has secured to each state the Prerogative of granting nothing."[55] The mere ability to request resources from the state proved inadequate for the nation's expenditures.

Settling State Accounts

To improve compliance with requisitions, Morris began the long process of settling accounts between Congress and the states.[56] Many states

---

[53] Charles Pinckney, Speech before the New Jersey Assembly, March 13, 1786, ibid., 8: 329.

[54] Ibid., 8: xxi–xxii. Tensions between New York and New Jersey continued through other mediums, however. In 1787 New York increased its duties and placed entrance fees on coasting vessels. New Jersey retaliated by levying a tax of 30 pounds per month on New York's lighthouse at Sandy Hook, New Jersey. Other retaliations were exchanged as well (see Nevins, *The American States*, 561–562; Spaulding, *New York*, 156–157).

[55] To the President of Congress, February 11, 1782, Morris, *Papers*, 4: 209. For similar sentiments, see Edmund Randolph, Constitution Debates, June 6, 1788; and A Native of Virginia: Observations upon the Proposed Plan of Federal Government, April 2, 1788, Jensen, ed., *Documentary History*; 9: 986 and 656–657, respectively.

[56] The process of settling state accounts began in 1782, but was not completed until 1793. Under the Articles, it was presumed that revenues would be pooled into a common treasury and current expenditures paid out of this pool. The amount each state legally owed

incurred costs on behalf of the nation for which they did not receive credit because the expenditures were unauthorized. States paid for the supplies needed for the Continental army when the army was near their state, the salaries of their own Continental soldiers, and even part of the debt owed to creditors residing within their borders. Morris believed that settling state accounts would show exactly how much each state owed and encourage requisition payments by showing that each state was behind in its payment.

During the Revolution, many states complained that they could not meet federal requisitions because they did not have enough time to raise taxes or that the perils of war prevented them from complying. During the Morris years, however, the dominant explanation was that each state had already paid its share of the national expense by supplying the army directly or by paying national expenses that the nation did not properly credit.[57] More than one state argued that it had already paid its quota, when direct payments were included. A grand committee reported to Congress that "almost every State thinks itself in advance."[58] The truth was that no state paid more than it owed. When Congress settled its accounts in favor of the states in 1793, all the states were in arrears.[59]

The authors of the confederation assumed that only the expenses authorized by Congress or its officers would be admitted as part of the common expense. However, shortly after final settlement began, Congress had problems distinguishing between authorized and unauthorized expenditures, partially because many of them served both excludable and nonexcludable interests. To maintain its enlistments, Massachusetts offered higher wages for its troops than authorized by Congress. Higher wages aided the army and helped it complete its tasks. Although Con-

---

would be settled later, after the expenses directly incurred by each state were taken into account. States that contributed more than they were required would receive the difference at 5 percent interest in the final settlement, while states that contributed less than required would pay a 5 percent penalty for their debts. When state accounts were finally settled and each state's share of the common charges were known, debtor states were supposed to give the money they owed to Congress, which would then forward the money to creditor states (Ferguson, *Power of the Purse*, 204).

[57] See, e.g., William Samuel Johnson to the Governor of Connecticut, July 9, 1785, Burnett, ed., *Letters of Members*, 8: 161–163; and Governor Clinton to Captain Townsend, August 31, 1780, Clinton, *Public Papers*, 6: 156–157.

[58] *JCC*, 26: 192. Similar statements were made by others. See Circular to the Governors of the States, July 25, 1781, Morris, *Papers*, 1: 380–383; and Ezra L'Hommedieu to George Clinton, September 8, 1781, Smith, ed., *Letters of Delegates*, 18: 25.

[59] See *American State Papers*, 1 (finance): 54–62. Of course, some states were deemed "creditors," while others were labeled "debtors," but such classification reflects a division of the costs actually paid by the states, not the amount requested by Congress.

gress did not authorize the expenditures, offering higher wages clearly advanced national interests and helped Massachusetts meet its quota. Other expenditures were more precarious. Massachusetts had also launched an unsuccessful mission on a British outpost in Penobscot, Maine, which cost $387,000. Many believed that this mission served Massachusetts alone and that the union should not bear the cost. But despite the objection, Massachusetts charged the expenses to the union. Likewise, Virginia wanted credit for Clark's expedition to the Northwest Territory. Out-of-state residents believed that this expedition helped Virginia secure control over its territory without aiding the union. Virginians argued that the excursion helped survey state lands so that they could be ceded to the union. The distinction between state and federal expenditures was difficult to determine when the interests of the two governments overlapped.[60]

Drawing the line at authorized expenditures might have resolved some of the confusion, but it would have overlooked the expenses that states incurred on behalf of the union and placed heavy burdens on the South. Many southern states kept poor records of their expenditures and included federal expenditures with expenditures of their own. Admitting only authorized expenses would ignore the fact that many southern states paid for the union out of their own funds. A delegate from North Carolina wrote:

It is curious but not very pleasing to observe, that while some of the Northern States never turned out a serjeants guard of Militia without obtaining the sanction of Congress or some Continental Officer, our state in the true spirit of a patriot but not of an accomptant has been expending Militia & raising state troops without taking any heed concerning the day of retribution.[61]

Rather than base common charges on authorized expenditures and allow the virtuous deeds of the South to go unnoticed, Congress eventually decided to admit all expenses incurred on behalf of the union as part of the common expense. The list included many controversial claims, such as Penobscot and the Northwest expeditions.[62]

When state officials heard the news, they combed their provinces for additional vouchers and rehashed old records to increase their claims. Each state argued that it contributed more to the war than its constitutional share. These were not the actions of magnanimous states. They

[60] Ferguson, *Power of the Purse*, 204–206.
[61] Hugh Williamson to Alexander Martin, September 30, 1784, Smith, ed., *Letters of Delegates*, 21: 799.
[62] Ferguson, *Power of the Purse*, 207, 213–214, 216–217; JCC, 29: 685–688; To the President of Congress (Elias Boudinot), August 12, 1783, Morris, *Papers*, 8: 415–424; James Monroe to James Madison, July 12, 1785, Burnett, ed., *Letters of Members*, 8: 163–165.

were the actions of states bent on reducing their own costs and protecting the interests of their constituents.

Requisition payments and the settlement of state accounts were greatly intertwined. States that fell behind in requisition payments claimed that they were in advance on their accounts. Many paid for the nation's defense directly and assumed federal quartermaster, commissary, and loan office certificates in expectation that Congress would credit their accounts. When unauthorized expenditures were admitted as part of the common charge of the union, such states were credited for larger contributions than they had actually contributed, particularly in the South. However, withholding requisitions in the name of unsettled accounts crippled the nation's cash flow and made Congress incapable of carrying out its constitutionally defined tasks. It was clear that the union was a group of individual states, not a bonded whole.

The Pursuit of Local Interest

States had no incentive to treat common interests as their own. They paid little to the federal treasury and pursued acts that struck at the very integrity of the union. States preferred withholding their payments until Congress settled state accounts rather than to help with the immediate needs of the union. They paid monies when it advanced local campaigns and withheld their monies when it was applied to the general interests of the union. They opposed the impost amendment when it advanced local interests and favored the measure when it gave them local gain. They strived to reduce their shares of the national burden, and they pursued policies conditioned upon the decisions made by other states. In at least one case, state behavior emerged as outright defiance to the union. All these acts were reasonable from a state's point of view. However, they were detrimental to the confederation and prevented Congress from fully supplying the army and paying its debts. Such actions clearly demonstrated the free-rider problem that was inherent in the American confederation.

The failure to obtain a federal impost left Congress poor, but not desperate, during the Morris years. With the war's end in sight, the financial wizardry of Robert Morris covered most of the nation's immediate expenses and delayed debt payments until loans became due. The Nationalists made the most of the system of requisitions. They succeeded in gaining larger returns than their predecessors and prevented the army from completely disbanding. Although they failed to give Congress the power to lay import duties, they gave it the national debt. Assigning the debt to Congress strengthened the federal government by giving it a reason for peacetime existence. But nationalizing the debt without a means of paying for it was a recipe for disaster. The system of requisitions soon faced its most critical test, and Congress could do nothing to stop it.

WANING YEARS OF THE CONFEDERATION, 1785–1789

The System of Indents

Congress asked the states to pay large sums in specie during the Morris years. But specie was scarce and states needed it to pay the interest due on their own securities and foreign loans. Without adequate specie from the states, Congress needed a plan. Members of Congress knew that state legislatures wanted to pay creditors in their states and developed a system that took advantage of their interests. This plan, called the system of indents, attempted to tie requisition payments to local interests. Congress gave the states indents to pay local creditors, then received the same indents in payment of requisitions. Indents were notes issued to a holder of a loan office certificate as payment for interest due. The national treasury printed these notes in set denominations and deposited them in each state's loan office. Holders of loan office certificates would then receive the indents and return them in payment of their taxes in the same year. This paid off the interest due to local bond holders and produced something of a new currency. The fact that they were transferable and could be used to pay federal taxes gave indents their value and made them acceptable notes for creditors.

Since Congress was unable to field the army requested by the requisition of October 30, 1781, it consolidated the requisition of 1781 with the requisition of October 16, 1782, and reduced the amount by 40 percent. Congress then combined this requisition with the annual expenses needed for 1784 and issued a new requisition for the difference on April 27 and 28. Since roughly one fourth of the $2.9 million requested was budgeted for interest due on loan office certificates prior to 1782, states were allowed to pay one fourth of the 1784 requisition in indents. Congress requested the other three fourths in the specie needed to pay foreign obligations. It would accept indents only if a state paid the percentage requested in specie. Congress included this condition to encourage payments in specie, which would allow it to pay foreign debts. Indents themselves would pay state bond holders and give the economy a circulating medium.[63]

In 1785, however, none of the states complied with the terms prescribed by the 1784 requisition. Many had already paid creditors for

---

[63] *JCC*, 26: 297–309, 310–314; Ferguson, *Power of the Purse*, 224.

interest due through 1782 and started to issue indents for the payments due in 1783 – against the plan. Large sums of specie were still unmanageable. Many states failed to properly comply with the requisition of 1784 because they could not raise the amount required in specie in order to receive proper credit.

On September 27, 1785, Congress tried again. Since two thirds of the budget would be applied toward interest on the public debt, Congress agreed to receive two thirds of its requisition in indents, as long as states paid the other one third in specie. To encourage specie payments, Congress directed loan officers to withhold their indents until their state passed tax laws to pay off their specie quota.[64] Similar specifications governed the requisition of 1786 (see Table 4.2 for a list of general requisitions). Both requisitions asked for the minimum amount of money needed to sink the debt, pay for the administration of the small national government, and apply money toward foreign loans. No additional expenditures were included. But the stipulations surrounding the requisitions were too austere and the states barely complied again.

Part of the problem was that many states refused to issue indents to nonresidents and would not receive indents issued from other states.[65] They wanted to pay their own creditors directly and were unwilling to pay creditors in other states at almost any cost. This contradicted the wishes of Congress and prevented indents from circulating like a currency. If a state issued indents to citizens of other states, it would have to reduce the amount issuable to its own citizens. Paying creditors in other states limited the amount of cheap money that a state could tax from their economies to meet congressional quotas and prevented states from paying off their own creditors. States would not receive out-of-state indents, in contrast, because receiving them would only reduce the amount of specie or state currency that a state could raise. Merchants typically paid their taxes in specie or state notes. If states allowed them to pay their taxes in out-of-state indents, merchants would withhold their specie and pay their taxes in a less valued medium.[66] The receiving state would then have less income for state purposes. Without universal acceptance, indents lost their value as a national currency, unraveling Congress's plan.

[64] Ibid., 225; *JCC*, 29: 616–618.
[65] For an example, see Extracts from the Minutes of the Eleventh General Assembly of Pennsylvania, November 13, 1786, *Pennsylvania Gazette*, December 6, 1786, no. 2949, p. 2.
[66] For states to maintain the value of their currencies, the currency's supply had to be limited through taxation. States did not want to lose this opportunity by absorbing out-of-state indents that were not valuable to them.

Table 4.2. General Requisitions, 1780–1788[a]

Date requested	Amount ($)	Mode of payment
January 12, 1780	60,128,073	in-kind, valued in old money
February 25, 1780	~4,200,000	in-kind, valued in specie[b]
March 18, 1780	1,666,666	annually (refinancing)[c]
August 26, 1780	3,000,000	new bills[d]
November 4, 1780	6,000,000	in-kind, valued in specie[e]
March 16, 1781	1,500,000	new bills, quarterly[f]
October 30, 1781	8,000,000	specie[g]
October 16, 1782	2,000,000	specie
December 31, 1782	8,000,000	
April 27 and 28, 1784	2,986,952	1/4 indents[h]
September 27, 1785	3,000,000	2/3 indents[i]
August 2, 1786	3,777,062	3/7 indents[j]
October 11, 1787	1,700,407	unenforced[k]
August 20, 1788	1,686,541	unenforced[l]
Total	57,354,163[m]	

Source: *JCC*, 16: 44–47, 195–200, 260–268; 17: 780–786; 19: 267–268, 298–299; 21: 1087–1088, 1091; 23: 658–661; 26: 297–309, 310–315; 29: 765–771; 31: 459–466; 33: 632–636, 651–655; 34: 432–443.

[a] Special requisitions are not included. See Dougherty, "Collective Action under the Articles," for a list.

[b] The value of this requisition is approximated using the prices specified within the requisition.

[c] States were to continue remitting $15,000,000 of the old currency per month as established October 7, 1779, and to stop their payments by the end of April 1781. They then were supposed to pay one sixth of the new currency issued (up to $1,666,666 per year) starting January 1, 1781.

[d] Payments were due as soon as possible, but before December 31, 1780.

[e] Roughly eight elevenths of this requisition were receivable in-kind, three elevenths in specie or new currency. Goods were due on different dates depending on the needs of the army; the earliest deadline was January 1, 1781. Specie was due in four quarterly payments beginning May 1, 1781.

[f] The requisition of October 30, 1781, superseded this requisition. Payments were due June 1, 1786. Therefore, only one quarter of the $6,000,000 requested was ever active.

[g] Receivable in four quarterly payments beginning April 1, 1782.

[h] This requisition superseded the requisitions of October 30, 1781, and October 16, 1782. Congress specifically designed it to pay off previous debts.

[i] Although payments were technically due May 1, 1786, Congress later resolved that it would not accept indents received after January 1, 1787.

[j] Indent payments were due July 1, 1787. After this date, a state owed the remainder of its quota in specie.

[k] This was the amount due in interest on the domestic debt that year. Money previously received from Holland paid the interest due on foreign loans. In addition, this requisition repealed the time limits on the receipt of indents, allowing states to fill their quotas using indents issued in 1787 or any previous year.

[l] As in 1787, this was the amount due in interest on the domestic debt that year. Interest due on foreign loans was to be paid by money previously received from Holland and specie still due from previous requisitions. Payments could be received in indents issued in any year or received in final settlement certificates.

[m] The total includes $10 million for complete redemption of the March 18, 1780, emission and a reduction of the January 12, 1780, requisition by 1/40. I make no attempt to reconcile the differences in market value of specie, new currency, in-kind goods, or indents. Hence, the total is a rough and potentially misleading approximation.

To encourage states to honor out-of-state indents, Congress rated out-of-state indents at a value of $1.33 for every $1.00 of in-state indents. This was not worth the trade-off in taxation power and did not alter the policies of the states. Again, states did not want to pay debts owed by delinquent neighbors nor to obey congressional dictates that went against their interests.[67] They wanted to pay creditors within their borders and to keep local taxes to a minimum. States pursued such priorities with little regard to its effect on the union.

In August 1786, an address from Congress noted that only eight states had enacted legislation complying with requisitions in the previous fourteen months. As Rufus King wrote, "Connecticut & New Jersey have finished their Sessions without attending to the situation of the confederacy; the former took into consideration the Requisition of last year, and refused compliance with it. The latter in their late Session did not even treat the subject with the attention it received from Connecticut."[68] Of the $1 million requested in specie that year, only one tenth of it was ever collected from the states. This made Congress incapable of paying its foreign obligations, let alone its civil list. The authors of the address claimed that "it is proved that the Receipts of the last Fourteen Months were not adequate to bare the maintenance of the Federal Government on the most economical Establishment, and in time of profound Peace."[69] By 1786 half the states issued their own currencies despite provisions within the Articles explicitly forbidding it. This reduced their ability to tax specie for congressional purposes and made compliance levels drop even further. In addition, loan offices issued indents whether or not their states met the stipulations of Congress. States paid their quotas in any form they pleased and Congress was stripped of its discretionary funds.

With inadequate income, Congress defaulted on many of its foreign obligations. Lack of specie caused it to suspend interest payments due to France in 1785 and to default on the principal, due in 1787. By concentrating its efforts, Congress managed to pay its small debt to Holland, but it made no payment to Spain and continued to fall short of its debts to France for the remainder of the Confederation.

At summer's end Congress was broke. The federal treasury had no

---

[67] As William Grayson observed, "Congress annually vote requisitions for the foreign and domestic interest which are totally disregarded" (William Grayson to William Short, April 16, 1787, Burnett, ed., *Letters of Members*, 8: 581). For a discussion of the revaluation of out-of-state indents, see Ferguson, *Power of the Purse*, 225; *JCC*, 31: 465.

[68] *JCC*, 31: 615; The Massachusetts Delegates to the Governor of Massachusetts, October 28, 1786, Burnett, ed., *Letters of Members*, 8: 498–499; Rufus King to Elbridge Gerry, June 18, 1786, Smith, ed., *Letters of Delegates*, 23: 363.

[69] *JCC*, 31: 615.

funds to pay for Congress's immediate expenditures, and the nation lay vulnerable to foreign invasion. Just then, civil unrest broke out in Massachusetts in the form of Shays' Rebellion. Congress requested money from the states to pay for an army to quell the unrest; but with the exception of Virginia, no state complied. Without revenues, Congress could not field the army needed to suppress the rebellion. Shortly thereafter Madison wrote:

Indeed the present System neither has nor deserves advocates; and if some very strong props are not applied it will quickly tumble to the ground. No money is paid into the public Treasury; no respect is paid to the federal authority. Not a single State complies with the requisitions, several states pass them over in silence, and some positively reject them. The payments ever since the peace have been decreasing, and of late fall short even of the pittance necessary for the Civil list of the Confederacy. It is not possible that a government can last long under these circumstances.[70]

In 1787, Congress gave up. It removed all stipulations from the $1.7 million requisitioned that year and told the states to pay domestic debts in any manner they found appropriate. Congress asked the states to pay previous requests for specie, but it expected meager returns.

A committee report epitomized the situation. It declared that Congress could not depend on requisitions nor other revenue powers to service the debt. The only alternative was to distribute the debt between the states and hope for the best.[71] "Privatizing" the debt was consistent with the natural tendencies of the union. But it would have sapped Congress of its ability to pay foreign obligations and prevented it from providing additional public goods.

Congress extended its 1787 policy into 1788. Not surprisingly, the national treasury received a large number of indents during both years (recall Fig. 3.1a). Paying requisitions in indents alone benefited local creditors at almost no cost to a state. This was consistent with state priorities and states willingly complied. The national treasury received $370,257 in indents in 1787 and an additional $1,041,000 in 1788.[72] But the new policy forced Congress to surrender ownership of public securities and subjected the nation to the particular and local needs of

[70] Madison to Edmund Pendleton, February 24, 1787, Madison, *Papers*, 9: 294–295.
[71] *JCC*, 31: 521–523.
[72] The last large peak in Figure 3.1a and b should not be overstated. Part of the increase in payments was due to congressional acceptance of indents that had already been raised but not accepted because they were raised against Congress's stipulations. When the stipulations were removed in 1787, indent payments increased abruptly. For the figures reported in the text, see Ferguson, *Power of the Purse*, 227–228, and Board of Treasury, Account of Taxes, *PCC*, M. 247, r. 154, i. 141, 1: 277, 333; 2: 125, 491.

the states. Although the constitutional convention saved the union from collapse, the trend was clearly toward greater disunion.

The End of the Confederation

Indents were Congress's last attempt to make the system of requisitions work. Congress clearly designed them to take advantage of the nonexcludable benefits from paying requisitions. By conditioning payments to local creditors on state payments in specie, Congress hoped to raise the money needed to pay off foreign debts. Nevertheless, states ignored the conditions of Congress and paid off holders of loan office certificates without concern for their quotas in specie. Like requisitions in currency and specie alone, requisitioning the states in indents did not entirely work. States were not encouraged to raise the amounts required in specie nor to pay the amounts needed for the foreign debt. Indents paid holders of loan office certificates, but they did not pay debts to foreign lenders or foreign military personnel. Congress could not tie the nonexcludable benefits of paying these debts to local interests. In other words, the system of indents helped pay excludable debts – such as the debts Congress owed to American soldiers or the debts it owed in Commissary and Quartermaster certificates – but it could not pay off nonexcludable debts – such as foreign debts and debts owed to Canadian regiments. States did not have any incentive to pay nonexcludable debts unilaterally and would probably not pay them if the debt was privatized. These debts would have to be paid by the nation as a whole with some mechanism to encourage contribution.

CONCLUSION

A constant drain on specie during and after the war made it difficult for states to collect taxes. Without a medium of exchange, states frequently assessed taxes in their own currencies or in specific goods. But lack of specie is not the sole reason for poor compliance with requisitions. Without sufficient incentive to consider national interests, states frequently pursued policies that advanced their excludable concerns. "As if we were so many different nations," a writer in Pennsylvania observed, "each state is endeavoring to do something for its own benefits but seldom does [so] without injuring the one of the union."[73] When local priorities did not coincide with national interests, states were unlikely to surrender state interests for the common well-being of the union. Policies such as the printing of local currency, assumption of federal debts, and opposition to national imposts were reasonable from a state's point

[73] November 15, 1786, *Pennsylvania Gazette*, no. 2946, p. 2.

of view, but they weakened the nation's ability to pay its debts reliably and made it incapable of addressing unexpected contingencies.

These were the types of problems expected from states locked in a collective action problem. Congress passed policies that the states desired, but each state was unwilling to contribute to its policies on its own. Since nothing guaranteed that other states would pay their fair shares, states frequently conditioned their behavior on the compliance of other states. Combined with limited resources in the states, strategic behavior encouraged states to lighten taxes on the populace.

But states did pay part of their requisitions. They complied more diligently than the theory of pure public goods would predict and seemed to pay more diligently when payment advanced local interests. Considering that the framers designed the confederation to serve the interests of the states, it is not at all surprising that the states pursued their own interests and complied when it advanced their excludable and local concerns. Pursuing local rather than national interests was consistent with the maintenance of thirteen separate democracies and typified what we would expect from a system of voluntary taxation.

The next chapter evaluates the private benefits hypothesis more formally by empirically evaluating the relationship between requisition payments and the distribution of private benefits. States that had more private benefits at stake were more likely to pay their requisitions than states that did not, further supporting the joint products argument.

5

State Contributions and Private Interests

> While some States exposed to danger strain every nerve
> others removed from danger and at ease are remiss and neg-
> ligent, whereas all should make the proper exertions and
> furnish their proportions whether immediately or remotely
> affected and w[hi]ch can alone give energy to military oper-
> ations.
>
> – Joseph Jones[1]

Recall that the model of pure public goods outlined in Chapter 3 predicted that a state would contribute to the national treasury only if
it received the most nonexcludable benefits from the public goods
produced by Congress. Otherwise, each state would withhold its contribution. A quick look at requisition payments made during the confederation shows that states behaved in a manner that was inconsistent with
that model. More states contributed to the national treasury than predicted by the theory of pure public goods. If we presume that states faced
strong incentives to withhold their contributions, then some additional
factor must explain why the states contributed. I suggest that private
goods, produced both consciously and unconsciously by Congress, gave
the states the incentive to contribute.

This chapter evaluates the private benefits hypothesis by testing two
relationships: (1) the relationship between state contributions and the
proximity of the Continental army, and (2) the relationship between state
contributions and the amount of public debt held by citizens within each
state. Both sets of data include direct measures of private benefits and
both suggest that the states were more likely to fill their quotas when
they received private benefits than when they did not. These results

---

[1] Joseph Jones to Pendleton, Wythe, and Jefferson in James Madison to Thomas Jefferson, April 16, 1781, Smith, ed., *Letters of Delegates*, 17: 158–159, n. 1.

explain a large portion of state contributions made during the confederation and corroborate the joint products argument.

AN EMPIRICAL EVALUATION

Fortunately, the goods produced by each state's contribution can be easily identified and were well known at the time. Although Congress engaged in foreign treaties, settled state disputes, and managed the postal service, the bulk of its monies were spent on two items: national defense and debt maintenance. As pointed out in the first chapter, Congress spent almost all of its monies on the Continental army from 1775 to 1781, then redirected its energies toward the debt between 1784 and 1789. States must have known that Congress would apply their contributions toward the Continental army during the war and toward reduction of the debt after the war, giving them a fairly clear idea of what benefits they should expect. Circulars from the committee of correspondence, Schedules of Receipts, and personal correspondences kept the states well informed of the contributions made by other states as well.[2]

The private benefits hypothesis can be evaluated systematically by comparing state compliance to the amount of private benefits received by each state. States that received more private benefits from the national government should contribute a greater percentage of their requisitions than states that received less. The general format of the test uses the following equation:

$$\text{COMPLIANCE} = \alpha + \beta \,(\text{PRIVATE BENEFITS}) + \in$$

where COMPLIANCE is the amount contributed by a state divided by the amount requested from it, α and β are unknown coefficients, PRIVATE BENEFITS is a measure of the excludable and rival benefits received by a state, and $\in$ is an error term.

The private benefits hypothesis can be tested by applying a one-sided t-test on the private benefits parameter, β. The t-test corresponds to the following null and alternative hypotheses:

H_0: $\beta \leq 0$ evidence against the private benefits hypothesis
H_1: $\beta > 0$ evidence in favor of the private benefits hypothesis

If private benefits do not affect state contributions or the effect is negative, the private benefits hypothesis would be rejected. If state

---

[2] When Congress requisitioned the states for money, it sent a budget of annual expenditures to the states along with documents indicating how much each state paid. After these documents were sent to the states, delegates repeatedly informed state officials about national expenses and policy in their personal correspondences. Such sharing of information kept state legislators well informed about how Congress spent their money. It also helps to justify the complete information model assumed here.

contributions increase with private benefits, the private benefits hypothesis would be corroborated. Since the theory we wish to evaluate is consistent with the alternative hypothesis, the reader should be cautioned about the possibility of a false positive. Rejecting the null hypothesis should not be interpreted as confirming the alternative hypothesis. Instead, we should merely claim that states contributed "as if" they responded to private benefits.

The advantage of using compliance figures rather than paid figures on the left-hand side of the equation is that it normalizes the contributions of each state by the state's ability to contribute. Each state's quota, the denominator of the dependent variable, is based on congressional estimates of white population. For requisitions in men, this figure was readjusted according to the number of loyalists, casualties, and economic conditions within each state, making the measure closely reflect the number of men available for contribution to the Continental army and the ability to contribute.[3]

For requisitions in money, the denominator again accounts for differences in ability to contribute. Monetary requisitions were based on congressional estimates of white population after the war, but the apportionment was fixed in 1783 and not adjusted to reflect changes in ability to pay after that time. State revenues, gross domestic product, or aggregate state wealth would provide a better measure of a state's ability to pay; but without such figures, white population acts as a reasonable indicator of ability to pay. Presumably, larger, more populous states were more capable of fulfilling their quotas than smaller ones. These states would have larger denominators in the dependent variable.[4]

Since the major goods produced by Congress, national defense and debt reduction, were produced during separate periods of the confederation, the private benefits hypothesis is evaluated during both periods

---

[3] The correlation between state quotas and white population figures recorded by the Census Bureau was .872, suggesting that quotas are a good approximation of each state's white population. The relationship should be of little surprise since population figures gathered by the Census Bureau were based partially on congressional apportionment of requisitions (*Historical Statistics*, series A 195–209, 1: 24–37; Greene and Harrington, *American Population*). For those who object to the interpretation of ability to pay in the dependent variable, I ran all of the regressions reported in this chapter using white population figures as an additional independent variable. This had little or no effect on the relationship between the dependent and explanatory variables, further corroborating the private benefits hypothesis.

[4] Of course, black and indigenous populations would help a state fulfill its quotas as well. But since white population is correlated with total population at .902, states with larger white populations were also more populous and more capable of fulfilling their quotas. In other words, ignoring nonwhite populations should not bias the results (table Z 1–19 in United States, Bureau of the Census, *Historical Statistics of the United States*, 1168).

separately. Poor record keeping and fires in the Treasury building destroyed any hope of gathering data on monetary requisitions prior to 1781. After 1783, Congress made almost no requisitions for men. This makes it virtually impossible to test the relationship in money during the war or to test the relationship in men after the war. As a result, the private benefits hypothesis is tested using requisitions for men from 1777 to 1783 and requisitions for money from 1784 to 1789. These results should give us a good idea of the overall effect of private benefits on state contributions.

State Contributions and the Distance of the Continental Army, 1777–1782

The relationship between compliance in men and private benefits from the Continental army is tested using two measures of state compliance and two measures of private benefits in the same empirical model. Combining these measures creates four regressions that look like the first version:

$$COMPREG_{it} = \alpha + \beta_1(DISTCAP_{it}) + \beta_2(THREAT_t) + \epsilon_{it},$$

where subscript i denotes the ith state ($i = 1, \ldots, 13$, from north to south), subscript t denotes the year ($t = 1777, \ldots, 1782$), $COMPREG_{it}$ is the number of regulars contributed by a state in a given year divided by the total number of men requested from that state in that year, $DISTCAP_{it}$ is the average weighted distance between each regiment in the Continental army and a state's capital (the measure of private benefits), $THREAT_t$ is the total number of British troops in North America each year, and ϵ_{it} is a disturbance term such that $\epsilon_{it} \sim IID(0, \sigma^2)$.

The most notable difference between this equation and the one stated in the previous section is the addition of $THREAT_t$ on the right-hand side. $THREAT_t$ measures public benefits. It is included in the troop regressions to more fully test the joint products hypothesis. It is not included in the monetary case because monetary regressions do not vary by year. $THREAT_t$ indicates the amount of damage that the British can inflict on the union as a whole. It varies only by year (not by region) to capture the nonexcludable benefits of defending the confederation against the British – such as expelling British forces. Presumably, the nonexcludable benefits from national defense are greater when British threats to the nation are greater. If the theory of joint products accurately describes state behavior, there should be no relationship between a state's compliance and $THREAT_t$. In other words, state contributions should not respond to public benefits; they should respond only to private benefits. To test the effect of $THREAT_t$, I assume a null hypothesis of $\beta_2 = 0$ and conduct a two-sided t-test on the null hypothesis. An insignificant relationship is consistent with the theory of joint products. A significant relationship which is positive or negative refutes the theory.

THREAT$_t$ was measured by the British army's strength reports listed in Katcher, *British Provincial and German Army Units*, Appendix D. These figures include all effective officers and other ranks in the British regular, provincial, and German army units in North America, based on Lord North's return books. They represent the total number of soldiers fielded by the British and provide a nice measure of the nonexcludable benefits from national defense each year.

Although the war lasted from 1775 to 1783, Lord North's return books did not include reports for the final year of the war. In addition, Congress began its annual troop requisitions in 1777. Without quotas from the first two years of the war nor British strength reports for the final year, the analysis was restricted to the years 1777 to 1782.[5]

The data for men requested and supplied in the left-hand-side variable were obtained from Report of the Secretary at War, May 10, 1790, *Statement of the Receipts*. This report contains separate listings for regular soldiers and militia attached to the Continental army. To take full advantage of this information, two data sets were created. The first data set counts regulars as a state's contribution to the confederation's defense, with the understanding that militia attached to the army were not part of the army's permanent force and should not be counted as part of a state's compliance with requisitions. Compliance in this data set is captured by the variable COMPREG$_{it}$. The second data set includes regulars and militia in Continental pay, with the understanding that every soldier sent to the Continental army was part of a state's contribution. Compliance in the second data set is measured by the variable COMPIPAY$_{it}$. Data based on regulars alone, the first data set, is presented in Table 5.1.[6]

Private benefits are measured by the average distance of each Continental regiment from a state. Presumably, Continental divisions that were closer to a state were more capable of providing private benefits than divisions farther away. Regiments closer to a state were more capable of

[5] Testing the relationship between state compliance and private benefits without the THREAT$_t$ variable produced similar results – with and without 1783 figures.

[6] The number of men requested and supplied from Georgia in 1777 and 1778 were excluded from both data sets. Georgia was authorized to raise two regiments of infantry and two companies of artillery (fifty men each) in Virginia, North Carolina, and South Carolina during those years. Since it is not clear whether these men were included in Georgia's quota, and Georgia's 1777 and 1778 returns almost certainly contained troops raised in other states, both observations were excluded from the analysis.

Table 5.1. State Compliance with Requisitions for Soldiers, 1777–1783

State	Number of soldiers supplied[a]	Quota	Compliance (paid/quota, %)
New Hampshire	6,653	10,194	65
Massachusetts	33,008	52,698	63
Rhode Island	3,917	5,698	69
Connecticut	21,142	28,336	75
New York	12,077	15,734	77
New Jersey	7,533	11,396	66
Pennsylvania	19,689	40,416	49
Delaware	1,778	3,974	45
Maryland	13,275	26,608	50
Virginia	23,503	48,522	48
North Carolina	6,129	23,994	26
South Carolina	4,348	16,932	26
Georgia	2,328	4,174	56
Total	155,380	288,676	54

Source: Henry Knox, "Report of the Secretary of War," May 10, 1790, *Statement of the Receipts.*
Note: Soldiers supplied include the number of regulars supplied by each state from 1777 to 1783, excluding the number supplied from Georgia in 1777 and 1788. See footnote 6 for why Georgia's contributions were excluded those years.

warding off local threats, trading with local citizens, and preventing the British from quartering in state homes than divisions farther away. Hence the private benefits received by a state are measured inversely proportional to the state's distance from the Continental army. The closer the Continental army was to a state, the more private benefits a state would receive.[7]

Calculating the distance between the Continental army and each state requires knowing the location of the army and the distance between the

---

[7] The location of British troops would be a less appropriate measure of private benefits because private benefits must come from contributing to the Continental army and because the British were in areas that the Continentals were not. Presumably, the bulk of the Continental army was close to the British throughout the war, making it a good indicator of local British threats. The British, however, were not always close to the Continentals. States frequently fought the enemy without the aid of Continental forces, and when they did, the location of the British would not indicate the private benefits a state would receive from contributing to the Continental force. The Continentals had to be close in order to bestow private benefits, suggesting that the location of the Continentals, not the British, is the appropriate measure. Using British troop movements is further limited by the fact that the British maintained no strength reports at the regimental level, despite continued requests from their generals.

army's location and each state. Locations came from Washington's strength reports in Lesser, *Sinews of Independence*. These records list the location of troops at the regimental level for most months during every year of the war. Distances were measured in two ways, using Cappon, *Atlas of Early American History*. DISTCAP$_{it}$ was calculated as the annual, average weighted distance between each regiment in the Continental army and a state's capital. DISTBOR$_{it}$ was calculated as the annual, average weighted distance between each regiment in the Continental army and a state's closest border. Both measures were weighted by the relative size of each regiment and the number of months a regiment remained in a given location.[8] Since the army was in more than one state during every month of the analysis and both measures were based on averages, neither measure could contain a zero value. These measures indicate the relative distance between the army and each state, inversely proportional to each state's private benefits. Distances were reported in miles.

Applying ordinary least squares (OLS) to the data with compliance in regulars and distance from capitals produces a slope coefficient of −.001 for DISTCAP$_{it}$, significant at the .01 level (see Fig. 5.1a and Table 5.2).[9] The negative value of the parameter reflects the theorized relationship between private benefits and the distance of the Continental army. States increased their compliance by a little more than 10 percent for every 100 miles of decreased distance between the army and a state. States were very responsive to the location of the Continental army and very responsive to the British threats implied by its location. States responded to private benefits as predicted.

States responded to the measure of public benefits as predicted as well. The coefficient for THREAT$_t$ was .000003, which was insignificant at the .05 level (see Fig. 5.1b and Table 5.2). Though the slope is slightly positive, there is no reason to reject the null hypothesis that the actual

---

[8] With the exception of the Southern army, no attempt was made to locate regiments missing from reports. For example, a regiment might be stationed at West Point in January and in Danbury in March, but no attempt was made to extrapolate the regiment's location for February. Lesser notes that returns from the Southern Department were incomplete. In these cases, the size and location of divisions were inferred from southern engagements (Morrill, *Southern Campaigns*; Peckham, *The Toll of Independence*). This provided a more complete picture of the Southern army's strength and location, which only weakened the results. Capitals used in the distance measure from north to south were Portsmouth, Boston, Newport, an average of New Haven and Hartford (since Connecticut periodically switched capitals between the two locations), New York, Burlington, Philadelphia, Dover, Annapolis, Williamsburg, New Bern, Charleston, and Savannah.

[9] A Tobit estimate with the dependent variable censored at zero produced similar parameter estimates and similar standard errors in all four versions of the model.

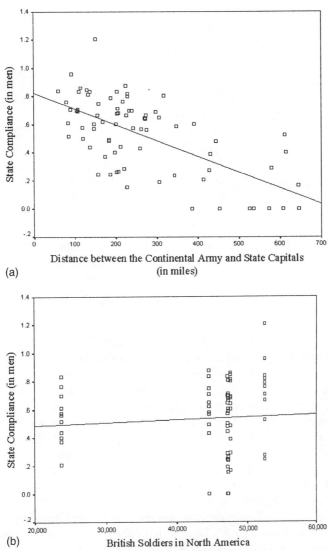

(a)

(b)

Figure 5.1. Compliance (in regular soldiers) and the distance of the Continental Army (*a*) and number of British soldiers (*b*), 1777–1782. *Sources*: Quotas and men supplied are drawn from Henry Knox, "Report of the Secretary at War," May 10, 1790, *Statement of the Receipts*; troop locations are compiled from Lesser, *Sinews of Independence*; distances are measured from Cappon, *Atlas of Early American History*; Boatner, *Landmarks*, and Morrill, *Southern Campaigns*, provided support.

Table 5.2. Regressions of State Contributions and the Distance of the
Continental Army

Model	$COMPREG_{it} = .684 - .0011(DISTCAP_{it}) + .000003(THREAT_t) + \varepsilon_{1it}$
t-values	5.63 −7.35 1.23
$R^2 = .428$	
$N = 76$	
Model	$COMPREG_{it} = .618 - .0013(DISTBOR_{it}) + .000003(THREAT_t) + \varepsilon_{2it}$
t-values	5.03 −6.88 1.32
$R^2 = .396$	
$N = 76$	
Model	$COMPIPAY_{it} = .667 - .0014(DISTCAP_{it}) + .000007(THREAT_t) + \varepsilon_{3it}$
t-values	2.74 −4.38 1.40
$R^2 = .291$	
$N = 76$	
Model	$COMPIPAY_{it} = .589 - .0015(DISTBOR_{it}) + .000007(THREAT_t) + \varepsilon_{4it}$
t-values	2.43 −4.17 1.44
$R^2 = .203$	
$N = 76$	

relationship is zero. The slight and insignificant slope is probably due to random variation, not an underlying relationship between the two variables. In other words, state contributions did not change in response to the total number of soldiers fielded by the British. State compliance was affected by local threats, as captured by $DISTCAP_{it}$, not confederation-wide threats as captured by $THREAT_t$. Substituting distance to a state's closest border for distance to a state's capital and including militia attached to the Continental army rather than regulars alone produced similar results (see Table 5.2). All four regressions indicate a relationship between state contributions and private benefits consistent with the private benefits hypothesis.

Contemporaries observed states responding to local threats as well. A delegate from Connecticut claimed that "the muster rolls would show that [Connecticut] had more troops in the field than Virginia. We strained every nerve to raise them. . . . If she has proved delinquent through inability only, it is not more than others have been, without the same excuse."[10] Connecticut contributed large portions of its levies during the war, but a quick glance at Table 5.1 suggests that Massachusetts and New York supplied large portions of their quotas as well. Considering

[10] Oliver Ellsworth, Yates' Notes on Debates, June 30, 1787, Farrand, *Records of the Federal Convention*, 1: 497–498.

that one third of the American casualties were taken in the state of New York and the largest armies were maintained northeast of Pennsylvania, there is good reason to believe that states closer to the action gained more private benefits from contributing to the army than states farther away. They certainly contributed more men to the cause.

Similar relationships may have existed at the local level. In a letter to Colonel Atlee, Joseph Reed, the President of Pennsylvania, wrote, "The Treasurer informs us that only Three Townships have paid off their Fifteen Million Taxes, while the Counties here which have been invaded, distressed & plundered, have paid off their Fifteen Million, their Forty Five, and Three of their Monthly Taxes. Is not this melancholy?" Melancholy indeed: Not only were the counties of Pennsylvania raising taxes in proportion to the local threat of the enemy, but the counties that were less capable of paying their taxes were contributing more than counties that were more capable of paying. The observation was directly the opposite of what most Anti-Federalists were claiming. Counties that were less capable but under more distress were contributing more than counties with greater resources. Though similar observations were made in Virginia, both observations were probably isolated cases. States and counties contributed more when their local interests were stake, but their ability to contribute undoubtedly limited their contributions.[11]

State Contributions and the Domestic Debt, 1784–1789

The relationship between state compliance in money and private benefits from debt reduction can also be tested using two different versions of a model that differs from that of troops. Each version contains different dependent and independent variables, creating two regressions that are treated separately. The first model is written

$$\text{COMPMONEY}_t = \beta(\text{DEBT}_i) + u_i,$$

where COMPMONEY_i is the money contributed by state i from July 1, 1784, to March 1, 1789, divided by the money requested during the same period; δ is an unknown parameter; DEBT_i is the value of national debt held within each state from roughly 1781 to 1791 in millions of dollars; and u_i is a disturbance term such that $u_i \sim \text{IIN}(0, \sigma^2)$. The constant term

---

[11] David Ross, a wealthy Virginian, wrote, "I observe that the County of Gloucester is delinquent for the princip'l part of the taxes from the year 1782 to this time, while many counties not possessing one-tenth of their wealth, nor anything like their natural advantages, have punctually paid up their taxes." (Reed quoted in William Henry to President Reed, July 3, 1780, *Pennsylvania Archives*, 8 (series 1): 380; David Ross to Governor Randolph, January 23, 1787, *Calendar of Virginia State Papers*, 4: 230–231).

was omitted from the equation for three reasons: (1) the theory implies that states without private benefits would not contribute; (2) thirteen observations makes each degree of freedom crucial; and (3) the constant term was insignificant when it was included in the analysis (both versions).

Although the Treasury Board kept quality records of monetary requisition payments after 1782, they did not know how much debt was owed to Continental soldiers or to citizens for conscripted wares until after the confederation had ended. The treasury board aggregated debt figures across time periods; hence I aggregated paid and requested figures across time to make them comparable. This caused the t subscript to be dropped from the equation and limited the analysis to thirteen observations. Without annual variation, a measure of public benefits could not be employed. Instead, the relationship between state compliance and private benefits was tested across states by itself.

Data on the amount of money requested and paid after the war come from the *Statement of the Accounts*. These statements record quarterly receipts from the thirteen states from June 1782 to March 1789, not including special requisitions. Special requisitions were kept in separate ledgers and often served separate purposes. Since Congress refinanced its outstanding requisitions in June 1784 and focused its budget on debt payments around that time, July 1, 1784, was used as a natural starting point for requisitions in money.

The private benefits for each state after the war were measured by the total value of debts held within each state during the postwar confederation. Congress spent 58 percent of its budget on the reduction of domestic debts and 88 percent of its budget on debts in general during this period.[12] Presumably, states with larger debt holdings would receive more excludable benefits from reducing the debt than states with fewer debt holdings. The more debt held within a state, the more private benefits a state would receive from reducing domestic debts.

Data on the debt held within each state were taken from Hamilton's report in the *American State Papers*.[13] This report contains separate figures for loan office certificates (public bonds), Pierce's certificates (debts owed to Continental soldiers), and quartermaster, commissary, hospital, clothing, and marine certificates (notes issued like I.O.U.s to citizens for conscripted belongings). They also contain debts not attributable to a particular state, such as debts to Hazen's Regiment, foreign

---

[12] The first figure is the average annual expenditure budgeted for *domestic* debts from 1784 to 1789 (*JCC*, 26: 186–187; 29: 765–766; 31: 462; 33: 578–579; 34: 433–436). The second was previously cited.

[13] *American State Papers*, 1 (finance): 239.

Table 5.3. State Compliance with Requisitions for Money, 1784–1789

State	Amount paid ($)	Compliance (paid/quota, %)	Amount of debt held ($)	Debt held per white population
New Hampshire	107,305	18	706,348	8.09
Massachusetts	995,741	42	5,245,030	16.79
Rhode Island	18,571	5	992,457	19.79
Connecticut	196,473	14	2,482,970	12.36
New York	706,655	64	3,080,050	14.44
New Jersey	35,486	4	2,121,930	16.43
Pennsylvania	1,086,190	51	6,368,130	19.93
Delaware	103,249	46	278,413	6.57
Maryland	348,109	22	1,351,730	8.20
Virginia	962,522	38	1,614,280	5.09
North Carolina	45,226	4	508,263	2.84
South Carolina	71,871	8	451,155	5.40
Georgia	0.00	0	215,395	6.11
Total	4,677,398	30	25,416,151	10.93[a]

Sources: Population figures come from "Estimated Population of American Colonies: 1610 to 1780," Series Z 1–19, *Historical Statistics*, 2: 1168. Requisition payments were found in *Statement of the Accounts*, RG 39, M-1014, roll 23, June 1, 1784, to March 1, 1789. Quotas and domestic debt come from *American State Papers*, 1 (finance): 57 and 239, respectively.
[a] Debt held per white population in the bottom row is the average debt held per state.
Note: Data for money requested and supplied by each state are from June 1, 1784, to March 1, 1789 – the period when Congress focused its expenditures on the national debt.

officers, and the Hospital Department. Debts that could not be associated with a particular state, such as these, were excluded from the analysis.[14] The dollar value of all other debts was then combined. The distribution of the domestic debt indicated the relative amount each state privately benefited from the reduction of the debt, making it a good indicator of the private benefits of paying requisitions after the war. Figures were reported in millions of dollars.

Table 5.3 lists the amount each state paid, its compliance with requisitions, and domestic debt held per white population from 1784 to 1789. If we assume that the error term is drawn from a normal distribution,

[14] Also excluded was information about the transfer of debts to holders outside of a state as well as the number of loan office certificates canceled. Neither of these factors is of major concern, since less than one twenty-fifth of the domestic debt was transferred prior to 1789 and few loan office certificates were canceled before the end of the confederation.

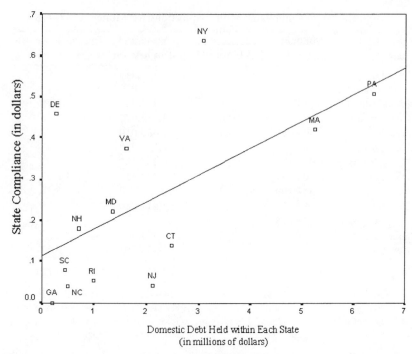

Figure 5.2. Monetary compliance and the public debt, 1782–1789. *Sources*: See Table 5.3.

we can test the relationship between state compliance and debt owner-ship using ordinary least squares.

Applying OLS to the model and running a one-tailed *t*-test produces a parameter estimate of $\hat{\beta} = .096$, significant at the .01 level (see Fig. 5.2 and Table 5.4). The positive value of the parameter reflects the direct relationship between private benefits and the amount of debt held within each state. The significance of the relationship provides further evidence in favor of the private benefits hypothesis. State legislators increased their compliance an average of 9.6 percent for every million dollars of addi-tional debt held within their states. Considering that half the states held more than one million dollars of the debt, the effect of debt ownership on state compliance appears strong.[15]

[15] To control for the percentage of creditors (or creditor sympathizers) within each state legislature, I added the percentage of wealthy legislators and the percentage of legisla-tors living within a city to a twenty-six–observation model of compliance on BOND holdings. Bond holdings were based on the value of loan office certificates in each state in 1783 and 1790. When controls for wealthy legislators and urban dwellers were

Table 5.4. Regressions of State Contributions and the
Public Debt

Model	$COMPMONEY_i = .096 \ (DEBT_i) + u_{1i}$
t-value	4.95
$R^2 = .671$	
$N = 13$	
Model	$COMPSPEC_i = .277 \ (BONDS_i) + u_{2i}$
t-value	4.25
$R^2 = .601$	
$N = 13$	

The second version of the debt model (shown at the bottom of Table 5.4) focuses on the special requisition of September 10, 1782. The special requisition requested funds for the explicit purpose of paying the interest due on the loan office debt (public bonds). Congress applied the money received from the special requisition to pay the interest on public bonds in proportion to the receipts from each state. It paid bond holders in non-contributing states only after loan office debts in the contributing state were eliminated. In this requisition, a state's requisition payment went to its bond holders. The procedure assured that each dollar received from a state went directly to the state's citizens and tied the excludable benefits of debt reduction to the act of paying. This made the special requisition of 1782 a particularly good requisition for testing the private benefits hypothesis. State contributions translated into private benefits directly and state legislators knew it. Not surprisingly, their response to the special requisition is again consistent with the private benefits hypothesis.

The dependent variable, $COMPSPEC_i$, is the money contributed by state i to the special requisition of September 10, 1782, divided by the amount requested from the state in that requisition. $BONDS_i$ is the value of the loan office certificates held within each state in 1783, scaled in millions of specie dollars.[16]

included, the significance and standardized coefficient of the bonds variable strengthened. In other words, controlling for the residential and economic composition of each state legislature did not have an adverse effect on the relationship between requisition payments and debt ownership. The controls added further support for the private benefits hypothesis (see Main, *Political Parties*, for state legislative variables, and "An Estimate of the Loan Office Debt," March 3, 1783, PCC, M247, r149, i137, 2: 205, for the additional bond figures).

[16] The amount requested and supplied to the special requisition of September 10, 1782, came from *JCC*, 23: 564, and *Statement of the Accounts*. The value of loan office certificates held within each state came from "An Estimate of the Loan Office Debt," cited in the previous note.

Applying OLS and running a one-tailed t-test produces a parameter estimate of $\hat{\delta} = .277$, significant at the .01 level (see the bottom of Table 5.4).[17] The positive value of the parameter reflects the direct relationship between private benefits and the amount of debt held within each state. The significance of the parameter corroborates the private benefits hypothesis. For every million dollars of loan office certificates held within a state, state compliance increased 28 percent. Considering that holdings ranged from $7,000 to roughly $4 million, this again suggests a strong positive relationship between compliance and debt held.

Table 5.3 suggests that the average person in the North held three times as much federal debt as the average person in the South and had a greater interest in seeing his or her state pay off debts than did southerners. Citizens north of Delaware held 76 percent of the domestic debt per capita and paid 44 percent more of their quotas than southern states. Their diligence was not due to greater patriotism. Instead, it was due to the greater private benefits that the north could obtain from paying requisitions. Citizens North of Delaware gained more excludable benefits from their requisition payments. It is not at all surprising that they paid a higher percentage of their requisitions as well.

The regressions of state compliance on the proximity of the Continental army and state compliance on the ownership of the domestic debt corroborate the private benefits hypothesis. States that stood to gain from protecting their borders or from paying their citizens contributed more of their resources than those that stood to gain less. They did not respond to public benefits as indicated by the threat of the British. Both relationships are consistent with the historical narrative and with the empirical analysis. In all, private benefits mattered, and they explained a large part of state contributions made during the confederation.

MANIPULATING PRIVATE BENEFITS

The relationship between state compliance and private benefits was not abstract. Contemporaries understood these relationships and tried to use them to make the system of requisitions work. Robert Morris attempted to tease money out of the states by withholding payment on the debt until the states complied, and members of Congress created the system of indents to take advantage of the same incentives. Indents encouraged

---

[17] The data contained one outlier that caused nonnormality in the distribution of errors. Removing the outlier only strengthened the relationship ($\beta = .274$, t-value = 8.20, and $R^2 = .859$). This was the payment from Delaware. Since there was no theoretical justification for removing Delaware from the study, the weaker of the two results was reported.

compliance by relating the restitution of state creditors with a state's payment. Both policies, however, achieved limited success.

As the war was coming to a close, Robert Morris began the arduous task of reducing the confederation's foreign and domestic debt. To increase compliance with requisitions, Morris withheld payments due on loan office certificates until states complied with their requisitions. He figured that withholding payments would bring creditors on his side and encourage them to lobby their legislatures to pay their requisitions. When creditors demanded the interest due to them, Morris wrote, "I must candidly declare to every public Creditor that while the Wealth of the People is in the Hands of the several state Legislatures, Redress must come from them and from them only."[18] Morris hoped that creditors would lobby their legislatures for stricter taxes and get them to pay their requisitions, but his plan backfired. Public creditors pushed the states to assume federal loan office certificates and demanded that states pay them directly. Many state legislatures easily succumbed to the pressure and assumed federal debts held by their citizens. After all, it was a cheaper and more effective way of paying creditors than using the system of requisitions.

A portion of state payments went to foreign governments, Canadian regiments, and debts owed to other states. Considering that part of each state's requisition payment would be applied to these debts, it is hard to see how private benefits could encourage compliance with requisitions. It would be always cheaper for states to pay federal creditors directly than for them to pay creditors indirectly through the system of requisitions.

State legislators recognized this advantage and took advantage of it. Many states assumed federal debts owed to their veterans in the early 1780s and debts owed to bond holders shortly thereafter. This provided the same private benefits for a state as a requisition payment, without the risk of transferring wealth to other states. Though the practice violated the Articles of Confederation, direct payment of creditors was a cheaper and more effective way of paying constituents than the system of requisitions.

Morris recognized that debt assumption would undermine the confederation and sternly objected to the practice. He pointed out that direct

---

[18] To John Lloyd, Jr., September 18, 1781, Morris, *Papers*, 2: 294–295. Also see Alexander Hamilton to George Washington, March 17, 1783; and North Carolina Delegates to Alexander Martin, March 24, 1783, Smith, ed., *Letters of Delegates*, 20: 37–38 and 91–93, respectively. Pennsylvania adopted the 1786 funding law which assumed federal debts owed to Pennsylvanians because of the "imbecility of the present Confederation" (James Wilson's Speech in the Court House Yard, October 6, 1787, Jensen, ed., *Documentary History*, 2: 171).

payments legally violated the Articles of Confederation and refused to credit state accounts for direct payments. In his eyes, direct payments were "free gifts." The salaries of Continental soldiers must come from "one common Treasury [replenished] by the common Contributions of all according to established Principles."[19] If a state paid Congress, Congress would pay its creditors. Morris did not care for the system of requisitions but he realized it was the only source of confederation revenue. If states pooled their funds rather than pay debts directly, Morris might have enough money left over to reduce foreign obligations and to provide other nonexcludable goods. Morris's efforts were an earnest attempt to use moral commitments and social sanctioning to encourage state contributions. His terse words reminded states of their legal obligations to requisitions, and his publication of state accounts in local newspapers provided some embarrassment for noncontributing states. But moral obligations and social sanctions were weak incentives for government. In combination with private benefits they encouraged some payments, but they were unable to prevent state payments from heading into decline after the war had fully ended.

When Morris retired, the Treasury Board also tried to use excludable benefits to their advantage in establishing the system of indents. Indents reduced requirements in specie and allowed the states to pay their requisitions in a less valued medium. More important, indents paid powerful political constituents directly. State legislatures could use the system of indents to meet their legal obligations and pay their creditors without paying the creditors in other states. When states issued indents to their citizens and reaccepted them in taxes, they ensured that every dollar spent came back to local constituents and provided an excludable benefit for their state. States with a large number of creditors had an incentive to use the system of indents, and this explains a large portion of the requisition payments made after the war. Some 46 percent of the requisitions received between June 1784 and March 1789 were in indents.[20] States paid their indents because they wanted their creditors paid. The system made requisitions more desirable from a state's point of view and tempered the incentive to pay creditors directly.

---

[19] JCC, 23: 624–626. Also see to George Olney, June 24, 1782; to the Governor of Rhode Island, William Greene, June 26, 1782; to Daniel of St. Thomas Jenifer, March 12, 1782; and Circular to the Receivers of Continental taxes, October 5, 1782, Morris, *Papers*, 5: 472–473, 484; 4: 396–398; and 6: 497–498, respectively; as well as *JCC*, 23: 629–631.

[20] If we count the twelve quarters in which indents were actually received, March 1786 to March 1789, 61 percent of all requisitions were paid in indents (*Statement of the Accounts*).

But indents failed to induce full compliance as well because Congress required a portion of each state's payment in specie.[21] Congress's focus on excludable benefits was the right formula for preventing the union from complete collapse, but its restrictions on specific due dates and conditions on specie limited returns considerably. Indents tied requisition payments to the benefits of paying citizens. They bound the union together and helped the confederation receive part of the money it requested. But Congress could not tie local interests to nonexcludable aspects of the debt. Private benefits encouraged compliance, but they did not, and could not, provide all the money the confederation needed for its expenses.

CONCLUSION

Combined with inadequate institutions, the pure public goods model introduced in Chapter 3 predicted that few or no states would contribute to the national treasury. In actuality, however, states consistently paid more than the model predicts. This chapter suggests that states paid their requisitions when payments produced local benefits, and they withheld their requisitions when payments did not. Such behavior is consistent with states seeking out the private benefits associated with joint products.

In claiming this we should not conclude that private benefits explain all of state contributions. Surely other factors encouraged states to contribute as well. One of these might be civic duty. But without further analysis, we cannot determine which factors had an effect, nor whether such factors outperform the one offered here. Instead, we can only conclude that part of the reason state legislatures contributed to the confederation was to provide for the individual interests of their states. In the words of Hamilton, "The States near the seat of war, influenced by motives of self-preservation, made efforts to furnish their quotas, which even exceeded their abilities; while those at a distance from the danger were for the most part as remiss."[22]

The next chapter illustrates the argument in greater detail by focusing on a single case. In the special requisition to suppress Shays' Rebellion, the pattern of contribution does not reflect the distance measures developed here. The rebellion occurred in Massachusetts, but Virginia was the only state to comply. This might lead us to believe that the theory does not apply in this particular case. Surprisingly, however, states again contributed according to their private benefits. Virginia complied because

---

[21] Ferguson, *Power of the Purse*, 223–228.
[22] Federalist 22, Rossiter, ed., *Federalist Papers*, 145–146.

it wanted other states to support its efforts against the Indians, and states closer to the rebellion took independent actions of their own. Both were consistent with local interests. The remaining states free-rode on the requisition as predicted by the theory of public goods. After careful examination, this seemingly contradictory pattern of state contribution again supports the joint products argument.

6

Reacting to Rebellion

Few circumstances could give me more pleasure than to see these Governments answer the ends that were expected, but my doubts go far beyond my hopes. The confederal Government was always an object of division rather than anything else with me – its like a man's attempting to walk with both legs cut off – all our Executives are water mixed with water – wishy washy stuff.

– John F. Mercer[1]

In September 1786, Daniel Shays led an angry mob toward the state supreme court house in Springfield, Massachusetts.[2] Forced to pay off property debts accrued while serving in the Revolutionary War, these men attempted to stop court proceedings in Springfield and to suspend additional foreclosures on their homes. The insurgents succeeded in obstructing the court for days and created additional bedlam throughout western Massachusetts for several months. The insurrection climaxed on January 23, 1787, when Shays followed through with his threat to seize the national arsenal at Springfield. The assault was repelled by a small detachment stationed at the arsenal, but the rebellion was not quelled until state troops, financed by donations from private businessmen in the eleventh hour, confronted Shays in Petersham.[3]

---

[1] John Mercer to James Madison, March 28, 1786, Madison, *Papers*, 511–512.

[2] This chapter is based on Dougherty, "Collective Action under the Articles" and Cain and Dougherty, "Suppressing Shays' Rebellion: Collective Action and Constitutional Design under the Articles of Confederation," *Journal of Theoretical Politics*, 1999, 11(2): 233–260, with permission from Sage Publications. The argument presented here differs from both in one important respect. It applies a joint products model to the Shays' requisition rather than a pure public, step-goods game. The most accurate description of state reactions to Shays' Rebellion may be a combination of the two, but step-goods are an unnecessary complication for the present discussion of joint products.

[3] Szatmary, *Shays' Rebellion*; Middleton, *Revolt*.

The Continental Congress was informed of rebellious activity as early as August 1786. The Secretary at War, Henry Knox, initiated a national response to the rebellion in late September and explicitly requested federal troops.[4] Congress perceived Shays' Rebellion to be a threat of grave national concern. The committee assigned to the matter declared:

> [I]t appears to the committee that the aid of the federal government is necessary to stop the Progress of the insurgents . . . and that there is the greatest reason to believe that, unless speedy and effectual measures shall be taken to defeat their designs, they will possess themselves of the Arsenal at Springfield, subvert the government, and not only reduce that Commonwealth to a State of Anarchy and Confusion, but probably involve the United States in the Calamities of civil war.[5]

Congress quickly responded to Secretary Knox's request and agreed to raise 2,040 soldiers for the purpose of suppressing Shays' Rebellion. Under the Articles of Confederation, Congress could raise the army with approval from nine of the thirteen state delegations; however, all of the delegations present at the October session approved the resolution. Congress followed its unanimous agreement to raise an army with a requisition to fund it.

But despite a commonly held belief among local and national politicians that Shays' Rebellion posed a serious threat, and despite a unanimous agreement to put down the insurrection, Congress was unable to raise the money needed to suppress the insurrection. With the exception of Virginia, states which had unequivocally supported military action now failed to pay for the army their delegates demanded. With such a serious menace to the security of the United States and with Virginia so far from the action, why was Virginia the only state to pay its requisition?

This chapter examines state decisions to contribute to the suppression of Shays' Rebellion. Although state responses were characterized by strong incentives to free-ride, the pattern of state contributions was consistent with the joint products argument. States closer to the rebellion, such as Massachusetts and New York, waited to see whether other states would contribute to the federal force before they committed their resources. When it became clear that other states would not comply with the special requisition, these states raised their own militias to carry out independent offensive actions. Virginia, in contrast, wanted federal assistance with its military expedition against the Indians and complied with the Shays requisition to ensure that federal troops would be applied to

---

[4] To the President of Congress, September 28, October 1, 3, and 8, 1786, *JCC*, 31: 698–700, 739–740, 751–753, and 875, respectively. Despite the countless corrections from my colleagues, Knox was the Secretary *at* War, not the Secretary *of* War.

[5] *JCC*, 31: 895.

its own cause. The remaining states did not receive enough private benefits to contribute to the affair. They withheld their resources and free-rode, as the theory of joint products would predict.

SIGNIFICANCE OF THE SHAYS REQUISITION

The requisition to suppress Shays' Rebellion is a particularly interesting case because it contradicts the distance measure developed in the previous chapter. As the story is told, Virginia was the sole contributor to the federal requisition to suppress Shays' Rebellion. The New England states did not pay any money to the federal effort. This seems somewhat odd since Massachusetts, Connecticut, and New York were closer to the action than Virginia and should have gained more private benefits than any of the southern states. Virginia was too far away to worry that the Shaysites would wander across its borders, yet Virginia was the sole contributor to the federal requisition to suppress the rebellion. How can this pattern of contribution be reconciled with the private benefits hypothesis?

The answer is simple. Even though Virginia was the only state to raise *money* for the federal force, Massachusetts and Connecticut did attempt to raise *troops* for the federal force. This reflected a cheaper, partial contribution that was consistent with the distance measures of the previous chapter. More important, Massachusetts and New York raised, and funded, their own state militias after the federal requisition had failed. State militias allowed Massachusetts and New York to pursue the insurgents according to local interests, when it was clear that the union would not come to their aid.

Virginia contributed because it gained private benefits as well, though its benefits were not captured by its distance from the insurrection. Politicians in Virginia wanted federal troops to help them fight the Indians in Virginian territory. The Wabash and Shawnee Indians attacked settlers along the Ohio River in the summer of 1786, and several tribes made an offensive alliance against the United States in September. Though the traditional story of Shays' Rebellion describes Indian troubles as little more than an excuse to raise troops,[6] Virginians wanted their western frontier protected and had reason to believe that such troops might be sent to Virginia after the troops completed their duties in Massachusetts. They also wanted to avoid transferring federal troops from the Indian frontier to Massachusetts. No other state gained private benefits from

---

[6] Szatmary, *Shays' Rebellion*; Freer, *Shays' Rebellion*; Patterson, "Nationalist Reaction to Shays"; and Warren, "The Confederation" all argue that the forces were raised for use in Massachusetts and neglect the possibility that they would be used against the Indians as well.

protecting the settlers in the Ohio Valley as Virginia did, and no other state had this reason to contribute to the federal army. States such as Massachusetts wanted to see the rebellion suppressed but they disliked the idea of a standing army. Virginia, on the other hand, wanted a standing army to protect Virginian settlers in the Ohio Valley. It had no *excludable* interests in suppressing the rebellion; it gained excludable benefits only from the raising of a federal force.

The point should not be misunderstood. All states gained public, nonexcludable benefits from the suppression of Shays' Rebellion. Shays threatened to seize a federal arsenal and to disrupt the courts in nearby states. Avoiding these dangers was a public good. But only Virginia and the New England states received the private, excludable benefits needed to encourage contributions. Virginia contributed to the federal force because the federal force served Virginia's private interests in the Ohio valley. Massachusetts and New York raised their own forces to prevent the rebellion from disrupting their courts. Massachusetts and New York chose to raise state militias to suppress the rebellion because state militias better served their private interests than a poorly funded federal force. The other states free-rode on the endeavor because they received only nonexcludable benefits from suppressing the rebellion and had no reason to contribute when Massachusetts was successfully engaged.

Suppressing Shays' Rebellion produced at least two public benefits. First, members of Congress and local leaders were legitimately concerned that the insurgents would seize the federal arsenal at Springfield. The depot contained roughly 450 tons of military stores, including 700 small arms, 1,300 barrels of powder, a large quantity of shot and shell, and a small supply of rations.[7] It also maintained a foundry for the production of brass cannon and a solid magazine. Losing this facility would have delivered a serious blow to the union.

Second, there were fears that rebels might overthrow the governments of Massachusetts and other nearby states. Agrarian unrest stirred periodically throughout the states. With a general outcry for tax relief, the Massachusetts uprising threatened to gain momentum and to spill over into New Hampshire, New York, Rhode Island, and Connecticut.[8]

---

[7] Henry Knox, Report to Congress, *JCC*, 31: 675–676.

[8] On September 20, 1786, some 200 farmers closed the statehouse in New Hampshire, detaining the governor and assembly for five hours. Likewise, plans were made to disrupt the New Haven court in Connecticut in late October, while farmers disrupted proceedings at the Windsor County courthouse in Vermont (part of New York at the time). Finally, a member of Virginia's house of delegates noted similar commotions in the Carolinas. Although these disruptions were not caused by Shaysites, they were related to the same plight. The insurrection in Massachusetts could have gained momentum and potentially caused a civil war (Szatmary, *Shays' Rebellion*, 59; From John Dawson, April 15, 1787, Madison, *Papers*, 9: 381).

Rumors of British involvement with the Shaysites made the threat even more severe. Newspaper accounts blamed the unrest on British sympathizers, and a delegate from Virginia informed his governor that "a direct offer has been made to the [insurgents] of the protection and Government of Great Britain."[9] Although rumors of British involvement remained unconfirmed, contemporaries found the idea plausible because open rebellion would have provided the perfect opportunity for Great Britain to regain its territory in North America.

Recognizing the severity of the threat, Congress voted to raise the funds needed to suppress the rebellion. The consensus among members attending Congress on October 20 and 21, 1786, indicated that sending a federal army to western Massachusetts was in the interest of the states.[10] The states wanted the rebellion suppressed, but only one state paid its share of the federal effort. This explicitly marked the direct conflict between common concerns and state incentives that characterized the confederation. Shays' Rebellion showed both the demand to take action and the subsequent lethargy of the states. Most states withheld their resources despite their common interests, while others contributed only to serve their independent interests. The special requisition of 1786 demonstrated both the free-riding behavior associated with public benefits and the pattern of contributions associated with private benefits.

TWO UNRESTS

The Indians

The traditional story of Shays' Rebellion describes hostilities with the Indians as little more than a cloak for true purpose of raising an army to suppress Shays' Rebellion. Although hostilities with the Indians served as the perfect foil, fighting on the frontier was more than a useful fiction. During the summer of 1786 small skirmishes had broken out between Kentucky settlers and the Wabash Indians, primarily in the vicinity of Vincennes. Most of these attacks were precipitated by settlers encroaching upon Indian territory, but aggressive movements were taken by both sides. British agents in Detroit were assisting Indians with munitions and

---

[9] For newspaper reports, see the *Hampshire Gazette*, September 20 and October 18, 1786. For the letter to the Virginia governor, see Edward Carrington to Governor Edmund Randolph, December 8, 1786, Virginia, *Calendar of State Papers*, 4: 197. The matter was also mentioned by Massachusetts representative Elbridge Gerry and others (to Rufus King, November 29, 1786, King, *Life and Correspondence*, 1: 197).

[10] Rufus King agreed with this point in his address before the Massachusetts House of Representatives, October 11, 1786, Burnett, ed., *Letters of Members*, 8: 478–481. However, it should be noted that New Hampshire, Delaware, and North Carolina were not represented during the vote (*JCC*, 31: 891).

encouraging them to attack American settlers. Later in the summer, several hundred Shawnee warriors assembled near the confluence of the Miami and the Ohio rivers to carry out a concerted action. They sent out small raiding parties on the settlements south of the Ohio River and took several prisoners. When the state militia prepared to respond, the Shawnee made an offensive alliance with several other tribes at Lower Sandusky, further aggravating the threat.[11]

Prior to 1784, Virginia laid claim to the entire Ohio valley from the state's current border west to the Mississippi and Illinois rivers and north to the Great Lakes. Virginia's territory included the area under attack and the modern-day states of West Virginia, Kentucky, Ohio, Indiana, Michigan, and most of Illinois and Wisconsin. Virginians controlled most of the American garrisons in the region during the Revolutionary War, and they felt responsible to its inhabitants. In 1784, the state ceded the land northwest of the Ohio to the union and removed its garrisons. But it still claimed the entire Kentucky district south of the Ohio River as part of its land. Most of the attacks occurred on Virginia settlements along the Ohio River. Since Congress could not afford a standing army to protect the northwest region, the area north of the Ohio was controlled solely by Indians and the menacing forts of the British along the Great Lakes. The forts were supposed to be surrendered to the confederation according to the Anglo-American peace treaty, but the British refused to surrender them over disputes about American debts. Without a military presence, the Indians moved south across the Ohio to attack various settlements while the settlers retaliated north across the Ohio to attack the Indians.

On May 16, 1786, Governor Patrick Henry informed the President of Congress of the attacks and asked for a review of the entire Indian department. He warned that "the necessity of the Case will enforce the people, for the purpose of self-preservation, to go against the offending Towns." In a separate correspondence he further instructed his delegates to formally request federal troops for the purpose of attacking the Indians. He thought that stationing the militia in or around the settlements would be ineffective and stressed that "experience clearly proves that attacking their towns is the only mode of effectual defence against hostile Indians." Offensive action would require movements into federal

---

[11] Helderman, "The Northwest Expedition"; Warren, "The Confederation." For some firsthand accounts, see Samuel McDowell to Governor Henry, April 18, 1786, *PCC*, M247, r. 69, i. 56, 271–272; Levi Todd to Patrick Henry, July 12, 1786, Virginia, *Calendar of State Papers*, 4: 155; John May to Patrick Henry, July 14, 1786, Henry, *Correspondence*, 3: 369–370; Joseph Martin to Patrick Henry, August 14, 1786, ibid., 3: 372–373; and Richard Butler and Samuel Parsons to the President of Congress, June 19, 1786, *JCC*, 349–351, among others.

territory. Henry believed the federal government should share the expense and send the federal army to aid the Kentucky militia. Besides, Article VI specified that states should petition Congress for military assistance before engaging in military actions, unless they were under imminent attack.[12]

On May 29, the Virginia delegates in Congress proposed that Congress raise 400 Continental troops under the command of Colonel Josiah Harmar and that these forces combine with as many Kentucky militia in the region as necessary to "destroy [the Indians] if they do not make concessions." Virginia officials wanted offensive action against the Indians but realized that such an expedition was almost exclusively in the interests of their state. Even though Virginia planned to protect federal lands that would be sold to pay for federal debts, they were also protecting their own settlers. Virginia delegate William Grayson expected "opposition from the circumscribed States who being themselves in no danger, will reluctantly yield assistance to those who are exposed." Unlike Virginia, no other state gained excludable benefits from protecting the region. They gained only the nonexcludable benefits from the sale of western lands. As Governor Henry confessed, "I am far from claiming idle or vain preeminence to Virginia when I say it appears to me she is more at stake as to Indian Affairs than any or perhaps all the other states in the union."[13]

On May 30 Congress assigned Henry's letter to a committee of William Grayson, James Monroe, and Nathan Dane – two delegates from Virginia and one from Massachusetts. A week later the committee recommended raising two companies under Harmar's command and the Kentucky militia "for the purpose of treating with the said Indians, or making war on them." Virginia wanted an offensive action, but other members of Congress delayed debate until June 28.[14]

---

[12] Patrick Henry to Congress, *PCC*, M247, r85, i71, 2: 427–431; Patrick Henry to the Virginia Delegates in Congress, May 16, 1786, Henry, *Correspondence*, 3: 350–352.

[13] Both Henry quotes come from Patrick Henry to Congress, *PCC*, M247, r85, i71, 2: 427–431. The measure was discussed among the delegates and the governor in William Grayson to James Madison, Smith, ed., *Letters of Delegates*, 23: 321–322; Virginia Delegates in Congress to Patrick Henry, June 8, 1786, Henry, *Correspondence*, 3: 357–358; and Patrick Henry to the Virginia Delegates in Congress, July 5, 1786, ibid., 3: 362–368. An additional statement of opposition to the measure can be found in Rufus King to Elbridge Gerry, June 8, 1786, Smith, ed., *Letters of Delegates*, 23: 340. For a general discussion of Congress's review of the Indian department during the same period, see James Monroe to John Jay, April 20, 1786, ibid., 23: 246 n. 1; and 23: 322 n. 7.

[14] William Grayson to James Madison, ibid., 23: 322 n. 7; *JCC*, 30: 330, 368–370. On September 14, Arthur St. Clair, a delegate from Pennsylvania and friend of the Indians, furthered opposition to the expedition. He motioned that "the State of Virginia do abstain from committing Hostilities against, making Reprisals upon, or entering into

Growing impatient with the delay, Grayson motioned on June 15 that Congress should order Colonel Harmar toward Vincennes to protect the inhabitants of the Kentucky district, should the need arise. Instead of offering immediate action, Congress referred the motion to the Secretary at War for report. When the secretary returned his report on June 21, Grayson and Richard Henry Lee proposed doubling the size of the requested force before the final measure was passed. They wanted more troops in the field than the expedition warranted but their substitute was quickly rebuffed. Other members did not want more troops, particularly if they had to pay for them. The measure passed only after the delegates from South Carolina arrived. Congress agreed to raise two companies under Colonel Harmar's command and to deploy them to the rapids of the Ohio River, near modern Louisville, without authorizing the use of force.[15]

A week later Congress debated the recommendation of the Grayson, Monroe, and Dane committee, which was trying to determine the intent of Congress. Were the troops to take an offensive action or a defensive one? Would they be held in readiness or sent with discretionary orders? After the debate had ended and several amendments were passed, it was clear that Congress did not have the same intention as Virginia. An opponent wrote that "the whole Report was negatived by a large Majority as being more hostile than we conceived existing Circumstances would warrant. . . . A soothing answer however is to be given to the Governor of Virginia." On June 30 Congress replied to Governor Henry's request by asking him to order Virginia's frontier militia to "hold themselves in readiness to unite with the federal troops, in such operations as the officer commanding the troops of the United States may judge necessary."[16]

The request was sent to Governor Henry on July 3, but it was not what he or the Virginia assembly had in mind. Virginia officials wanted action. They did not want their militia held in "readiness" under federal command. Placing the militia under federal command with orders to "hold" prevented their state from aiding the settlers, which was worse than not requesting the aid of Congress at all. As James Monroe wrote,

War with all or any of the Tribes or Nations of Indians with which the united States are in Peace or any other" (*JCC*, 31: 656–658). The committee assigned to the motion reported on October 30 that Virginia's actions were in conformity with the Articles of Confederation and that "offensive operations . . . were authorized by self-preservation" (*JCC*, 31: 916–18). For more on the St. Clair motion, see Timothy Bloodworth to Richard Oswell, September 29, 1786, Smith, ed., *Letters of Delegates*, 23: 574 n. 4.

[15] *JCC*, 30: 340 n. 1, 346–349, 353–354.

[16] Charles Pettit to James Wilson, July 2, 1786, Smith, ed., *Letters of Delegates*, 23: 381; *JCC*, 30: 367–382. The final resolution is written in *JCC*, 30: 381.

"the ultimate decision of Congress . . . hath been contrary to the sense of the State . . . the present State of the confederacy derang'd & out of order as it is, being rather irritating than conciliating spirit."[17]

Upon receipt of the request from Congress, Governor Henry immediately wrote Colonel Harmar that he had received a resolution of Congress ordering two of his nine companies of federal troops to protect the settlers near the Ohio and that these troops were "intended to cooperate with such numbers of militia in the district as the occasion shall render proper."[18] Henry conveniently omitted the phrases "hold themselves in readiness" and engage in "operations as the officer commanding the troops of the United States may judge necessary." Without these phrases, or a direct order from the Secretary at War, Harmar misunderstood the intent of Congress and ordered two of his companies under Captain Finney's command to "act in conjunction with the militia" in the region. Governor Henry's omission, and Harmar's subsequent failure to wait for direct orders, placed federal troops under the command of the state militia. As Henry Knox later described it, "His Excellency Governor Henry . . . appears to have been mistaken . . . As this arrangement places Capt. Finny and his troops under the command of the militia." Whether Henry's omission was intentional or not, his letter served the interests of Virginia. The Kentucky militia was allowed to go on the offensive as originally planned, and it appeared that federal troops would assist them.[19]

On August 2, settlers along the Ohio voted to send out a strong expedition against the Indians under the command of George Rogers Clark. Clark called the militia to the rapids of the Ohio and garrisoned it with Finney's federal troops. In mid-September, Virginians from the Kentucky district raised enough men to send two expeditions against the Indians. One, under the command of Benjamin Logan, moved east along the Ohio River with 790 men. The other, under Clark, moved west to Vincennes

---

[17] Charles Thompson to Patrick Henry, July 3, 1786, Smith, ed., *Letters of Delegates*, 23: 383; James Monroe to Elbridge Gerry, July 14, 1786, ibid., 23: 397–399.

[18] The nine companies under Harmar's command were protecting federal surveyors further to the east, near modern-day Parkersburg in West Virginia. Had the requisition for Shays' Rebellion been successful, Harmar's seven companies would be called to Massachusetts where they would combine forces with newly raised troops. The combined army would then confront Shays in western Massachusetts.

[19] Governor Henry to Colonel Harmar, July 12, 1786, PCC, M247, r164, i150, 2: 159; Colonel Harmar to Captain Finney, October 11, 1786, PCC, M247, r164, i150, 2: 207; Extracts of a letter from the Secretary at War to Lieutenant Colonel Harmar, January 22, 1787, PCC, M247, r164, i150, 2: 151–154. It is interesting to note that the privy council used the same wording as Congress when it advised the governor to send a letter to the Kentucky militia (July 18, 1786, Virginia, *Journals of the Council*, 3: 568). Intentional or not, Henry appears to be responsible for the omission.

and up the Wabash River toward Wabash Indian encampments. He had closer to 1,200 men. Both were committed to the offensive, but the two expeditions were not equally successful. Logan destroyed several Shawnee towns near the Miami River, killed ten chiefs (including one friendly to the United States), captured thirty-two prisoners, and destroyed a wide variety of Indian provisions. Clark faced supply problems as he moved northward, which caused nearly half of his men to desert him. With inadequate supplies, he had to call off the attack and return to Vincennes without engaging the Indians.[20]

Although well-disciplined Continentals would have strengthened both expeditions considerably, the two companies under Captain Finney never left the garrison at the rapids of the Ohio. Harmar did not receive the letter from Governor Henry for some time and he did not order Finney to combine with the militia until October 11. When Finney finally received his orders, the expeditions under Clark and Logan were already completed. Virginia continued to demand federal troops in the region to protect their inhabitants, but the northwest expeditions of Clark and Logan were conducted without federal aid.

Shays' Rebellion

Before hearing of Clark's expedition or Logan's success against the Indians, state leaders turned their attention toward another uprising, Shays' Rebellion. Angry mobs in western Massachusetts were beginning to interrupt court proceedings and to transform themselves into an organized opposition. Although the agitation in western Massachusetts began in the summer of 1786, the idea of raising a federal army to face the insurgents most likely originated in a meeting between Secretary at War Henry Knox, Governor James Bowdoin of Massachusetts, Massachusetts delegate Rufus King, and others in October 1786.[21] This meeting determined the course of federal action. The first question addressed at the meeting was whether the munitions at Springfield should be protected or moved to another location. Everyone preferred the former because it

---

[20] Extracts of a letter from Colonel Harmar to the Secretary at War, November 15, 1787, PCC, M247, r164, i150, 2: 163–165; Helderman, "The Northwest Expedition," 325–331.

[21] Exactly who attended this meeting remains uncertain. Most likely it was a gathering of representatives from all three branches of the state government. Such conferences were held previously when Massachusetts raised troops to protect its courts (Warren, "The Confederation"; Freer, *Shays' Rebellion*). For firsthand accounts of the meeting, see Henry Knox to the President of Congress, *JCC*, 31: 875, 886–887; and Rufus King to Elbridge Gerry, October 19, 1786, King, *Life and Correspondence*, 1: 191–192. Knox warned Bowdoin that federal troops already in service were ordered to the frontier (Henry Knox to James Bowdoin, PCC, M247, r. 164, i. 150, 1: 551–553).

showed the strength of government and it would have required just as many men to move the munitions as it would to defend them. After deciding to protect the arsenal, the next question was whether state or federal troops should be applied. Those attending the meeting wanted to raise an army quietly to avoid provoking an attack on the arsenal. Some legislators in the Massachusetts assembly sympathized with the insurgents, so it was agreed that the federal government would gather troops. To maintain further disguise, members of the committee also agreed to request federal troops under the pretense of an ensuing war with the Indians. Tensions with the Indians were clearly on the rise, and such hostilities provided the perfect cover for a federal operation.

On October 18, Congress received a letter from Henry Knox regarding the outcome of his meeting with state officials. The letter informed Congress that those attending the meeting unanimously determined that "a force would be obtained only in consequence of a requisition of Congress." It further recommended that the federal government should augment its army by 1,500 men to guard the arsenal for the winter. "If they should not be requisite for the same purpose the next spring, they might be marched to the frontiers, or disbanded, as Congress should think most proper," Knox wrote. The report was assigned to a committee of five, who had just received a report from Knox on the hostilities in Kentucky.[22]

On October 20, the committee reported on the threat of the Indians along the Ohio and officially requested federal troops to meet the threat.[23] After hearing the report, members of Congress unanimously

---

[22] Knox reported his meeting with Massachusetts officials in Henry Knox to the President of Congress, October 18, 1786, *JCC*, 31: 886–888. He reported hostilities with the Indians by forwarding two letters from the frontier: Information of Captain Teninese, a Delaware Indian, July 6, 1786, and Extract of a letter from Lieutenant Colonel Harmar, September 7, 1786, in *PCC*, M247, r. 164, i. 150, 2: 75–76, 79–80, respectively. The former was used as the basis for the committee report on October 20.

[23] The committee reported that Shawnees, Pottawattamies, Chippewas, Tawas, and Twightwees were agitated and gathering warriors in Shawnee towns near the confluence of the Miami and Ohio rivers. This report was based on the letter from Captain Teninese, who anticipated that roughly 1,000 warriors would attack settlers of the United States. Although the Indians were clearly gathering for war, Harmar wrote that they were probably preparing to defend themselves against Clark's expedition rather than readying themselves for an attack, as Captain Teninese had suggested. Given Congress's previous reluctance to send troops to the region and knowing that the Kentucky militia was preparing its own expeditions, the committee would not have requested an addition 1,340 men solely for the purpose of sending them to the West. Since the requisition was laid almost exclusively on New England states, it is clear that the committee had western Massachusetts in mind when it laid its report before Congress. Tensions with the Indians were the perfect guise for the requisition, but not the primary purpose (*JCC*, 31: 891–893).

resolved to add an additional 1,340 men to the 700 soldiers currently standing – presumably under Colonel Harmar. These soldiers would be enlisted for three years, the same duration as the troops on the Ohio. Combined, the force of 2,040 men would give the federal government exactly three brigades and provide it with the means to protect the "frontiers of the states." The resolution further specified that almost all troops should come from New England. Congress ordered almost half of the total from Massachusetts (660 men) and assigned another 560 to New Hampshire, Connecticut, and Rhode Island. The remaining 120 were requested in cavalry from Maryland and Virginia. Governors were asked to raise their levies quickly and to call their legislatures to session if they were not already meeting. The fact that Congress focused its requisition on the New England states strongly suggests that it had the insurrection in western Massachusetts in mind when it approved the new force. The new troops were raised for the suppression of the insurrection in western Massachusetts, but once they had served this purpose they could also be used to protect settlers in Kentucky.[24]

The following day, Congress heard the committee report on the commotions in western Massachusetts and requisitioned the states for the money needed to fund the force (see Table 3.1 for the apportionment). The committee suggested that Congress apply the troops requisitioned the previous day to the insurrection in Massachusetts while maintaining the secrecy of their primary intent. The report continued that "as these troops are proposed to be raised chiefly in the eastern states, they may probably effect these salutary purposes before they are moved to the Western Country." This made it clear that the new troops were intended for the rebellion in western Massachusetts, but that they could be redeployed to Kentucky after the rebellion was subdued. Congress unanimously agreed to the report.[25]

The same day, Congress authorized an immediate loan of $500,000 to finance the new force and backed the loan by a special requisition of $530,000 on the states. The requisition was paramount to the loan. Without receipts from the states, Congress could neither pay the loan nor expect investors to lend it the necessary cash.

---

[24] *JCC*, 31: 891–893; Rufus King to James Bowdoin, October 20, 1786, Smith, ed., *Letters of Delegates*, 23: 606–607; Rufus King to Elbridge Gerry, October 20, 1786, ibid., 23: 607–608. Congress further resolved that if the requisition was not met, Congress would not "hazard the perilous step of putting arms into the hands of men whose fidelity must in some degree depend upon the faithful payment of their wages." In other words, Congress would not send a Continental army without the funds needed to pay for it (*JCC*, 31: 896).

[25] *JCC*, 31: 896.

GOVERNMENTAL RESPONSES

Federal officials spread the news of their decision quickly and secretly, using hostilities with the Indians as their façade. On October 30, eight days after Knox informed Bowdoin of his state's quota for soldiers, both houses of the Massachusetts general assembly passed a bill authorizing the immediate recruitment of troops.[26] The bill designated Major General Henry Jackson of the Massachusetts militia to command and recruit Massachusetts's contingent of the federal force. The assembly gave him £2,500 to recruit 660 soldiers, but provided no money to pay or supply his militia.[27] Massachusetts was deeply in debt and the general assembly made no attempt to support Jackson financially nor to pay the special requisition for money. This made it difficult, if not impossible, for Jackson to recruit his troops. By December 11 he recruited only eighteen or twenty men and realized that he could enlist few more without the money needed to pay their wages.[28]

To secure the necessary funds, Jackson was authorized to obtain loans from private businessmen. But businessmen were not interested in an unbacked offer. They did not want to lend money at a low rate of 6 percent interest without some guarantee that Congress would pay back its debt. Congress had backed loans with airy requisitions before and investors expected little return from such a venture.[29] Without adequate loans, Jackson's recruiting effort was delayed. By the end of February, Jackson reported just under 200 recruits – still less than one third of his state's quota.

Connecticut faced similar problems. It brought recruits into Hartford during the dead of winter without rations or supplies. Like Massachusetts, Connecticut authorized the raising of soldiers but provided no money for its portion of the federal requisition. Governor Samuel Huntington explained that the expenses of the late war, the heavy fiscal

---

[26] Henry Knox to Governor Bowdoin, October 22, 1786, Knox, *Henry Knox Papers*, reel 19, frame 29; Resolve for Raising Six Hundred and Sixty Men, October 30, 1786, Massachusetts, *Massachusetts Resolves*, 124–126.

[27] The amount of 2,500 Massachusetts pounds equaled roughly $8,333 U.S. dollars. All subsequent figures are reported in U.S. dollars.

[28] Henry Jackson to Henry Knox, December 11, 1786, Knox, *Henry Knox Papers*, reel 19, frame 84.

[29] The pretense of raising federal troops for an Indian war did not last long. By the end of October, Major William North wrote from Boston, "The people here smell a rat, that the Troops about to be raised are more for the Insurgents than the Indians" (to Henry Knox, October 29, 1786, Knox, *Henry Knox Papers*, reel 19, frame 36). Also see Elbridge Gerry to Rufus King, November 28, 1786, King, *Life and Correspondence*, 1: 191–192.

burden of his people, and the arrears in taxes prevented Connecticut from paying its portion of the monetary requisition. Officially, the state claimed it could not pay the requisition nor supply the men left in Hartford.[30]

Without supplies from the states, the commander of the Connecticut contingent, Lieutenant Colonel David Humphries, turned to Congress for the subsistence of his men. After considerable grumbling, the designated purchaser for the continental Board of Treasury, Jeremiah Wadsworth, provided the men with blankets, fuel, and shelter out of his own pocket, but proclaimed that "the Treasury Board must find the warrants to refund my present advances – or I shall immediately stop."[31] Without proper provisions, Wadsworth eventually withdrew his support and the Connecticut contingent shrank over the course of the winter. Connecticut attempted to comply with the requisition for troops, but failed to provide the supplies needed to fully do so.

Virginia responded to Congress's request quite differently. Legislators in that state agreed to raise their quota of sixty cavalry and to back them financially. This helped Virginia recruit its cavalry. Virginia also passed taxes to pay for its requisition in money, which was a stronger stance than that of Connecticut.

Politicians in Virginia were more preoccupied with the possibility of British involvement than politicians in other states. Virginia delegates warned that the British had contacted the insurgents and that the insurgents were "contemplating a reunion with G. Britain."[32] Virginia officials took these letters seriously and Governor Randolph secretly read part of Edward Carrington's letter before the house of

---

[30] Not everyone believed that Connecticut was unable to pay its quota. James Davenport, a member of the Connecticut General Assembly, "chided" the House for ordering Governor Huntington to inform Congress that the state had no money (Jensen, ed., *Documentary History*, 13: 111 n. 4). Concerning the resolve, Madison later lamented, "Congs. recd. a letter a few days ago from the Govr. of that State inclosing a noncompliance of the Assembly with the requisition of Congs. In fact payments to the treasy. are ceasing every where, and the minds of the people are losing all confidence in our political system" (To James Madison, Sr., February 25, 1787, Madison, *Papers*, 9: 296–297, 297 n. 4; Connecticut, *Public Records*, 6: 232–233; *JCC*, 32: 80 n. 1). Neither believed that lack of resources was the full explanation.

[31] Jeremiah Wadsworth to Henry Knox, December 11, 1786, Knox, *Henry Knox Papers*, reel 19, frame 85. Also see February 10, 1787, reel 19, frame 161.

[32] From Henry Lee, November 11, 1786, Washington, *Papers*, 4: 357–358; From Henry Lee, October 17, 1786, ibid., 4: 295–296; From William Grayson, November 22, 1786, Madison, *Papers*, 9: 173–174; Edward Carrington to Governor Edmund Randolph, December 8, 1786, Virginia, *Calendar of State Papers*, 4: 195–199; Jay to Jefferson, December 14, 1786, Jefferson, *Papers*, 10: 596; Jefferson to Jay, August 11, 1786, ibid., 10: 221, 222 n.

delegates four days before the house signed the Shays requisition into law.[33]

But avoiding the British would not have provided the type of excludable benefit that could spur Virginia into action. Other states received more excludable benefits from preventing the British involvement in New England than Virginia, even though the British had agitated the Wabash Indians and other tribes in the Northwest Territory for years. Virginia's politicians must have known that their contribution would not provide an army alone. Virginia's prompt response to the requisition was motivated by something else. Politicians in Virginia wanted federal troops for a military expedition of their own. Federal troops would legitimate their actions in the Ohio valley, strengthen the militia by providing well-disciplined troops, and spread the cost of Indian affairs across the union. If the troops did not make it in time, Virginia could still gain from a standing army that protected its unstable western territory.

Since the expeditions would engage Indians in lands ceded to the union, Virginia tried to place the expense of these expeditions on Congress. On December 6, Governor Randolph requested that Congress supply 500 stands of arms, 3,000 pounds of powder, 1,200 pounds of lead, and 20,000 flints for the continuing problems in the Kentucky district. The request was ordered by the Virginia general assembly, but the Virginia delegates in Congress quickly informed Randolph that such a request would never be granted.[34]

On January 24, 1787, twenty days after the Virginia house of delegates agreed to pay the Shays requisition, Governor Randolph tried again. This time he attempted to reimburse his state for the expeditions of Clark and Logan. He sent a letter to the President of Congress requesting credit on Virginia's accounts for its expedition against the Indians and for the confederation to take control of their prisoners. When the letter was finally referred to a committee on July 30, the committee recommended the denial of federal support, "the said expedition not having been authorized by or conducted under the knowledge or direction of the United States."[35]

[33] For some controversy around Carrington's letter read before the Virginia General Assembly, see Rufus King to William Grayson and James Madison, March 11, 1787, Smith, ed., *Letters of Delegates*, 24: 137–138; and James Madison and William Grayson to Rufus King, March 11, 1787, ibid., 24: 138.

[34] Virginia, *Journals of the Council*, 4: 5; Virginia Delegates to Edmund Randolph, December 24, 1786, Smith, ed., *Letters of Delegates*, 24: 56–57.

[35] On August 2, 1787, the committee reported unfavorably on Virginia's request because Congress did not authorize the expenditure, but through the politicking of Grayson and Carrington the report was amended to avoid official denial. Congress never credited Virginia's account for its 1786 expedition, and the issue apparently died on the floor

But it was this hope of securing assistance with raids against the Indians that encouraged Virginia to pay its requisition. On November 3, 1786, the Virginia house of delegates unanimously agreed to write a bill calling for the sixty cavalry requested from the state, which passed both houses on the 24th. To pay for the cost of recruiting soldiers the bill appropriated money from the taxes raised for the requisition of 1785.[36] This would not pay the requisition in money but it would raise Virginia's contingent of the federal force. On December 20, the house further appointed a committee to write a bill that would pay for its portion of the monetary requisition. This bill called for an additional tax of 6 shillings per hogshead on exported tobacco. As the bill was considered, the legislature also heard complaints about attacks made by the Indians in the Kentucky district. On January 4, the bill passed the house of delegates moments after the house liquidated expenses for its expeditions against the Indians. It passed the senate the next day.[37] Payment of the special requisition and Virginia's Indian affairs appeared inexplicably intertwined.

Although politicians in Virginia clearly knew that the federal force would be applied to the insurrection in Massachusetts, they also hoped that the force could be dispatched to the Ohio valley after it had dealt with Shays. Crises in the Kentucky district were recurring and Virginia could always benefit from a federal force in the region. A successful requisition would also prevent Congress from moving Harmar's forces eastward in pursuit of the insurgents. The benefits from both possibilities encouraged politicians in Virginia to pay their requisitions.

By the summer of 1787, Virginia's affairs with the Indians had become tenuous once again. Virginia wanted to undertake another expedition against the Indians and requested federal involvement before it took action. The lieutenant governor, under advice of the legislature and privy council, asked the federal government to combine its forces with Virginia's militia and to fund Virginia's part of the force out of the federal treasury. The issue was assigned to the Secretary at War for a report on July 6, debated before Congress on July 19, and passed in a weaker form

---

that day (Edmund Randolph to the President of Congress, January 21, 1787, *PCC*, M247, r. 85, i. 71, 2: 467; Virginia Delegates to Edmund Randolph, February 12, 1787, Madison, *Papers*, 9: 266; *JCC*, 430 n. 2, 441, 448–450).

[36] Virginia, *Journals of the Council*, 4: 2; *Journals of the House of Delegates*, 18, 22, 54, 56, 60; Hening, ed., *Statutes at Large*, 12: 255.

[37] *Journals of the House of Delegates*, 111, 119, 135, 137, 140; Hening, ed., *Statutes at Large*, 12: 288–289. On February 12, Knox informed Governor Randolph that Congress did not receive the funds needed to deploy the Virginia contingent (General Henry Know to Governor Edmund Randolph, February 12, 1787, Virginia, *Calendar of State Papers*, 4: 236).

on July 21. Congress decided to apply six companies to the defense of the frontier and gave Virginia full credit on its account for the pay and rations of the Virginia militia. Virginia's compliance with the special requisition for suppressing Shays' Rebellion helped it obtain federal support for military actions of its own. Even though it did not help out in 1786, Congress unanimously agreed to support Virginia's 1787 expedition.[38]

Unlike Virginia and the New England states, the Pennsylvania assembly did not find the disturbances in Massachusetts especially threatening to the confederacy, nor to their own interests. The low threat to Pennsylvania may explain why the state did not respond quickly to the special requisition of Congress. There was no mention of Shays' Rebellion during the fall session of the Pennsylvania assembly, and Benjamin Franklin, the newly elected governor of the state, wrote in November of 1786 that "the little Disorders you have heard of in some of the States, rais'd by a few wrong Heads, are subsiding and will probably soon be extinguish'd."[39] Pennsylvanians were well aware of the disorders in New England; but unlike their fellow Virginians, they did not have any excludable reasons to comply.

Pennsylvania did consider paying its portion of the special requisition, however. In a report by the Ways and Means Committee in December 1786, Pennsylvania's portion of the special request, $72,504, was listed as a debt owed to the confederacy.[40] But the Pennsylvania legislature never issued taxes to pay for the special requisition and the bill never got out of the Ways and Means Committee. Paying for the special force would require Pennsylvania legislators to use monies raised for other purposes or to issue new taxes. Pennsylvania legislators could have paid their quota out of monies raised for the general requisition of 1784 or 1785, but this would take money away from federal creditors in their state who were receiving one of the largest portions of general requisition money in debt payments. If Pennsylvanians wanted to pay a requisition, it would be better for them to pay one designated for Pennsylvanians than to pay one designated for the stability of western Massachusetts. Raising money in new taxes would also be undesirable. These considerations made the decision to withhold financial support for the special requisition an easy one. Pennsylvanians preferred to

---

[38] Virginia, *Journals of the Council*, 4: 104–106; William Grayson to the Lieutenant Governor of Virginia, July 7, 1787, Burnett, ed., *Letters of Members*, 8: 617; *JCC*, 32: 327–332, 370–375; 33: 385–387.

[39] Benjamin Franklin to Edward Bancroft, November 26, 1786, Franklin, *Writings*, 9: 550–551.

[40] Proceedings of the General Assembly of the Freemen of Pennsylvania, December 26, 1786, Jenkins, ed., *Records of the States*, a.1c, r.2, u.3, p. 94.

contribute toward federal efforts that benefited their citizens rather than those of other states. Following much of the same motives as Virginia but heading toward different conclusions, Pennsylvania legislators never complied with the special requisition.

Other states appeared equally remiss. Many state legislatures simply passed over the requisition as if it were never ordered. For example, after receiving a motion to adjourn from the Maryland house of delegates, the Maryland senate wrote back, "you have not taken any measures to comply with raising a troop of horse" or "passed an assessment bill to bring any money into the state or continental treasury." To this the house replied, "We shall only say in reply that we have paid every possible attention to the public affairs of the union, and the interest and happiness of our people . . . we repeat our request to close this session this evening."[41] Contributing to the federal force was not in the interest of Maryland, even though protecting the federal arsenal or avoiding a widespread insurrection clearly was. Later that night, the Maryland legislature adjourned without raising its quota of money or men.

State Forces

By January, the lack of revenue brought the federal endeavor to a close. Recruitment ceased in Massachusetts, Connecticut, and Virginia, while lack of federal funds prevented it from ever starting in Rhode Island and New Hampshire. Falling short of the number needed for deployment, no contracts were made for the subsistence of the soldiers. Without the money requested from the states, federal involvement in Shays' Rebellion ground to a halt.

As the shortcomings of federal effort became clear, Governor Bowdoin proposed raising the Massachusetts militia on January 4. He ordered Benjamin Lincoln to command 4,400 soldiers for the express purpose of rounding up the insurgents throughout western Massachusetts and for defending the debtor courts in Worcester.[42] He did not plan to defend the federal arsenal nor to redeploy his troops toward the western frontier. Realizing the added benefits of maintaining control over the militia, as well the advantages of showing the state's ability to quell its own domestic unrest, Massachusetts raised state troops instead of paying for the federal effort on its own. If politicians in Massachusetts had to fund an entire army by themselves, they preferred to raise a state militia, capable of carrying out state objectives, than to pay for the national army on its own.

---

[41] Votes and Proceedings of the Senate of the State of Maryland, January 20, 1787, ibid., a.1a, r.7, u.2, pp. 37–39. All revenue bills originated in the house.

[42] James Bowdoin to Benjamin Lincoln, January 19, 1787, Washington, *Papers*, 4: 422–423.

When it became clear that Massachusetts would raise its militia, Shays and his men tried to augment their arms by attacking the federal arsenal on January 25. A local militia deterred the assault, but if there was any question about the need for a force, Shays and his men answered it. A state force would be raised, it would require money, and it would act independently of the federal government. Of course there were no funds in the state treasury to pay for a state militia, either, but state guarantees to back loans with new revenues allowed Lincoln to obtain loans more quickly than Jackson. Wealthy investors realized that the moment was dire and that the money needed to raise the force would come from them and them only. As Lincoln pointed out, they had to become "loaners of part of their property if they wished to secure the remainder."[43] The immediacy of the situation was clear, but the real reason that investors supported the loan was because the general assembly backed it with state impost and excise taxes. On February 6, the general assembly passed an act which backed the 6 percent bonds with these revenues.[44] This gave investors the security they needed to lend the money required by the state.

With loans from investors, Lincoln had no problem paying his soldiers and raised the requisite force quickly. As Rufus King noted, it was "natural for men to prefer [state] service in which they would stay at home & be sure of their pay, to [federal service], in which they might, with little prospect of it, be sent to the Ohio to fight the Indians."[45] The secure payment and local purpose of the army drew ample men to the cause.

Before state troops departed, Jackson proposed merging his contingent with the state militia and argued that such an act would help Massachusetts fulfill its quota with Congress. But Knox wanted federal forces applied toward federal purposes, and he would not approve Jackson's proposal. On January 19, Lincoln marched his men toward Worcester, without the additional forces under Jackson's command.

The state senate then passed a resolution on February 5 requesting that Governor Bowdoin inform Congress of the rebellion, tell the federal government that Massachusetts was successfully suppressing it, and suggest that the United States allow Massachusetts to call on the federal government in the event of an emergency. But the house refused to concur with this measure, and after a conference meeting between the two chambers, it further stipulated that Congress should protect its property

---

[43] Lincoln to Washington, February 22, 1787, ibid., 4: 422. For the effect of rebellious activity on loans, also see Stephen Higginson to Henry Knox, November 25, 1786, Knox, *Henry Knox Papers*, reel 19, frame 58.

[44] An Act providing for the Pay and Subsistence of the Militia, Massachusetts, *Session Laws*.

[45] Notes on Debates, February 19, 1787, Madison, *Papers*, 9: 277.

at Springfield without state assistance. The proposal was debated in both houses, but finally passed in this form on the ninth.[46] Governor Bowdoin obeyed the decree and informed Congress that he would apply state forces toward state purposes only. The arsenal was a confederative concern that needed to be protected by the confederation.

On the same day, Knox was convinced that he should station federal troops at Springfield and ordered the federal forces under Jackson and Humphries to march to that location. He gave them strict orders to protect the arsenal and not to help state troops round up the insurgents. In addition, he stipulated that Jackson should not start off before receiving adequate resources from Massachusetts to pay for his men. Knox was angry at the Massachusetts government for redirecting its resources to the state militia and made it clear that Massachusetts was partly responsible for Congress's inability to fund the federal force. As anticipated, however, no supplies were appropriated and Knox later countermanded his order. The differences between state and national priorities were increasingly apparent, and they prevented Jackson's force from being deployed. On February 14, Humphries reached Springfield with 124 men and relieved the local militia stationed at the arsenal. This was the closest that federal forces ever came to suppressing the rebellion.

When the Massachusetts assembly directed Bowdoin to restrict state forces to state purposes, it also instructed him to issue a reward for the capture of Daniel Shays and other leaders of the insurgents. The assembly requested that Bowdoin ask the governors of nearby states to issue similar rewards and assured them that any money they paid would be reimbursed by Massachusetts. On February 9, Governor Bowdoin issued the proclamation and a reward of $500 for the apprehension of Daniel Shays and another $333 each for Luke Day, Adam Wheeler, and Eli Parsons.[47]

New York entered the game only at that point. The governor of New York, George Clinton, was a strong Anti-Federalist who chose not to call the legislature to session during the fall of 1786 for the emergency requisition.[48] Suppressing a rebellion in Massachusetts did not appear to be

---

[46] Journal of the Senate, Jenkins, ed., *Records of the States*, a.1a, reel 17, p. 8; Message from the Governor to the Senate and House, March 2, 1787, Massachusetts, *Resolves of the General Court*, 209.

[47] Ibid., 182–183. Rhode Island actually refused to issue such a bounty because of the large number of legislators in the state who sympathized with the insurgents (James Varnum to Samuel Wood, Jr., April 2, 1787, Smith, ed., *Letters of Delegates*, 24: 198–199).

[48] The Ninth Assembly of New York ended on May 5, 1786, and the Tenth Assembly began on January 12, 1787. The New York legislature never considered funding the federal requisition in between.

in New York's interest, yet Governor Clinton and members of the New York legislature wanted to prevent Shays' Rebellion from spreading into their state. On February 24, Clinton issued a reward for the apprehension of the leaders of the insurrection. When it became clear that the agitators might flee to New York, the New York legislature authorized the governor to call out the militia, and Governor Clinton quickly raised three regiments. By early March he personally went to New Lebanon "in very ungenial weather for the purpose of chasing away Captain Shays."[49] Concerned that the rebellion could spread to their state, the New York government raised state troops and coordinated military plans with Massachusetts independently of the federal government. New York had no intention of providing money for the federal effort nor of raising troops that could be ordered west. It carefully protected its own interests and became involved only when it was clear that other states would not intervene on its behalf.[50]

The End of Federal Involvement

Convinced that Massachusetts and New York were quelling the rebellion, Charles Pinckney of South Carolina proposed that Congress suspend any additional efforts to raise federal troops. He stood before Congress on February 19 and noted that an army could not be raised without the money needed to pay for it. To this point Massachusetts delegate Rufus King argued that his state needed federal assistance to disarm the Shaysites and that if Congress rescinded its measures now, Congress would appear to disapprove of his state's actions. Pinckney and others clearly disapproved. He replied that "if fresh commotions should spring from them, that the State of Massts. alone should be at the charge, and abide by the consequences of their own misconduct."

Congressional delegates were divided over the debate between Pinckney and King based on their proximity to the threat, with one exception. Before the votes were cast, James Madison of Virginia rose from his chair and spoke in favor of maintaining the federal force. He argued that Congress should not suspend the enlistments because "[w]henever danger was apprehended from any foreign quarter which of necessity extended

---

[49] To General Benjamin Lincoln, March 6, 1787, Clinton, *Public Papers*; New York, *Journal of the Senate*, 35–36; *Journal of the Assembly, 1787*, 62.

[50] The tenth session of the legislature of New York opened with a letter from the governor proposing that the legislature take early notice of the requisitions of October 20 and 21. On January 17, the Senate replied that it would "duly attend" to the requisition "since our national credit and honor depend upon a punctual compliance with every requisition." But the bill bogged down in the Ways and Means Committees of both Houses shortly thereafter. Many of these statements appeared like public orations (New York, *Journal of the Senate*, 4, 6, 7; *Journal of the Assembly, 1787*, 6, 11).

itself to the federal concerns, Congs. were bound to guard agst. it." Madison wanted the federal government to continue with the enlistments in hope of raising an army for the stipulated term of three years. If Congress were obliged to defend other states, it would also be obliged to help Virginia. Madison presented other reasons for his position, and when the vote was taken, he sided with the New England states. Pinckney could not obtain the votes needed to rescind additional enlistment of the federal troops.[51]

On March 28 Congress appointed a committee to resolve the matter of enlistments. On April 4 the committee recommended a repeal of the October 20 requisition and the discharge of all officers appointed but no longer required. After debate on the floor, Congress restricted the policy even further and ordered that only two artillery companies remain at the arsenal. It decided to pay and discharge all other men enlisted under the resolve of October 20, 1786. The measure passed with a vote of seven states to two, with Massachusetts and Rhode Island the only states dissenting. The next day, Congress determined that all monies paid toward the Shays requisition should be credited toward a specie requisition of the contributing state's choosing. Loans requested to fund the federal force were also revoked.[52] This officially ended federal involvement in Shays' Rebellion exactly six months after it began on October 21, 1786.[53]

Without a guarantee that the requisition would be paid, Congress could not sell the bonds needed to fund a federal army. As a result, federal troops were never sent against the insurgents. The nation relied on loans from wealthy businessmen and state actions to address the insurrection. But the armies raised were state militias ordered to capture the insurgents rather than to defend federal property. Fortunately for the union, state purposes were fairly consistent with the interests of the union. Massachusetts suppressed the rebellion and ended the insurrection for the union.

DISCUSSION

Massachusetts attempted to free-ride. It requested federal troops to reduce the costs to its citizens, then chose not to commit money to the

---

[51] *JCC*, 32: 61–64; Notes on Debates, Madison, *Papers*, 9: 275–279, 279 n. 5.

[52] *JCC*, 32: 153–154, 227–228. On December 14, 1787, the Virginia legislature applied the remainder of the money it received from its duty on exported tobacco to the state sinking fund. It used this fund to pay both state and federal debts owed to individuals within their state (an act providing a sinking fund; Hening, ed., *Statutes at Large*, 12: 453–454).

[53] Massachusetts stopped chasing the insurgents when the General Court resolved on May 30, 1787, to reduce the number of soldiers assigned to the western counties to no more than 800 men (Nathan Dane to Nathaniel Gorham, June 22, 1787, Smith, ed., *Letters of Delegates*, 24: 339 n. 1).

federal force unless the federal force would be deployed. Waiting to see the outcome of the requisition, Massachusetts reserved its resources for a state militia instead. This was a prudent policy for a state which gained more from quelling the rebellion than any other state and was likely to repel the rebellion alone if the requisition failed. As it turned out, Massachusetts was right in its skepticism. Problems of collective action dissuaded other states from contributing their shares and prevented Congress from deploying a significant force. If Massachusetts sent its money under these circumstances, it would have received a less effective force than originally intended – as described in Chapter 3. Massachusetts would pay virtually the same amount for a force that was not under its command.

Of course, the Articles of Confederation and financial hardship in Massachusetts bolstered the request for federal involvement, but Massachusetts did not withhold its resources purely because of its revenue problems. It was fully capable of funding a state militia more than ten times as expensive as its portion of the federal requisition. The impost and excise taxes used to back state loans were under consideration in early November, and Jackson's force was eventually supplied from the money appropriated for the annual requisition of 1785.[54] Both of these resources could have been applied toward the federal requisition had the Massachusetts assembly chose to do so. But it did not. Massachusetts used the guise of destitution to gain assistance from other states. When it could not gain enough support, it raised its own force under a separate command. Waiting gave the state a better estimate of the contributions of other states and the severity of the threat. It provided state decision makers with a more accurate picture of the expected benefits from a federal army compared with a state militia. For the federal

---

[54] On March 2 Governor Bowdoin informed the General Assembly that Knox would order the Massachusetts contingent to Springfield as soon as the state provided the money needed for him to do so. The General Court responded by appropriating $16,666 for the pay, clothing, and subsistence of the federal force (21% of the money requested on October 21), but the appropriation stipulated that federal troops would have to aid the state in pursuit of the insurgents beyond its borders. Congress never agreed to the conditions, but raising a sum indicates that the state was not entirely strapped for money. In addition, the Massachusetts senate was working on a bill to raise $510,667 by the lottery of eastern lands. This bill appeared as early as October 28 and could have been applied toward federal requisitions by February (Message from the Governor to Senate and House, March 2, 1787, 209; Resolve requiring the Governor to write to Delegates at Congress, March 8, 1787, 237; and Resolve granting pay out of Specie tax . . . , March 8, 1787, 239, all in Massachusetts, *Resolves of the General Court*; Journals of the Senate, November 8, 1786, Jenkins, ed., *Records of the States*, a.1a. reel 17, p. 54; and March 8, 1787, Massachusetts, *Resolves of the General Court*, 239; Journals of the Senate, October 28, 1786, Jenkins, ed., *Records of the States*, a.1a, reel 17, unit 1, pp. 240–241).

government, such strategic interaction represented the failure of the articles themselves. States refused to fund a requisition that they had unanimously ordered only six months before.

Now it is interesting to note that Virginia raised money for the special requisition fairly quickly. This is because the Virginia assembly did not have the luxury of waiting to see how many states would donate before committing its own resources. If Virginia were going to send any money at all, the assembly would have to send it early enough for the federal army to form in Massachusetts.

Virginia's politicians did not have a unique sense of national patriotism. They contributed to the Shays requisition but ignored other requisitions at the same time.[55] Such pick-and-choose behavior was not consistent with a predilection for payment. Virginia paid the special requisition to signal other states that this requisition was going to be a success and to show that it was committed to national defense. More important, by contributing to the Shays requisition, Virginia hoped that the troops (mostly from New England) might be sent to protect the settlers on the western frontier on a more permanent basis and that Harmar's forces would not be called away from the Ohio River, where they had been partially defending the state. These private incentives encouraged Virginia to contribute both the money and men requested by Congress.

Outside New England and Virginia, however, no additional attempts were made to meet the quota. States south of New England lacked the private incentives needed to send their shares, while the New England states waited to assess the progress of the requisition. By the time Massachusetts and New York allocated resources toward state troops, Connecticut, Rhode Island, and New Hampshire had no reason to contribute any troops of their own. Political leaders in Massachusetts and New York restored order to advance local interests, not to provide for the union.

Now the question may arise about why Massachusetts and Connecticut attempted to raise federal troops even though they made no attempt

---

[55] In the summer of 1787 the Virginia Council openly defied the general requisitions of 1785 and 1786 by refusing to pay either one until it was fully credited for its initial payments to the general requisition of 1786. Congress would not credit Virginia for compliance with the requisition because the Virginia House of Delegates did not raise its full portion in specie. Without credit for its payment in 1786, the Virginia Council refused to pay any of its subsequent general requisitions (Hening, ed., *Statutes at Large*, 12: 323–329; Virginia, *Journals of the Council*, 4: 76, 102, 132; Virginia Delegates to Edmund Randolph, February 26, 1786, Smith, ed., *Letters of Delegates*, 24: 121–122 n. 1; and Richard Henry Lee to Edmund Randolph, September 1, 1787, ibid., 24: 419–421).

to raise money for the federal army. Perhaps the answer lies in the fact that recruiting troops was considerably cheaper than raising money. Enrollment in the federal army was voluntary in 1786 and few casualties were expected from a force that would be deployed only when it was large enough to defeat Shays' farmers. Combined with a widespread desire to suppress the rebellion, simply recruiting a state's contingent of the federal force created few political and social costs for these states. If men were paid out of the common treasury, the monetary cost of raising the army would be solely the cost of recruitment, which neither state really attempted to pay. Considering that men who enlisted in the infantry faced a high rate of unemployment at the time, recruiting an army had the potential of employing local residents at the union's expense. Paying and supplying the army, on the other hand, cost the states more than they wanted to bear. In addition, Massachusetts and Connecticut stood to gain more substantially from a federal force than states further away. Rebellion was on their doorstep; it threatened their courts and disrupted the collection of their taxes. Had the requisition succeeded, these states would have gained more private benefits from suppressing the rebellion than states farther away. The minimal cost of recruiting forces would have provided at least a small federal army to meet state purposes if other states raised the money needed to pay them.[56]

CONCLUSION

The events surrounding state reactions to Shays' Rebellion were consistent with the private benefits hypothesis and the joint products model. As that model predicts, states that gained private benefits from a requisition were more likely to pay their shares than states that gained less. Massachusetts, Connecticut, and New York made contributions consistent with local interests and their proximity to the threat. Virginia did not gain the same type of benefits from quelling domestic unrest, but it did gain private benefits from contributing to the federal effort. Fortunately, state interests were fairly consistent with the interests of the union. Massachusetts and New York raised forces to stop the insurrection near their borders. They pursued the insurgents, made a number of

---

[56] The low cost of supplying men may not generalize to earlier requisitions. Levies filled during the Revolutionary War assigned men to armies that were already standing and likely to engage well-trained opponents whether sufficient numbers were raised or not. In other words, more casualties were expected during the Revolution than in 1786. This made the socioeconomic costs of raising men for the Revolution much higher than those for the Rebellion. Considering that men were frequently conscripted during the Revolution, political costs from raising an army were larger during the war as well. Raising troops in 1786 was uniquely economical.

arrests, and provided general security for the union. But neither state protected the arsenal at Springfield, and neither state put its troops in a position where they could be redeployed toward the western frontier. The rebellion was quelled, but in a manner slightly different from the interest of the union.

The failure of the Shays requisition set the stage for the federal Constitution of 1789. After 1787, Americans knew that the system of requisitions was not giving states incentive to contribute to the union. Requisitions would not provide for national defense, and they would not help Congress discharge its debts. The nation's weak response to Shays' Rebellion helped ardent New England radicals such as Paul Revere, Samuel Adams, and John Hancock to seek a new set of institutions and a new constitution. As a representative to the Massachusetts general assembly wrote, "I never saw so great a change in the public mind on any occasion as has lately appeared in this state as to the expediency of increasing the powers of Congress."[57]

The problem of collective action surrounding the Shays' requisition was not new. It typified state responses to federal requisitions from 1775 to 1789. What was new about the Shays requisition was its clear demonstration of the conflict between common state interests, on the one hand, and local incentives, on the other. States that had unanimously declared their common interests in Congress openly defied their own decisions when it was time to pay their shares. Those that withheld men or money faced problems of cooperation that extended beyond mere resource constraints. Those that contributed resources did so for reasons other than their common obligations. The failure of the October 21 requisition clearly demonstrated what many had suspected. The confederation could not raise federal revenues effectively through the system of requisitions, and some state sovereignty would have to be sacrificed to galvanize the union.

---

[57] Stephen Higginson to Henry Knox, November 25, 1786, Knox, *Henry Knox Papers*, reel 19, frame 58.

7

A New Constitution

[T]he difficulty certainly is, how to give this power in such manner as that it may only be used to good, and not abused to bad purposes. Whoever shall solve this difficulty will receive the thanks of this and future generations.

– Richard Henry Lee[1]

If revenues would have permitted it, some members of Congress would have voted to maintain a small standing army in the summer of 1787, rather than to repeal the special requisition outright. Crises like Shays' Rebellion could occur again, particularly with American settlers moving westward into Indian territory. With a small standing army, the federal government could demonstrate its energy and react more effectively to military necessities. But without the perpetual consent of nine state delegations or a means of financing a force, the federal government could not defend the West.

The Nationalists used the nation's poor response to Shays' Rebellion to illustrate the defects of the union and to push for institutional reform. They observed that states withheld requisitions according to the particulars of each request and realized that requisitions in their original form would work only partially. Reliance on requisitions prevented Congress from raising the men and money it needed to provide public goods for the states. By the summer of 1787, the federal government had no funds to protect American shipping from the Barbary states, it could not dislodge the British from their garrisons along the Canadian border, and it could not breach the Spanish blockade of the Mississippi – let alone suppress a domestic insurrection. Each problem affected the United States and threatened its interests. Congress cajoled the states for money and for men, but it could not get the system of requisitions to

[1] Richard Henry Lee to George Mason, May 15, 1787, Lee, *Letters*, 2: 420.

work completely. For the Nationalists, old institutions based on a confederation of civically minded republics would never be the solution. New institutions had to be developed.

Nationalists, including those who supported the Constitution and those who wanted something more, tried to give Congress the power to enforce requisitions or other sources of revenue throughout the 1780s. This was not new in 1787. What became new by 1787 was an increasingly widespread admission that the confederation was deficient and that the central government needed to be more effective. Many Americans no longer believed that civic virtue would encourage politicians to contribute resources to the federal government. They believed that the federal government needed new institutions to induce cooperation from the states or that Congress should have an independent source of revenue. The confederation had failed to provide an efficient amount of public goods for the states, and in 1787 they were ready for wholesale reform.

This chapter introduces the institutions that Americans proposed to solve the collective action problem among states. The first proposals were amendments to the Articles of Confederation, motivated by the goals of promoting common state interests and protecting state sovereignty. As soon as the framers discovered that increasing efficiency implied substantial trade-offs in state sovereignty, they changed their tack and sought an entirely new design. The Virginia Plan and subsequent Constitution allowed the federal government to act directly upon the people and to raise excise and impost taxes directly. Although it addressed a wide variety of problems, the Constitution also can be seen as a solution to the collective action problem among states.

But treating the Constitution as one of many solutions to the collective action problem presents a problem. With several institutional solutions under consideration, why did the framers choose to reconstitute the government?[2] Certainly, one of the amendments considered, or some combination of them, would be adequate for solving the problems of the confederation. In addition to introducing proposed reforms, this chapter suggests that one of the reasons that Nationalists tried to reconstitute the government was to circumvent established rules for reform. Madison,

---

[2] This question was explicitly addressed by Merrill Jensen in *A New Nation*. Jensen argued that the Nationalists reconstituted the government to strengthen their own interests. Rakove, *Beginnings of National Politics*, 380–396, suggests that incremental amendments were avoided because passing some reforms would weaken the chance of other reforms being passed. Rakove's argument that the framers were trying to shape a take-it-or-leave-it option has been extended by Riker, *Strategy of Rhetoric*. Beard, *An Economic Interpretation*; Crosskey and Jeffrey, *Political Background of a Federal Convention*; and others have addressed this question as well.

and other reformers, realized that an entirely new constitution might be ratified more easily than an amendment to the Articles of Confederation, and this is part of the reason that they chose this new approach.

The irony of reconstitution being easier than amendment stems from the fact that all amendments to the Articles of Confederation had to receive the unanimous consent of state legislatures to be ratified. A new constitution, in contrast, could be proposed by a federal convention and possibly ratified by a super-majority of popularly elected state conventions. What Madison needed was a proposal that would justify such a process. The Virginia Plan fit that bill nicely. In other words, the chicken did not come before the egg. New ratification procedures were not proposed because they were appropriate for the new government; a new government was created to legitimize a new procedure for ratification.

MORE EFFICIENCY

The authors of the Articles of Confederation did not understand the forces that bound their union together, wrote Benjamin Rush. "Although we understood perfectly the principles of liberty, most of us were ignorant of the forms and combinations of power in republics." The Stamp Act, Intolerable Acts, and war with Great Britain made authors of the confederation adverse to anything that resembled centralized authority. They wanted to protect state sovereignty and gave the power of enforcement to the states to promote that goal. As Jackson Turner Main wrote, the fact that "the Articles of Confederation denied to Congress the right to raise money by taxation was no accident, nor a product of ignorance, but a recognition that control of the public's money could be 'faithfully watched' only if the individual states had their separate treasuries."[3] Maintaining state authority over confederation revenue helped protect state sovereignty and local democracy. The idea might have worked if state politicians were as virtuous as the authors of the Articles of Confederation had anticipated. But state politicians were responsive to the interests of their constituents and were not willing to surrender state resources to the common good. Whether this meant that they were protecting thirteen separate conceptions of the common welfare or trying to serve the material interests of their constituents did not matter.[4] State

---

[3] Rush, "Address to the People of the United States," January 1787, Jensen, ed., *Documentary History*, 13: 46; Main, *Antifederalists*, 79. For an interpretation similar to Main's, see Hoffert, *A Politics of Tensions*.

[4] Note that the collective action problem described throughout this book has more to do with interstate behavior than with the self-interest of state politicians. Politicians who pursue the interests of their states are not likely to abnegate to the union whether they are self-interested or state-interested.

politicians would not abnegate local interests for the needs of the union in either case. The framers knew that they needed to do something more than promote civic virtue. They believed new institutions were the best solution.[5]

INSTITUTIONAL SOLUTIONS

The institutions that they proposed attempted to increase the efficiency of the central government without overly infringing upon state sovereignty. Although historical accounts have focused on the impost amendments and the Constitution as the major attempts to alter the confederation and give Congress greater revenue power, other proposals were certainly considered. Benjamin Tupper, a Massachusetts state legislator, and Peregrine Foster, a citizen from Rhode Island, proposed replacing the confederation with a monarchy. James Monroe proposed a three-branch design similar to the Constitution with both legislative chambers representing the states and the system of requisitions maintained. Monroe believed that a more complete national government would encourage states to comply with requisitions without an enforcement mechanism. Others believed that the union should be broken into regional confederations, while still others entertained the idea of dissolving the union altogether and leaving government entirely to the states.[6] Certainly there were countless more proposals, but Congress gave serious consideration to only four ideas after the Articles of Confederation were adopted in 1781: the coercive powers amendment of 1781, the impost amendment of 1783, the amendment for conditional direct tax-

---

[5] As L.F.E. Oppenheim observed, "[i]t is an indisputable fact that [sovereignty], from the moment that it was introduced in political science until the present day, has never had a meaning which was universally agreed upon" (*International Law*, 1 (1905): 103, quoted in Hannum, *Autonomy, Sovereignty, and Self-Determination*, 14). For a survey of the various conceptions of autonomy and sovereignty, see ibid., 14–49, and Dworkin, "The Concept of Autonomy." For its effect on shaping the Constitution, see Onuf, "State Sovereignty and the Making of the Constitution." Although economists typically define efficiency using the Pareto criteria, doing so here would present a problem. The impost amendment would place Rhode Island, and later New York, in a worse situation because the amendment threatened to reduce revenues from state import taxes. Hence, the impost amendment would not be a Pareto improvement over the Articles of Confederation. Contemporaries, however, clearly believed the impost amendment would be an improvement of efficiency, suggesting that the Pareto criteria would not capture the contemporary perspective. A more suitable definition might be the easy-rider index described by Cornes and Sandler, *Theory of Externalities*, 159–161. See Stokey and Zeckhauser, *Primer for Policy Analysis*, 270–273, for a definition of the Pareto criteria.

[6] Brown, *Redeeming*, 176–177; and Some Observations on the Constitution, Monroe, *Writings*, 1: 307–343. Zuckert, "Federalism and the Founding," analyzes six federal designs considered at the federal convention. Others are described by Rakove, *Beginnings of National Politics*, 382–388.

ation of 1786, and the fully drafted Constitution of 1787. These plans represent the most serious attempts to revise the Articles of Confederation and to solve the collective action problem among states. Each was proposed in response to a failed requisition system that left the national government wanting for more efficiency but still demanding a protection of state sovereignty.

The Coercive Powers Amendment

Unlike the impost amendment, the coercive powers amendment originated with the states. As described in Chapter 4, the New York legislature introduced the idea when Washington was asked to liberate New York City without resources to attack. In October 1780, the legislature resolved that whenever a state was deficient in its quota of men, money, or supplies, Congress should "compel it to furnish its deficiency" through military force. The legislature further instructed that the resolution should be sent to Congress and discussed at the Hartford convention where New York commissioners were directed to "propose and agree to" the plan.[7]

The Hartford convention agreed to the New York proposal with few revisions. Though it toned down the language of marching the army into delinquent states, it maintained the power of coercing compliance and allowed the commander of the armed forces to coerce the states without consulting Congress. John Witherspoon, preacher and delegate from New Jersey, reacted to the news of the Hartford convention with disgust: "[T]hat resolution is of such a nature that I should never give my voice to it . . . and I have that opinion of Gen. Washington that I do not think he would accept or act in consequence of such powers." James Warren, speaker of the Massachusetts assembly, agreed. He believed the idea ignored "the Principals on which our Opposition to Britain rests. . . . General Washington is a Good and a Great Man. I love and Reverence him. But he is only a Man and therefore should not be vested with such

---

[7] The Hartford convention met on November 8, 1780. It was attended by commissioners from the five northeastern states to consider several flaws in the union, including the New York proposal. The convention resolved "that the Commander in Chief of the army of the United States be authorized and empowered to take such measures as he may deem proper and the public service may render necessary to *induce* the several states to a punctual compliance with the regulations which have been or may be made by Congress for supplies for the years 1780 and 1781." The Hartford convention restricted coercive authority to two years and allowed the Commander in Chief to act without the consent of Congress, but it made few revisions to the original New York version (see Resolutions of the New York Assembly, October 10, 1780, New York, *Journal of the Assembly, 1780*, 43; John Witherspoon to the Governor of New Jersey (William Livingston), December 16, 1780, Burdett, ed., *Letters of Members*, 5: 487–88, emphasis in the original).

powers." Witherspoon and Warren both recognized the deficiencies of the requisition system, but neither was willing to fix it by sending an army into a delinquent state. They were conscious of its effect on state sovereignty and would not accede to the plan. The prospect of assigning such powers to Washington's successor, who might be a less prudent man, was even more disturbing.[8]

Others favored the proposal with Congress deciding whether to coerce. Madison believed "the necessity of arming Congress with coercive powers arises from the shameful deficiency of some of the States which are most capable of yielding their appropriate supplies." Root claimed that requisitions allowed states to individually defeat the most important measures of Congress and that the power of coercing delinquent states "is so far from infringing upon the rights or sovereignty of the particular States that it is as necessary for the preservation of them as the union itself." Independence was necessary for state sovereignty, Root argued. Though he favored the coercive powers amendment over the Articles of Confederation in its unamended form, Root further confessed his preference for the impost amendment over the other two.[9] Both amendments were considered at the same time, which weakened support for the coercive powers amendment.

The proposal was assigned to a congressional committee, debated, and offered to the floor on February 23.[10] Five days after the Articles of Confederation were enacted and one month after Congress passed the first impost amendment, James Mitchell Varnum proposed that Congress give itself "full and explicit powers for effectually carrying into execution all

[8] John Witherspoon to the Governor of New Jersey (William Livingston), December 16, 1780, ibid., 5: 487–488; James Warren to Samuel Adams, December 4, 1780, Lodge, ed., *Warren-Adams Letters*, 2: 151. Despite Witherspoon's claim, Washington favored the proposal. He wrote that "the non compliance with the reccmns. of Congress in some States; the unseasonable compliance in time and manner by others; the heavy expence accumulated thereby to no purpose . . . are alone sufficient to prove the necessity of a controuling power" (George Washington to Joseph Jones, March 24, 1781, Washington, *Writings*, 21: 371–374).

[9] *JCC*, 18: 1141; James Madison to Thomas Jefferson, Madison, *Papers*, 3: 71; Jesse Root to the Governor of Connecticut (Jonathan Trumbull), December 27, 1780, Burnett, ed., *Letters of Members*, 5: 504; Amendment to Committee Report on Hartford Convention, Madison, *Papers*, 2: 318–319.

[10] The proceedings of the Hartford Convention were laid before Congress on December 12 and assigned to a five-man committee consisting of John Mathews (SC), James Madison (VA), Jesse Root (CT), Joseph Montgomery (PA), and John Witherspoon (NJ). Madison and Root favored the idea of compelling compliance with requisitions rather than leaving the system in its current form. Montgomery and Witherspoon opposed the measure. Mathews, who later became a Federalist, acted as the swing vote and must have favored softening the measure. The five-man committee proposed a bill without the compulsory clause on February 23.

acts or resolutions passed agreeably to the Articles of Confederation."
The motion carried and Congress appointed a three-man committee of
Varnum, Madison, and James Duane to prepare amendments to the
Articles of Confederation. The committee favored the proposal and a
strong coercive clause. Varnum and Madison were clear advocates of
enforcing requisitions and Duane represented the very state that presented the idea.[11]

The product they produced was laid before Congress on March 16,
1781. They proposed that Congress be given the authority to "compel"
delinquent states into compliance by employing "the force of the United
States as well by sea as by land." Congress could distrain "the effects of
Vessels and Merchandizes of such State or States or of any of the Citizens thereof wherever found, and to prohibit and prevent their trade and
intercourse as well." The proposal would give Congress the ability to
use economic sanctions, as well as coercive force, to obtain compliance
with requisitions.[12]

Madison envisioned that the amendment would be carried out as a
small embargo against offending states. "The situation of most of the
States is such that two or three vessels of force employed against their
trade will make it their interest to yield prompt obedience to all just
requisitions on them." Madison not only favored the coercive powers
amendment, he was one of its biggest advocates in Congress. He included
a similar institution in his Virginia Plan and did not completely surrender the idea until the Constitutional Convention. The reason that he later
created the Virginia Plan could not have been that he found coercive
powers unprincipled. On the contrary, he found them sufficiently effective to include them in his own plan and explicitly defended them in
1781. The push for a new constitution in 1787 was for reasons other
than disliking coercive designs.

The Varnum, Madison, and Duane report was debated in early May
and referred to a grand committee, consisting of one member from
each state, on May 2. While the three members favored coercion, the
preponderance of delegates did not share their sentiments. The grand
committee delivered a milder version on July 20 which suggested that

[11] JCC, 19: 236; James Mitchell Varnum to the Governor of Rhode Island (William
Greene), March 16, 1781, Burnett, ed., Letters of Members, 6: 28; and James Mitchell
Varnum to the Governor of Rhode Island (William Greene), April 2, 1781, ibid., 6:
41–42. In the latter, Varnum further advocates a constitutional convention "to revise
and refraim the Articles of Confederation."

[12] Amendment to Give Congress Coercive Power over the States and their Citizens, March
16, 1781, Jensen, ed., Documentary History, 1: 141–143; "The Articles of Confederation," Ketcham, Anti-Federalist Papers, 364; Proposed Amendment of the Articles of
Confederation, March 12, 1781, Madison, Papers, 3: 17–20.

Congress be given the power to lay temporary, uniform embargoes during a time of war and that states should keep separate accounts for the taxes they raised to pay requisitions. The report did not mention coercion, and the new embargoes were more for the regulation of trade than for gaining compliance with requisitions. Trade reforms were always less controversial than enforcement mechanisms, even though they were not more central to reform. Even though the grand committee softened the report, the coercive powers amendment was left to die as a controversial measure.[13]

A year later Hamilton expressed the dilemma underlying the whole idea. Using the pseudonym "the Continentalist" he wrote:

A mere regard to the interests of the confederacy will never be a principle sufficiently active to curb the ambition and intrigues of different members. Force cannot effect it: A contest of arms will seldom be between the common sovereign and a single refractory member; but between distinct combinations of the several parts against each other.[14]

Many believed that requisitions were not effective in their present form, but they also believed that giving Congress the power to coerce states was a worse idea. Congress did not have a supreme standing army to coerce compliance from the states. It had to depend on state militias to carry out acts of coercion. If a few states failed to comply with a requisition, Congress would pit troops from complying states against troops from noncomplying states. In such an environment, the coercive powers amendment might lead to civil war. This was Hamilton's point. The coercive powers amendment would create instability, not efficiency. Members of Congress did not want the trade-offs in state sovereignty and the clashes between state forces that the coercive powers amendment implied. The idea would have solved the collective action problem among states, if congressional forces were supreme,[15] but it would entail large

---

[13] The grand committee report was turned over to yet another three-man committee which later included a coercive powers clause among a laundry list of additional powers for Congress. The new three-man committee submitted its report on August 22, 1781, and Congress made it the order of business the next day. There is no evidence, however, that Congress ever considered the report (for the report of the grand committee, see *JCC*, 20: 469–471, 773; and Report of the Grand Committee Delivered July 20, 1781, *PCC*, M 247, r. 31, i. 24, p. 15–16. For the report of the three-man committee of Randolph, Ellsworth, and Varnum, see Committee Report on Carrying the Confederation into Effect and on Additional Powers Needed by Congress, August 22, 1781, Jensen, ed., *Documentary History*, 1: 143–145; and *JCC*, 21: 893–896).

[14] The Continentalist No. VI, July 4, 1782, Hamilton, *Papers*, 3: 105.

[15] The efficient production of a public good requires both an accurate estimate of state demands as well as an enforcement mechanism that ensures these estimates will be fully enforced. In claiming that the coercive powers amendment would improve efficiency, I

trade-offs in state sovereignty. Such a proposal was unlikely to obtain support from any legislature that was asked to subjugate itself to congressional rule. Reformers needed to wait for the results of the first impost amendment before proposing a second, more controversial amendment to the states. Unfortunately, the impost amendment failed to be ratified and the coercive powers amendment died in its wake.

The Amendment for Conditional, Direct Taxation

Since the impost amendment of 1783 was already introduced in Chapter 4, it will not be elaborated on here. Instead, we skip to the third amendment deliberated on by Congress – the amendment for conditional direct taxation. This measure developed shortly after the New Jersey affair in 1786. In the spring of that year, Congress sent Charles Pinckney to New Jersey as head of a congressional envoy. He proposed that the New Jersey legislature seek redress for its grievances against New York by calling a general convention of the states, rather than officially declaring that New Jersey would not comply with requisitions. Many members of the New Jersey legislature liked the idea, and on May 3, roughly two months after Pinckney spoke in Trenton, Pinckney proposed that Congress assign a day to sit as a "committee of the whole to take into consideration the state of public affairs." Pinckney thought the grand committee should either appoint a convention to discuss greater powers for Congress or consider greater powers themselves and propose these powers as amendments to the Articles of Confederation in the usual fashion.[16]

James Monroe favored the idea of compelling state compliance, but responded that there was no need for a convention. He believed that the thirteenth article of confederation gave Congress the right to "Compel a Complyance in every case." He also believed the second impost amendment would soon pass. Monroe saw no need for a convention with both possibilities on the horizon. Despite Monroe's objection, however,

---

implicitly assume that Congress would estimate roughly efficient demand through a Lindahl mechanism. Even with a fully functioning Lindahl mechanism, however, these estimates would be imperfect. Efficiency would improve, but it would not be optimal (see Mueller, *Public Choice II*, 43–49; and Cornes and Sandler, *Theory of Externalities*, 201–205, for more on the Lindahl mechanism; and Dougherty, "A Public Choice Comparison," for its application to the current setting).

[16] For a general overview of Pinckney's proposal, see Introduction, Commentaries on the Constitution, Jensen, ed., *Documentary History*, 13: 31–33; and Bancroft, *History of the Formation of the Constitution*, 1: 253–266. For a description of the New Jersey affair and early proposals for a federal convention, see Nathaniel Gorham to Caleb Davis, March 1, 1786, Smith, ed., *Letters of Delegates*, 23: 166–167; and William Grayson to Richard Henry Lee, March 22, 1786, ibid., 23: 200–203. The quoted passage comes from *JCC*, 30: 230.

Congress assigned the following Tuesday to sit as a committee of the whole and to discuss possible amendments. This was Congress's last attempt to alter the confederation before it considered the fully drafted Constitution.[17]

After sitting in grand committee, William Grayson became "apprehensive" that the committee "will produce nothing & that Congress will never be able to agree on the proper amendments even among themselves." Proposed reforms always seemed to be entangled with local interests. Grayson believed the states from New England wanted nothing more than to "carry the commercial point" because "our affairs are not arrived at such a crisis as to insure success to a reformation on proper principles." Without such a crisis, delegates would be reluctant to propose more difficult reforms. In the words of Rufus King, every man who proposed strengthening the federal government was accused of being "unfriendly to the liberties of the People." Protecting state sovereignty and defending individual liberty were legitimate goals of the confederation, and accusing delegates of violating liberty was an effective way of dissuading delegates from backing reforms.[18]

On July 3, Congress appointed a grand committee to report such amendments and to draft such resolutions as might be necessary to "render the federal government adequate to the ends for which it was instituted." A month later, the grand committee laid seven amendments before Congress, numbered Articles XIV–XX, as proposed additions to the original thirteen.[19] These amendments touched on a wide variety of commercial, financial, judicial, and legislative reforms. Article XIV gave Congress the exclusive power to regulate foreign and domestic commerce, to levy import and export duties, and to make laws required to collect duties. Article XV directed Congress to specify a timetable when the states had to pass laws complying with congressional requisitions. States that failed to comply by a specified date would be assessed additional charges. Article XVII awarded interest to states that paid surpluses to Congress and fined them for arrears. Article XVIII altered the system of amending the Articles of Confederation. It allowed the assent of only eleven state legislatures to pass amendments that dealt with new systems of revenue or finance. Article XIX allowed Congress to appoint a federal court with specific powers and Article XX was designed to improve

---

[17] Thomas Rodney's Diary, May 3, 1786, Smith, ed., *Letters of Delegates*, 23: 262–263.

[18] William Grayson to James Madison, May 28, 1786, ibid., 23: 320; Rufus King to Elbridge Gerry, June 18, 1786, ibid., 23: 364. On Grayson's disposition toward constitutional reform, see William Grayson to William Short, November 10, 1787, ibid., 24: 550–551.

[19] Amendments to the Articles of Confederation Proposed by a Grand Committee of Congress, August 7, 1786, Jensen, ed., *Documentary History*, 1: 163–168.

attendance in Congress by disqualifying delegates who did not arrive on time or left without permission.[20]

The most significant alterations to the system of requisitions were laid out in Article XVI, which I refer to as the amendment for conditional, direct taxation. The Article read:

[I]f any State shall so Neglect as aforesaid to pass laws in compliance with the said Requisition . . . and it shall then or afterwards be found that a Majority of the States have passed such laws and adopted such measures, the United States in Congress Assembled shall have full power and authority to levy, assess and collect all sums and duties with which any such State so neglecting to comply with the Requisition may Stand charged.

Congress would have the power to assess direct taxes whenever a state was delinquent in a requisition for ten months and a majority of the other states had complied with the request. Rather than coerce delinquent states into compliance, as proposed by the coercive powers amendment, this amendment gave Congress the power to tax individuals directly using the same manner that taxes had been previously assessed. Avoiding the use of coercive force reduced the prospect of a civil war. Although the amendment would increase the power of Congress, it was also careful to protect the rights of states – something that state legislatures and delegates desired. A state was given every opportunity to willfully pay its requisition under the proposed system and Congress could tax directly only when a majority of other states complied. If the preponderance of states found a requisition tyrannical or unjust, they could still withhold their requisitions as the authors of the Articles of Confederation had originally intended. Congress could infringe on state sovereignty only when a majority of states concurred with its requisition. In this sense it was a milder version of the coercive powers amendment. The amendment for conditional, direct taxation would produce less efficient outcomes than the coercive powers amendment, but it would do a better job of preserving state sovereignty.

Congress planned to consider the amendments on August 14, but there was no evidence that Congress discussed the measure then or on any other day. The proposal was tabled because of the bitter dispute between North and South over the treaty with Spain. Spain had blockaded American ships from the Mississippi River, which affected southern trade. At the same time, northern states wanted the Secretary of Foreign Affairs, John Jay, to negotiate a commercial treaty with Spain that advanced their economic interests. Congress had instructed Jay to

---

[20] *JCC*, 30: 494–498; Introduction, Commentaries on the Constitution, *Documentary History*, 13: 31–33.

negotiate the treaty only if he was able to protect American rights to the free navigation of the Mississippi River. On August 3, four days before the grand committee reported the amendment for conditional direct taxation, Jay wrote a letter to Congress asking whether Congress would forbear navigation of the Mississippi for a period of twenty-five to thirty years so that he could close the deal with Spain. Southern delegates were stunned by Jay's request. After a bitter debate, Congress repealed Jay's earlier instructions to protect the Mississippi River in a vote of seven states to five. The vote split along sectional lines, with the northern states voting for the repeal and the southern states voting against it. Congress would now allow Jay to negotiate the treaty without protecting southern interests.[21]

Southern delegates would not support the amendment for conditional, direct taxation under such conditions. If the amendment passed, Congress would have the exclusive power to regulate foreign and domestic commerce, as well as the power of taxing conditionally. The amendment would force southerners to comply with the treaty and subjugate them to northern rule. The whole dispute endangered the movement to strengthen the national government and killed the amendment for conditional, direct taxation. The amendment would not obtain the nine-state majority needed to pass it to the states and it certainly would not receive ratification from all thirteen. More than three attempts to amend the Articles of Confederation had failed, and several started to consider more radical reforms.

The Constitution

The development of the Constitution followed a more circuitous path, though one of its principle motivations was the same – solving the collective action problem among states. The Articles of Confederation did not allow the national government to properly adjudicate disputes between states, to manage foreign affairs, or to regulate interstate commerce. "But the radical infirmity of the 'art[icle]s of Confederation,'" wrote Madison in his preface to the notes on the federal convention, "was the dependence of Cong[res]s on the voluntary and simultaneous compliance with its Requisitions, by so many independent Communities,

---

[21] Timothy Bloodworth to Richard Caswell, September 4, 1786, Smith, ed., *Letters of Delegates*, 23: 549–550; Amendments to the Articles of Confederation Proposed by a Grand Committee of Congress, August 7, 1786, Jensen, ed., *Documentary History*, 1: 163–168. For details on the Jay-Gardoqui affair, see The United States, Spain, and the Navigation of the Mississippi River, Jensen, ed., *Documentary History*, 13: 149–152; and Banning, *Sacred Fire of Liberty*, 66–75. A sample of southern objections can be found in James Madison to Thomas Jefferson, March 19, 1787, Madison, *Papers*, 9: 319–322.

each consulting more or less its particular interests & convenience and distrusting the compliance of others."[22] Requisitions embodied the fundamental problem of leaving enforcement with the states, and they were in dire need of reform. As Roger Sherman said midway through the federal convention, "I acknowledge there have been failures in complying with federal requisitions. Many states have been defective, and the object of our convention is to amend these defects."[23] The framers created a two-house legislature, altered the apportionment of representatives, and separated the powers of government into three branches only after they were committed to a new design. These, and other institutions, were created to protect the people from a strong national government. They were not the primary reason for discarding the Articles of Confederation. As it had been for years, one of the cardinal reasons for reform was to solve the collective action problem among states.[24]

Madison began analyzing the vices of the political system well before the Annapolis convention in September 1786. He set out to obtain treaties on past and present confederacies as early as 1784 and wrote his famous "Notes on Ancient and Modern Confederacies" in the spring of 1786. In it, Madison tried to determine what made confederations fail and what made them succeed. He concluded that confederations were frail forms of government and that the absence of a controlling central authority was the common vice. This caused failures with requisitions and allowed for interstate conflict. Madison later argued that the best solution to the problem was for the general government to obtain a negative, or veto power, over local legislation, which his colleagues rejected at the Constitutional Convention.[25]

In January 1786, the Virginia assembly invited states to send commissioners to Annapolis to discuss the issue of trade. Although Madison

---

[22] Preface, Madison, *Notes of Debates*, 7.

[23] Roger Sherman, Yates' Notes on Debates, June 30, 1787, Farrand, ed., *Records of the Federal Convention*, 1: 498.

[24] The most common explanation for the Constitution is that the framers were interested in commercial reforms but entered the federal convention relatively open-minded about what type of reforms they would enact (Banning, *Sacred Fire of Liberty*; Rakove, *Beginnings of National Politics*; and Zuckert, "Federalism and the Founding"). Others have argued that foreign affairs (Marks, *Independence on Trial*), sectional conflict (Davis, *Sectionalism in American Politics*), land disputes (Onuf, *Origins of the Federal Republic*), or the system of requisitions (Brown, *Redeeming*) brought about the need for constitutional reform. By claiming that the framers were primarily interested in resolving the collective action problem among states, I make a broader claim than stating that the impetus was merely the inadequacy of requisition. As stated in the conclusion, requisitions were one manifestation of the broader problem of leaving enforcement with the states.

[25] "Notes on Ancient and Modern Confederacies," Madison, *Papers*, 5: 3–24.

orchestrated the invitation and had larger reforms in mind, the Virginia legislature did not give its delegates full authority to propose amendments to the Articles of Confederation. Madison thought that the meeting could still be used to recommend additional powers for Congress. He wrote to Monroe, "the expedient is better than nothing; and, as the recommendation of additional powers to Congress is within the purview of the commission, it may possibly lead to better consequences than at first occur."[26]

On the surface, the Annapolis convention appeared to fail. Only five states sent delegates to the convention, and the state hosting it, Maryland, was not among them. Without more delegations, those attending did not conduct business. But Madison and Hamilton used the convention to their advantage. They convinced other delegates that a second convention would be needed to consider "important defects in the system of the Foederal Government." The delegates from New Jersey were given the power to discuss "commercial regulations and other important matters." Hamilton urged states to give their delegates to the second convention the same broad powers as New Jersey had given its delegates to the Annapolis convention. Anything that the federal convention should decide would be reported to Congress and, if confirmed, should be ratified by state legislatures. Members of the convention agreed to the proposal and asked their states to appoint delegates to a second convention in Philadelphia. They then sent a copy of their report to Congress out of "respect."[27]

Some members of Congress suspected that the delegates in Annapolis wanted wholesale revisions and tried to ensure that the Philadelphia

---

[26] The Annapolis convention sprang out of the Mount Vernon accords. In 1785, delegates from Virginia and Maryland met in Mount Vernon and agreed on a means of obtaining free navigation of the Potomac River. They also agreed to consider extending the headwaters of the Potomac to the Ohio River and to consider free navigation of the Chesapeake. Their compact required the assent of Pennsylvania and Delaware and perhaps another meeting. The Annapolis convention was that subsequent meeting (for quoted remarks, see Madison to Monroe, January 22, 1786, ibid., 8: 483; for evidence that Madison orchestrated the invitation to the Annapolis convention in Virginia, see Rutland's introduction, The Annapolis Convention, September 1786, ibid., 9: 115–119; for a fairly complete discussion of the Mount Vernon Compact, see Mason, *Papers*, 2: 812–823).

[27] Proceedings of the State Commissioners at Annapolis, Maryland, September 11–14, 1786, Kammen, *Origins of the Constitution*, 21, 20. Madison explained to Washington that a convention based on trade had fewer enemies than a convention granting revenue and regulatory powers, suggesting that this is why trade was discussed (James Madison to George Washington, December 9, 1785, Madison, *Papers*, 8: 439). For a different view, see Rakove, *Beginnings of National Politics*, and Banning, *Sacred Fire of Liberty*. Both authors argue that Madison and Hamilton entered the Annapolis convention with little more than commercial reform in mind.

convention worked within the framework of the Articles – in both content and procedure. Congress received the report from the Annapolis convention on September 20 and assigned it to a grand committee on October 11. Nathan Dane, a Massachusetts delegate and member of the grand committee, told the Massachusetts legislature that he suspected the Annapolis convention wanted to discard the federal system and to replace it with a different form of government. He believed that members of the convention were consciously vague about their intent.[28] Other members of the committee were suspicious of the proposal and hoped that Congress would propose adequate amendments of its own. Combined with frequently poor attendance, the committee was in no position to take action before Congress ended its session on November 3, 1786.

By the time Congress had reconvened the following January, the Virginia legislature had already taken the lead. They approved the report of the Annapolis convention and declared that a federal convention was "preferable to the discussion of the subject in Congress."[29] The Virginia legislature asked other states to pass similar resolves, and by the time Congress received representation of seven states to conduct business on January 17, 1787, Virginia, New Jersey, Pennsylvania, and North Carolina had already appointed delegates consistent with the resolve of the Annapolis convention. Other states soon followed. New Jersey agreed to the proposal but omitted all references to Congress's approval. Other states restricted their delegates from certain reforms.[30]

On February 13 Congress added two delegates to the grand commit-

---

[28] Nathan Dane's Address to the Massachusetts House of Representatives, November 9, 1786, Smith, ed., *Letters of Delegates*, 24: 20. For other discussions of the rumors about wholesale reforms, see William Pierce to George Turner, May 19, 1787, ibid., 24: 281–283.

[29] The Virginia legislature claimed that a convention was preferred to discussing the matter in Congress because Congress would be overly interrupted by ordinary business. The official invitation asked states to "join with them in devising and discussing all such Alterations and farther Provisions as may be necessary to render the Federal Constitution adequate to the Exigencies of the Union." Although the invitation did not explicitly mention it, Madison probably had *constitutional* convention in mind when he ushered the proposal through the Virginia legislature (see An Act Authorizing the Election of Delegates, November 23, 1786, Jensen, ed., *Documentary History*, 1: 196–198).

[30] Delaware forbade their delegates from accepting any alteration of equal votes in Congress; New Hampshire instructed its delegates to attend only if the convention received the approval of Congress; and Connecticut and New York instructed their delegates to consider revisions of the Articles of Confederation alone (Appointments of Delegates to the Constitutional Convention, November 23, 1786 – September 15, 1787, Jensen, ed., *Documentary History*, 1: 192–292).

tee, and six days later the committee endorsed the report of the Annapolis convention by one vote.[31] When the issue was presented before the floor on February 21, the New York delegation moved to postpone the report and to consider a motion from the New York legislature proposing a convention. Their proposal was similar to that of the Annapolis convention but contained the proviso that the convention meet "for the purpose of *Revising* the Articles of Confederation," not for considering a new government. If Congress adopted the New York proposal, the new convention would be working under the direction of Congress; it would limit itself to new amendments and it would not allow radical changes in design. The New York proposal would delay the measure as well. States that had already assigned delegates would have to reassign delegates with new instructions about the nature of their business. After some debate over the proper mode of proposing revisions, through Congress or through convention, members of Congress agreed to a compromise. They acknowledged the appointments previously made but declared that the meeting was "for the sole and express purpose of revising the Articles of Confederation." The former prevented New York from delaying the action, while the latter instructed the convention to work within the confines of the existing system.[32]

Several delegates seemed to ignore the point. Six days later, William Irvine, a delegate from Pennsylvania, wrote, "Some states have complied in part with the requisitions of Congress – some not at all, and others have flatly refused. There is therefore no alternative to giving up all at once for lost – but that of attempting to revise and mend the Confederation – or to frame an entire new Government – whether the proposed Convention will be able to affect either it is hard to say – but an attempt

---

[31] Adding two delegates to the grand committee helped the report onto the floor. A slight change in political climate may have affected it as well. In April 1786 a party of "Levelers" took control of the Rhode Island government, and by February 1787 they were considering a bill for redistributing private property every thirteen years. New Hampshire farmers had surrounded the New Hampshire state house less than six months before, and Shays' Rebellion reached its apex when the congressional committee was considering whether to endorse the federal convention proposed in Annapolis. The confederation may have appeared more ineffective at the time, with little hope of obtaining Rhode Island's consent to amendments. This was the backdrop from which Congress considered the Annapolis report, and it may have convinced several delegates to favor the proposal (The Calling of the Constitutional Convention, January 21 – February 21, 1787, Jensen, ed., *Documentary History*, 178–179).

[32] Resolve of the New York Assembly Regarding the Articles of Confederation, February 17, 1787, PCC, M 247, R 81, i 67, 2: 555; *JCC*, 32: 71–74; Madison's Notes on Debates, February 21, 1787, Smith, ed., *Letters of Delegates*, 24: 108–110; James Madison to Edmund Randolph, February 25, 1787, ibid., 24: 120–121; and James Madison to Thomas Jefferson, February 15, 1787, ibid., 24: 94 n. 5.

is necessary and the sooner it is made it will be sooner compleated." Congress stated that the convention could only propose amendments to the Articles of Confederation, but Irvine acted as if there were talk about ignoring the decree. With the authority given to the convention by the states, reconstituting the government might still be within their purview.[33]

Madison ignored the declaration of Congress as well. In the spring of 1787 he described the failures of the confederation in a note titled "Vices of the Political System of the United Sates" and outlined his own plan for government in letters to Jefferson, Washington, and Governor Edmund Randolph, senior delegate from Virginia. He noted that "sanction is essential to the idea of law, as coercion is to that of Government. The federal system being destitute of both, wants the great vital principles of a Political Constitution." This was the central problem of the Articles of Confederation. "[A] distrust of the voluntary compliance of each other may prevent the compliance of any," he wrote, "although it should be the latent disposition of all." Madison had recognized the collective action problem and was ready to propose a solution. At this point he was not alone.[34]

The federal convention began in Philadelphia on May 25, 1787. The first three days established the rules of the proceedings and the credentials of the delegates. On the fourth day, Randolph opened its business with a presentation of the Virginia Plan. Though Madison was its primary author, senior delegate Randolph was the more appropriate presenter. The Virginia Plan contained more than a few alterations to the Articles of Confederation. It proposed a whole new system of government. The plan described a federal government with three branches. The lower house of the legislature would be elected directly by the people and apportioned according to the number of free inhabitants within each state or the amount of revenue contributed by each state – apparently to be resolved at the convention. Other parts of the government emanated from the lower house. State legislatures would nominate members of the upper house, and the lower house would elect the upper house from those nominated. Both houses would then select members of the executive and judicial branches, which would carry out functions similar to those specified in the Constitution. The legislature also maintained the

---

[33] William Irvine to Josiah Harmer, February 27, 1787, ibid., 24: 123.
[34] Vices of the Political System of the United States, April 1787, Madison, *Writings*, 2: 363–364. Madison developed the Virginia Plan in three letters: James Madison to Thomas Jefferson, March 19, 1787, Madison, *Papers*, 9: 317–322; James Madison to Edmund Randolph, April 8, 1787, ibid., 9: 368–371; and James Madison to George Washington, April 16, 1787, Smith, ed., *Letters of Delegates*, 24: 228–232.

authority to nullify state laws, which was contested at the convention and quickly removed.[35]

As it was proposed, the Virginia Plan was ambiguous on the issue of federal revenue. The last clause of the sixth resolution authorized the legislature to "call forth the force of the Union against any member of the Union failing to fulfill its duty under the articles thereof," but no other provision was made for revenue. Presumably, this clause would give the government coercive authority similar to the coercive compliance amendment of 1781. If states failed to pay their requisitions, the legislature could apply military force against state citizens or blockade their ports. Madison was more explicit about the idea in his letter to Washington, but even then he seemed nervous about the use of force and hoped they could find a better source of federal revenue at the convention. If the Virginia Plan were allowed to act on the people, as proposed, several modes of taxation would be consistent with the doctrine of taxation by consent. Madison realized that alterations to his plan were inevitable, and as long as the government acted directly upon the people, adequate revenue could be found.

Despite differences in opinion about the nature of the proposed union, several provisions within the Virginia Plan quickly passed. Within two days, the convention agreed that the national government should contain three branches, that the legislature should have two houses, and that each house should have the power to initiate bills. The reason those measures passed quickly is because the convention clearly contained more proponents of a strong national government than opponents. According to political scientist William Riker, only six of the fifty-five delegates attending could be counted as true Anti-Federalists: Elbridge Gerry (Massachusetts), John Lansing and Robert Yates (New York), Luther Martin and John Mercer (Maryland), and Alexander Martin (North Carolina). Mercer showed up for a few days in mid-August and returned home when he realized he had no effect. Lansing and Yates went home on July 10 after realizing that the convention was going beyond the sanctions of Congress. Other delegates, such as George Mason, sat on the fence and would not be labeled true Anti-Federalists. They agreed with much of the proposed plan and sought only a few revisions. A super-majority of Nationalists is one reason that the convention easily passed measures where Congress had troubles in the past.[36]

---

[35] James Madison to George Washington, April 16, 1787, ibid., 24: 228–232; The Virginia Resolutions, Kammen, *Origins of the Constitution*, 22–25; The Resolutions and Draft Constitutions of the Constitutional Convention, May 29 – September 17, 1787, Jensen, ed., *Documentary History*, 1: 232–235.

[36] Yates and Lansing explained their reasons for leaving the convention in a letter to Governor Clinton (Robert Yates and John Lansing to Governor George Clinton, December 21, 1787, Bailyn, ed., *Debates on the Constitution*, 2: 3–6). Of course, other delegates,

In a debate on the sovereignty of the national government begun on May 30, George Mason argued that the system of requisitions had failed because the Articles of Confederation did not provide an enforcement mechanism, but he also remarked that punishment could not be applied to states as collectives. Coercion would fall on individuals if it were ever applied to states, he thought. This was one of the problems with the Virginia Plan. In Mason's mind, governments should only "punish those whose guilt required it," not everyone in a collective. Although little is made of Mason's argument, Hamilton and Madison must have taken note of it. Hamilton used it to defend the Constitution in Federalist 15 and 16 and Madison backed off the idea the next day.[37]

When the compulsory clause of resolution 6 was taken into consideration the following afternoon, Madison claimed "that the more he reflected on the use of force, the more he doubted the practicability, the justice and the efficacy of it when applied to people collectively and not individually." To him the use of force seemed more like "a declaration of war, than an infliction of punishment, and would probably be considered by the party attacked as a dissolution of all previous compacts by which it might be bound." He hoped that a system could be framed that would make this clause unnecessary and asked that the convention postpone consideration of the measure. If a national republic was framed, other revenues would become available. Madison wanted to hold off on the issue until something more palatable could be proposed. Other delegates agreed to postpone.[38]

As the committee of the whole made headway on the Virginia Plan, William Paterson presented his own plan of union on June 15. His plan, later known as the New Jersey Plan, maintained the confederation and the equal representation of the states in a single-house legislature. But it expanded the government to include an executive and a judicial branch

such as George Wythe of Virginia and William Pierce of Georgia, left the convention before its conclusion as well. This made the exact ratio of Federalists to Anti-Federalists vary on almost a weekly basis, though the ratio always favored the Federalists (Riker, "The Lessons of 1787," 12–15, and *Strategy of Rhetoric*, 148–150; Delegates Who Attended the Constitutional Convention, Jensen, ed., *Documentary History*, 1:230).

[37] For example, Banning recognizes that Mason is the first to see the effects of coercion on innocent individuals but does not connect the idea to the later arguments of the Federalists (*Sacred Fire of Liberty*, 141–142). Ostrom notes its importance to the Federalist debates but attributes its authorship to Hamilton (*Political Theory*, 38–41). The effect of the argument on the Federalist debates is revisited in the conclusion. For quoted remarks, see Madison's Notes on Debates, May 30, 1787, Farrand, ed., *Records of the Federal Convention*, 1: 33–34; and Yate's Notes on Debates, May 30, 1787, ibid., 1: 38–39.

[38] The first resolution passed on May 30 while the latter two passed on May 31, 1787 (Convention Journal, May 30 and 31, 1787, ibid., 1: 30, 45–46, respectively). Quotes from Madison come from his Notes on Debates, May 31, 1787, ibid., 1: 54.

that were responsible to Congress. The powers of Congress were then augmented to include the power to tax imports and the power to lay direct taxes on states that did not comply with requisitions. More than a third of the New Jersey Plan described new revenue powers, and it was obvious that overcoming the collective action problem was central to its design. The power to tax imports and the power to tax in noncomplying states were not new ideas.[39] They were modifications of earlier designs debated in Congress. Together these powers should have provided sufficient revenue for the union.

But Paterson was not trying to offer a more perfect union. He was trying to preserve the interests of the smaller states. The New Jersey Plan maintained equal representation in the legislature and would protect the voice of the smaller states. It was also a series of revisions to the Articles of Confederation, and if it passed, it would probably require the assent of Congress and the unanimous approval of thirteen state legislatures – as specified in the Articles of Confederation. With Congress explicitly stating that the convention should amend, not replace, Paterson had created the perfect counterproposal to Randolph's. His proposal was consistent with the instructions given by Congress, and it gained the support of delegates who did not want to overstep that line.

The debate on the New Jersey Plan turned on the issue of the convention's authority to reform. Paterson believed the convention could consider proposals such as his, but it did not have the authority to offer the Virginia Plan. He said, "If the confederacy is radically wrong, let us return to our States, and obtain larger powers, not assume them ourselves. I came here not to speak my own sentiments, but the sentiments of those who sent me." It was a reminder that his plan was within the purview of the convention. The Virginia Plan was not. Unless the convention preserved the interests of the smaller states, Paterson would press the issue and make sure that the convention failed. Although delegates from the larger states had their majority, they ultimately agreed to a compromise.[40]

---

[39] The New Jersey Plan and the amendment for conditional direct taxation differed in the condition under which Congress could interfere with state sovereignty. In the New Jersey Plan, Congress could tax in any noncomplying state, while in the amendment for conditional direct taxation Congress could tax in any noncomplying state only when a majority of other states had complied. There were other differences as well. See Madison's Notes on Debates, June 15, 1787, Farrand, ed., *Records of the Federal Convention*, 1: 242–245.

[40] Paterson, June 16, 1787, Madison, *Notes on Debates*, 122–123. For a similar argument made by John Lansing, see June 20, 1787, ibid., 155–157. Delegates from New Jersey did not oppose wholesale reforms. They eventually signed the Constitution, their state was the third to ratify it, and New Jersey was the only state to give its Annapolis dele-

When Mason spoke the next day, he first attacked the notion of a legislature with a single house, then derided the New Jersey Plan for proposing military coercion as the means of securing revenue from the states. "Will the militia march from one State to another, in order to collect the arrears of taxes from the delinquent members of the Republic?" he asked. Certainly slaying people for their government's failure to pay taxes was severe. "To punish the non-payment of taxes with death, was a severity not yet adopted by despotism itself: yet this unexampled cruelty would be mercy compared to a military collection of revenue, in which the bayonet could make no discrimination between the innocent and guilty." Coercing states implied force against citizens who paid their taxes and force against those who did not, according to Mason. But he could not "agree to abolish the State Govts'" or render them absolutely insignificant," despite the problems with coercive force. He would vote to preserve the states, as would Wilson, Martin, and Lansing. Now that coercive powers were proposed by Paterson, Madison was ready to abandon the idea. He would no longer defend what he had advocated in 1781 or proposed as part of the Virginia Plan. Instead, he would brand those who supported coercive powers as opponents to the Constitution and hope that attributing the idea to Paterson would swing delegates to his side.[41]

The great compromise of the convention came on July 16 when delegates overcame the impasse between the Virginia and New Jersey plans by creating a two-house legislature, one elected by the people, the other elected by the states. Merging the ideas of representation created a government that represented both the people and the states. Not only were the delegates planning a large republic against the better understandings of Montesquieu, they were now planning a republic where both people and states were represented. With members of the House of Representatives representing the people, the nation could tax the people directly, consistent with the doctrine of taxation by consent. With members of

gates the authority to discuss general reforms. Delegates from New Jersey presented the plan simply to preserve the voice of the smaller states. As Charles Pinckney put it, "[g]ive N[ew] Jersey an equal vote, and she will dismiss her scruples and concur in the Nati[ona]l system" (Madison's Notes on Debates, June 16, 1787, Farrand, ed., *Records of the Federal Convention*, 1: 255; for more on this view, see Roche, "The Founding Fathers," 805–808).

[41] Madison's Notes on Debates, June 20, 1787, Farrand, ed., *Records of the Federal Convention*, 1: 339–340. Luther Martin defended requisitions on June 27 based on the claim that states lacked the ability to comply. On June 30, Madison and Sherman attacked requisitions because the system implicitly assumed that states would fulfill their mutual compacts. In Madison's words, "experience shows that the confederation is radically defective, and we must in a new national government, guard against those defects" (Madison's Notes on Debates, ibid., 1: 437, 497–498).

the Senate representing the states, smaller states could protect some of their sovereignty.

Creating a national government, in itself, solved the collective action problem. A national government would not have to depend on the states to enforce its decisions nor to raise revenue, men, or supplies. It could enforce its own edicts and raise resources without the states. In other words, a national government solved the collective action problem by circumventing the states, not by fixing the problem itself. The methods for raising revenue – through head tax, excise tax, import tax, or other forms – were mere detail if an independent national government was to be enacted. Creating an independent government that acted directly upon the people, or was at least constituted by their consent, would lead to a variety of revenues that were consistent with the doctrine of taxation by consent.

In this sense, it did not matter whether the new government would represent the people only, as the Virginia Plan proposed, or a combination of the people and the states, as the Constitution proposed. As long as the national government obtained authority from the people, the national government would circumvent the collective action problem and raise resources of its own. The New Jersey Plan would not imply such revenue powers for the central government because it kept the government dependent on the states. This is why the New Jersey Plan had to specify solutions to the revenue problem, while the developing Constitution and the original Virginia Plan could leave these matters to detail. The New Jersey Plan had to specify fixes for a confederation that had problems, while the Constitution and Virginia Plan implicitly solved the problem by creating an independent national government. Resolving the collective action problem was a major part of all three documents; however, the specifics were needed up front in only one.

The proceedings of the convention were referred to the committee of detail on July 26. At this point taxation was not explicitly discussed, but everyone knew that an independent national government would require its own revenue. Two weeks earlier the floor determined that direct taxation was to be apportioned according to representation in the lower house. This implied that one of the forms of revenue would be direct taxation. The committee of detail incorporated the ideas of the floor and reported the first draft of the Constitution on August 6 with two new articles related to taxation – neither of which had been explicitly discussed on the floor. Article VII, section 1, of the draft stated that "the Legislature of the United States shall have the power to lay and collect taxes, duties, imposts and excises," similar to the ratified form of Article I, section 8, of the current Constitution. Article VII, section 5, further specified that "no capitation

[head] tax shall be laid unless in proportion to the census." These were the first explicit clauses about the mode of taxation since the compulsory clause had been abandoned two months before. The new legislature would have the power to raise a capitation tax, and they could collect additional revenues on duties, imposts, and excises. Combined, these would provide plenty of revenue for the new government and sidestep the collective action problem among the states.[42]

When the floor discussed Article VII on August 16, Luther Martin asked what the committee of detail meant by duties and imposts. If they were the same, why not delete the former? Wilson explained that duties applied to a variety of objects, such as stamps, which were not captured by imposts. With minor debate, the convention agreed to the clause that gave the legislature the power "to lay and collect taxes, duties, imposts and excises." Elbridge Gerry alone dissented. The requirement in Article VII, section 5, that capitation taxes would be apportioned according to the census passed without debate four days later. Lack of discussion reflected the virtual consensus on the issue and perhaps the limited thought put into the details. When Rufus King asked, "What was the precise meaning of direct taxation?" Madison noted that "no one answ[ere]d."[43]

The proceedings of the convention were assigned to the committee of style and arrangement on September 10, which rearranged the Articles and reported a final draft on September 12.[44] Members of the convention then gathered to sign the Constitution on September 17, 1787. At the time Franklin observed that artists were unsure whether the painting hanging behind Washington's head depicted a rising or a setting sun.

---

[42] Resolutions submitted to the Committee of Detail, July 24, 1787, Jensen, ed., *Documentary History*: 1: 255–260; Committee of Detail 1, July 23, 1787, Farrand, ed., *Records of the Federal Convention*, 2: 129–133; Convention Journal, July 12, 1787, ibid., 2: 589–590; Madison's Notes on Debates, July 12 and August 6, 1787, ibid., 1: 592 and 2: 181–183, respectively. Requiring that direct taxes be apportioned according to the population within each state hampered federal income taxes a century later. For the constitutional impact of the provision, see *Pollock v. Farmers' Loan & Trust Co.*, 157 U.S. 429 (1895).

[43] Madison's Notes on Debates, August 16, 1787, Farrand, ed., *Records of the Federal Convention*, 2: 305–308; Convention Journal, August 16, 1787, ibid., 2: 303–304; McHenry's Notes on Debates, August 16, 1787, ibid., 2: 311; and Madison's Notes on Debates, August 20, 1787, ibid., 2: 350.

[44] The committee of style moved Article VII, section 1 (giving the legislature the power to lay and collect taxes, duties, imposts, and excises), to Article I, section 8; and both Article VII, section 5 (apportioning all capitation taxes according to the census), and Article VII, section 4 (prohibiting the taxing of articles exported from a state), to Article I, section 9.

After the work of the convention had ended, he declared, "I have the happiness to know that it is a rising and not a setting Sun."[45]

The fact that new revenue and military powers were rarely debated at the convention does not mean that the collective action problem was not central to reform. Debates were more likely to go on at length over issues that were not agreed upon. Those that received a general concurrence usually received less debate. More important, requisitions were the central topic for reform in the coercive powers amendment, the two impost amendments, and the amendment for conditional direct taxation. The whole issue was central to the confederation and the push for institutional reform. Although delegates spent little time discussing revenue, they spent a great deal of time on the nature of the national government and indirectly addressed the collective action problem. In fact, the nature of the national government was the cardinal theme of debate. If members of the convention agreed upon an independent, national republic they would resolve the major problems of the Articles of Confederation. They would no longer have to depend on states to enforce common agreements or to raise common resources and could create a government that stood on its own.

In the end, the Constitution was a much more complex document than any of the amendments proposed by Congress in the 1780s. It would improve the efficiency of the government over the Articles of Confederation, but it also implied trade-offs in state sovereignty. The Constitution created a national government that could act directly upon the people, could raise armies and revenues independent of the states, and would reign supreme in interstate commerce. These were permanent

---

[45] Madison's Notes on Debates, September 17, 1787, ibid., 2: 648. The convention sent the Constitution to Congress for lawful submission to the states. As the public viewed it, Congress merely received and transmitted the document. What actually transpired was a heated debate. Nathan Dane argued that the convention did not have the authority to subvert the authority of Congress, but suggested that they transmit the document to the state *legislatures* for examination. Twelve states sent their delegates to the federal convention, and Richard Henry Lee believed this justified transmitting the document as well. But he too believed it should be examined by state legislatures, not state conventions. He then made examination by state legislatures a formal motion. William Grayson and Richard Henry Lee objected to ratification by nine states rather than thirteen and suggested that Congress should make alterations because several parts of it were flawed (for more details on the debate in Congress between September 26 and 28, see Introduction, The Confederation Congress and the Constitution, September 20–28, 1787, Jensen, ed., *Documentary History*, 1: 322–324; Nathan Dane's Motion, September 26, 1787, ibid., 1: 327–328; Melancton Smith's Notes, September 27, 1787, ibid., 1: 329; 331–333, 336–337; James Madison to George Washington, September 30, 1787, Smith, ed., *Letters of Delegates*, 24: 456–458; and Richard Henry Lee to George Mason, October 1, 1787, ibid., 24: 459).

overlaps between state and national jurisdictions that infringed on state sovereignty more than the amendment for conditional direct taxation, the impost amendment, or the Articles of Confederation. With such an assault on the interests of the state governments, it is no surprise that those who pushed for a national republic wanted their proposal ratified without requiring the consent of every state government.

THE PRAGMATICS OF RECONSTITUTION

Treating the Constitution as one of many solutions to the problems of the confederation brings up an interesting question: Why did the framers choose to reconstitute the government when reasonable amendments had already been proposed? There are several answers to this question that provide a partial or complete explanation. It is quite possible that the framers did not have the mindset needed to conceive of a national republic in the early 1780s. Changes in republican ideology have been documented by Bailyn and Wood, and both have claimed that the Constitution was created out of a new ideology. It is also possible that the framers believed amendments were inadequate for the job. Madison and Hamilton, early advocates of coercing the states, pointed out the problem with this idea and argued that the Constitution was necessary for reform. Crosskey and Jeffrey argued that the Constitution reflected the true sentiments of the people better than any of the previous proposals. Both sets of authors argued that a new Constitution was the best solution. Finally, reformers may have used the Constitution not only as a vehicle for solving confederation problems, but also as a mechanism for advancing their wealth and personal interests. Beard argued that the Constitution advanced the economic interests of the framers, and Jensen echoed the idea with respect to political power.[46]

All of these explanations focus on the content of the reform more than the method. The framers reconstituted the government because it would produce a more desirable government. But there is an additional explanation which seems to have been overlooked. Reconstituting the government may have been simply easier than amending the Articles of Confederation. Reformers had tried to amend the Articles before and they had failed. They knew that any revision which threatened state sovereignty was unlikely to obtain the consent of all the state legislatures. Even the innocuous impost amendment failed ratification. More contro-

---

[46] Bailyn, *Faces of Revolution*; Wood, *Creation of the Republic*; Rossiter, ed., *Federalist Papers*; Crosskey and Jeffrey, *Political Background of a Federal Convention*; Beard, *An Economic Interpretation*; and Jensen, *A New Nation*. Note that the Beardian thesis was weakened by empirical evidence from Brown, *Charles Beard*, and McDonald, *We the People*.

versial reforms were likely to meet the same fate. What the framers needed was another way of instituting reforms. Reconstituting the government allowed for wholesale revisions but also allowed reformers to circumvent the ratification procedures laid out in the Articles of Confederation. Reformers hoped that a new government could be proposed by a constitutional convention, ratified by the people, and, with a little luck, require approval from only a preponderance of states. Reconstituting the government was not only a way of handling a large volume of reforms, it was also a way of circumventing existing requirements for revision.

One of the first attempts to circumvent the reform procedures started when Congress developed the coercive powers amendment in 1781. Madison wanted the coercive powers amendment enacted, but he realized that it would probably not receive unanimous consent from the states. "If they should refuse," Madison wrote Jefferson, "Congress will be in a worse situation than at present; for as the confederation now stands . . . there is an implied right of coer[c]io[n] against the delinquent party, and the exercise of it by Congress whenever a palpable necessity occurs will probably be acquiesced in." Madison believed the proposal might be enacted whether or not it received the unanimous consent of the state legislatures because enforcement powers were implied by the thirteenth article. In its original form, Article XIII declared that "every state shall abide by the determinations of the United States in Congress assembled on all questions which by this Confederation are submitted to them. And that the Articles of Confederation shall be inviolably observed by every State." Madison, and a few other members of Congress, argued that omitting a means of enforcing this article was an oversight, not a conscious decision of the authors of the Articles of Confederation. At this very early stage he was thinking about how they could enact reforms without the consent of all thirteen state legislatures. He realized, however, that asserting such an implied right would have been dangerous, especially if some of the states explicitly noted their opposition to the measure when asked to ratify it.[47] Though the coercive powers amendment was unlikely to receive unanimous consent from the

[47] Some states had expressed their disapproval. Six months earlier, Duane noted that the Pennsylvania legislature directed their delegates "to consent to no Act of Coercion agt any people friendly to the Revolution," and Joseph Jones informed Edmund Pendleton that the Virginia legislature censured a similar measure in debate on December 24, 1779 (James Madison to Thomas Jefferson, April 16, 1781, Madison, *Papers*, 3: 71–73; James Duane to George Clinton, October 7, 1780, Smith, ed., *Letters of Delegates*, 16: 160–161; Joseph Jones to Thomas Jefferson, April 16, 1781, Jefferson, *Papers*, 5: 472 n.; and Joseph Jones to Pendleton, Wythe, and Jefferson in James Madison to Thomas Jefferson, April 16, 1787, Smith, ed., *Letters of Delegates*, 17: 158 n. 1).

states, it was even less likely to be imposed without their agreement. Madison was not alone in his idea for sidestepping the states, but he realized that asserting implied powers would not sit well with other members of Congress nor the states.[48]

Another idea was to propose reforms through a constitutional convention. The constitutions of Pennsylvania, Maryland, and Massachusetts were all written by popular conventions, and in the summer of 1782 both houses of the New York legislature requested that Congress call "a general convention of the states specially authorized to revise and amend the Confederation."[49] Revising the Articles through convention, rather than the usual mode of Congress, offered three clear advantages. First, a new government could be proposed in a constitutional convention while only amendments could be proposed by Congress. Congress was an institution of the Articles of Confederation and it had to work within its confines. A convention was more basic than the Constitution itself and could sit outside the Articles to discuss constitutional revisions. Second, any revisions proposed in a constitutional convention could be laid before the public rather than before state governments. The public might accept changes that state legislatures would reject. As William Pierce, a delegate from Georgia, noted, "it is certain that the confederation is very incompleat, and deficient in point of energy, but I fear we shall meet with great difficulties in amending it. The different States will not make such a surrender of their sovereignty as may be found necessary to give the federal head compleat weight in the Union."[50] Increasing the efficiency of the federal government would almost certainly reduce the sovereignty of states and threaten a proposal that had to gain the consent of state legislatures. If the state governments were made even slightly worse off by the proposal, it would be better for proponents to

[48] Joseph Jones, a Virginia delegate, found equal necessity in the measure. In a separate letter to Jefferson, he wrote that "it appears to me indispensably necessary for the general welfare in time of war that the Congress should be vested with a controuling power over the States sufficient to compel obedience to requisitions for Men and Money." Jones was not sure whether Article XIII implied the power, but he was sure that state governments were likely to oppose it. Both men wanted Jefferson's opinion on the matter before they acted, but Jefferson never replied (Joseph Jones to Thomas Jefferson, April 16, 1781, Jefferson, *Papers*, 5: 469–470; see also James Madison to Thomas Jefferson, May 1, 1781, Madison, *Papers*, 3: 97–98).

[49] Quoted in The Calling of the Constitutional Convention, January 21 – February 21, 1787, Jensen, ed., *Documentary History*, 1: 176–179. James Madison made no attempt to support a convention at this early stage, perhaps because he thought amendments would be adequate or a convention would be unsuccessful without a greater crises (Rutland, The Annapolis convention 1786, Madison, *Papers*, 9: 116).

[50] William Pierce to St. George Tucker, April 14, 1787, Smith, ed., *Letters of Delegates*, 24: 221.

seek ratification by popularly elected conventions than by state legislatures. Finally, if the constitutional convention was considered greater
than written law, the procedure for ratifying its proposals might extend
beyond the procedures outlined by the current constitution. Delegates to
the convention might be able to create a new covenant that required the
consent of only those states which adhered to it. This meant that any
proposed changes could be ratified with a super-majority of states, rather
than the usual unanimity. Unanimous consent had caused both of the
impost amendments to fail and prevented the coercive powers amendment and the amendment for conditional direct taxation from even being
congressionally proposed. The possibility of avoiding the unanimous
consent of thirteen separate bodies would help any reform.

The advantages of a constitutional convention (popular ratification,
by a super-majority of states) could be obtained only if a new constitution were proposed. If the federal convention proposed a few amendments to the Articles of Confederation as Congress had requested, the
convention would probably be treated as an aid to Congress rather than
an organic meeting that transcended the confederation. In that case, it
would be governed by the Articles of Confederation and confined to the
ratification procedures already established. In other words, a valid constitutional convention had to frame a new government in order for the
scheme to work.

Madison had toyed with the idea of a constitutional convention long
before he wrote the Virginia Plan. In December 1784 he wrote to Richard
Henry Lee, "I have not yet found leisure to scan the project of a Constitutional Convention with so close an eye as to have made up any
observations worthy of being mentioned to you." He believed the question was "in what mode, & at what moment the experiment for supplying the defects ought to be made. The answer to this question cannot
be given without a knowledge greater than I posses of the temper &
views of the different States." What Madison meant by "the experiment"
is unclear, but he probably meant proposing a constitutional convention.
The plan he drafted in the spring of 1787 was fitting of such a convention, and the political conditions of the year made the timing of the
proposal just about right. Reformers such as Madison, Randolph,
and Hamilton would try for a convention that worked outside of the
Articles of Confederation and in doing so they would justify a new
method of ratification.[51]

---

[51] James Madison to Richard Henry Lee, December 25, 1784, Madison, *Writings*, 2:
99–100. The idea of reconstituting the government was more Madison's idea than Randolph's. In Edmund Randolph to James Madison, March 27, 1787, Madison, *Papers*,
335, Randolph said that the alterations should be "grafted on the old confederation,"

Those who headed the reforms knew that a constitutional convention might not be authorized by Congress and they did not explicitly request one at the Annapolis convention. They left the nature of the federal convention vague to avoid unnecessary opposition. They explicitly wrote that the federal convention would propose revisions to Congress which would be ratified in the usual mode, but they left the nature of the convention (aid-to-Congress or constitutional convention) sufficiently vague, hoping that Congress would approve the plan.

Of course, members of Congress worried that such a plan was under way and did not want the convention in Philadelphia to subvert their authority. Delegates from New York succeeded in limiting the function of the federal convention to amendments, but these setbacks did not deter Madison. He got started on the Virginia Plan shortly after Congress declared the convention should limit itself to amendments. With delegates being appointed by the states, the convention might still have the authority to work outside the confederation.

Madison described the Virginia Plan in letters to Jefferson, Randolph, and Washington, but he seemed more concerned about how he could get a proposal passed than exactly what he put in it. "Radical attempts, although unsuccessful, will at least justify the authors of them," he wrote to Washington. Many items were left vague, as if they would be worked out at the convention.[52] What was less vague was how various items would aid the plan. In his first letter to Jefferson, Madison laid out three parts of his plan. These might be considered the most fundamental. He believed the new system should be ratified by the people themselves, the national government should be allowed the power to negate (or veto) state acts, and representation should be apportioned according to the size of each state.

In his words, ratification by the people would render the document "clearly paramount" to the authority of state legislatures. The new government would be affirmed by the people and reign supreme in states where the state constitution had not required popular ratification. Ratification by the people would also avoid any sticky problems the states

---

perhaps because Congress resolved that only amendments should be considered. In Madison's response on April 8 he wrote, "it may be best to work the valuable articles into the new system." In other words, Randolph wanted to amend and Madison wanted to create a new system. Madison then went on to describe a government that, in his words, was not a consolidated republic nor a confederation. The extent to which Madison and Randolph discussed this "new system" prior to Randolph's letter is unclear.

[52] James Madison to George Washington, April 16, 1787, Smith, ed., *Letters of Delegates*, 24: 228. For more on the idea that Madison was willing to concede points at the convention, see Banning, "Practicable Sphere of a Republic."

might have with their own constitutions. To give the system proper validity, Madison wrote Washington that "a ratification must be obtained from the people, not merely from the ordinary authority of the Legislatures. This will be the more essential as inroads on the *existing Constitution* of the States will be unavoidable." The "inroads" that Madison was thinking about were unclear, but the constitutions of Delaware, Massachusetts, and South Carolina all had passages that gave their legislatures the right to elect congressional delegates and the power to revise their state constitutions. If the convention proposed the direct election of representatives, or similar measures, these states might have to amend their constitutions before they could approve a new mode of electing congressional representatives. Popular conventions were organic bodies that did not have to confront such requirements. Obtaining ratification from the people gave the federal government more authority than state governments, but it also avoided the potential need to amend three state constitutions.[53]

With regard to changing the apportionment of representatives, Madison wrote Jefferson that changing the principle of representation was "just" but also "practicable." He thought a majority of states would gain from the new representation and have reason to support his plan. The eastern states were the more populous and with anticipated growth the southern states might become more populous as well. He believed that apportioning representation according to population would encourage states from both areas to support his plan. He then reasoned that "if a majority of the larger States concur, the fewer and smaller States must finally bend to them." In other words, changing apportionment would help gain support for his plan. Madison stressed this point with Randolph and made it explicit in his writing to Washington. He told Washington that the idea was necessary to "obviate the principle objections of the larger States to the necessary concessions of power." Madison spent as much time considering how his proposal would be accepted as he did on its content. He remained flexible enough to allow for alterations at the convention and was willing to support a wide range of proposals.[54]

---

[53] Quoted material comes from James Madison to Thomas Jefferson, March 19, 1787, Madison, *Papers*, 9: 318; and James Madison to George Washington, April 16, 1787, Smith, ed., *Letters of Delegates*, 24: 231 (emphasis in the original), respectively. See Thorpe, *Federal and State Constitutions*, 1: 564, 566; 3: 1906; 6: 3248, 3253, 3257, for constitutional conflicts in the states, and Rakove, *Original Meanings*, 96–108, for an argument that popular ratification provided national supremacy.

[54] James Madison to Thomas Jefferson, March 19, 1787, Madison, *Papers*, 9: 318–319; and James Madison to George Washington, April 16, 1787, Smith, ed., *Letters of Delegates*, 24: 229. Randolph wrote Madison that he thought they should propose "what is best in itself, not merely what can be obtained from the assemblies." This may have

The final provision of the Virginia Plan revealed Madison and Randolph's premeditated intent of circumventing the ratification procedures outlined by the Articles of Confederation. Rather than requiring thirteen state legislatures to ratify the proposal, provision 15 suggested that "after the approbation of Congress" the resolves would be submitted to "an assembly or assemblies of Representatives, recommended by the several Legislatures to be expressly chosen by the people." In other words, popular conventions, not state legislatures, would ratify the proposal. The people would elect representatives to the ratifying conventions and they would determine the fate of the new constitution.[55]

Other delegates liked the idea as well. When Ellsworth said, "And let it ever be remembered, that without" the approbation of the state legislatures "your government is nothing more than a rope of sand," Wilson snapped back, "I am not for submitting the national government to the approbation of the state legislatures. I know that they and the state officers will oppose it. I am for carrying it to the people of each state." The issue of ratification by state conventions or state legislatures was carefully discussed on July 23, but the focus was still more on whether the proposal would pass than on its philosophical merits. Gerry, Paterson, and Ellsworth spoke against it, while twice as many delegates spoke for it. Madison argued that the proposed changes would "make essential inroads on the States Constitutions" and that several state legislatures did not have the power "to concur in alterations of the federal Compact." He further reassured the members of the convention that they were creating a constitution that was founded on the people, not a league founded on states. If they were to propose a constitution that acted on people, the people's consent would be appropriate. Nathaniel Gorham saw the efficacy of the provision and was much more blunt. He preferred ratification by popular conventions because "men chosen by the people for the particular purpose, will discuss the subject more candidly than members of the legislature who are to lose the power which is to be given up to the Genl. Govt." Gorham's remarks were not the philosophical reasoning that needed to be laid out, but they probably represented the latent thoughts of most members who favored a national government. Ratification by the people would help the Constitution pass, and those friendly to the proposal wanted to establish such a procedure. Gorham noted that if the convention adhered to the thirteenth article of confed-

lessened Madison's remarks with Randolph about what reforms were obtainable, but it did not convince him to withhold his remarks altogether (Edmund Randolph to James Madison, March 27, 1787, Madison, *Papers*, 335; and James Madison to Edmund Randolph, April 8, 1787, ibid., 9: 368–371).

[55] The Virginia Resolutions, Kammen, *Origins of the Constitution*, 25.

eration they would not be able to ratify their proposal by a super-majority of states. "If the last art[icle] of the Confederation is to be pursued," he claimed, "the unanimous concurrence of the States will be necessary. But will any one say that all the States are to suffer themselves to be ruined, if Rho[de] Island should persist in her opposition to general measures[?]" Gorham saw the pragmatics of Madison's plan. The reforms created at the federal convention were more likely to succeed if they could be ratified by popular conventions. When the provision for ratification by popular convention was put to the vote, it easily passed, nine states to one.[56]

In writing the first draft of the Constitution, the committee of detail also included a clause stating the number of state conventions that would be sufficient to ratify the document. Article XXI read, "The ratifications of the Conventions of ____ States shall be sufficient for organizing this Constitution." The exact number was left blank for the floor to decide. When the issue was taken up on August 30, proposals were offered from seven states to thirteen, representing a simple majority to a unanimity of states. Randolph suggested that nine states were a respectable majority of the whole and that nine was "a number made familiar by the constitution of the existing Congress." Congress raised revenue, armies, and proposed amendments by nine states, so there was some precedent for this number. With some opposition, it was agreed that nine states would be sufficient to enact the Constitution. The clause was made possible because the delegates to the convention were not amending the Articles. They were creating a new compact and believed that states could freely choose whether to enter the compact or stay with the old. A preponderance of states was all that was needed to make a new compact viable.[57]

CONCLUSION

With Rhode Island's previous opposition to federal duties and recent election of Levelers, Madison and Randolph believed that they could not count on unanimous consent from the states. "What number of states ought we have said?" asked Randolph at the Virginia ratifying convention. "Ought we have required the concurrence of all thirteen? Rhode Island, in rebellion against integrity." Madison also thought the existing

---

[56] The exchange between Ellsworth and Wilson is in Yate's Notes on Debates, June 22, 1787, Farrand, ed., *Records of the Federal Convention*, 1: 379; other quoted material comes from Madison's Notes on Debates, July 23, 1787, ibid., 2: 88–94; also see Convention Journal, July 23, 1787, ibid., 2: 84–85.

[57] Madison's Notes on Debates, August 30–31, 1787, ibid., 2: 468–469, 475–479; Convention Journal, August 31, 1787, ibid., 2: 471–472.

system was unreasonable. He wrote of "the absurdity of subjecting the fate of twelve States to the perverseness or corruption of a thirteenth; from the example of inflexible opposition given by a majority of one sixtieth of the people of America to a measure approved and called for by the voice of twelve States." Both had recognized the need to circumvent the ratification process of the Articles of Confederation and both believed it was one of the major advantages of the Virginia Plan. Undoubtedly, reconstituting the government had certain advantages; among these was its ability to enable reform.[58]

It would be hard to claim that Madison had more content on his mind than method when he formulated the Virginia Plan. He did not know which provisions the convention would agree to and intentionally left many of them vague. The Virginia Plan did not surrender the content of earlier amendments. It contained an independent national government that contained the same provision for coercing the states as the coercive powers amendment. If all Madison cared about was presenting a sufficient solution to the confederation's problems, he would have proposed yet another amendment. Certainly, the volume of reforms was not the issue. The amendment for conditional, direct taxation and all of its surrounding provisions created an equal number of reforms. Part of the reason that Madison went further was because he wanted to work outside the confederation box, where popular conventions and supermajority ratification procedures might be found. He knew this would be much more efficacious than working within the box, where seemingly innocuous amendments had already failed. Reconstituting the government had as much to do with the probability of enacting reforms as with the content of the proposal.

The framers had several ideas that would work with an unvirtuous citizenry: the coercive powers amendment, the impost amendment, and the amendment for conditional direct taxation, to name only a few. Part of the reason they chose to reconstitute the government was because a new constitution was easier to enact than any of them. When they arrived in Philadelphia, they created a constitution that improved the effectiveness of the national government on one hand, while still protecting individual liberty on the other. The decision to reconstitute the government may have stemmed from the ratification process, but the exact content of the Constitution was determined by value judgments and political compromise. The Constitution that they created was a work of pragmatics, but it was also a work of improving the government's efficiency without infringing too heavily upon state sovereignty.

[58] Edmund Randolph in the Virginia Convention, June 4, 1788, ibid., 3: 308; Madison, Federalist 40, Rossiter, ed., *Federalist Debates*, 251.

8

Conclusion

> We are told that the Confederation carried us through the
> war. Had not the enthusiasm of liberty inspired us with una-
> nimity, that system would never have carried us through it.
>
> – John Marshall[1]

After enacting the Constitution the American Revolution had run its
course. In less than twenty years, Americans had moved from a principled opposition to centralized government to a new constitution that
strengthened centralized power. They secured independence from Great
Britain, experimented with a confederation of independent republics, and
were now ready to jump into a new form of democracy that had never
been tried before. They planned an enormous republic that would
encompass the diverse interests of the Massachusetts merchant and
the Georgia frontiersman, the New Hampshire craftsman and the
Virginian gentry. As no other republic had done before, government
under the Constitution would now represent both the people and the
states and allow state and national governments to coexist in different
spheres. "The federal Constitution forms a happy combination in this
respect," wrote Madison, "the great and aggregate interests being
referred to the national, the local and particular to the State." The idea
was radical, and it seemed to work against the initial goal of protecting
state sovereignty. Few would have risked it without experiencing the
failures of the confederation.[2]

The American confederation is rich with stories about the formation
of a nation. Although every good story is worth retelling, my intent has
not been to retell the story of the American confederation. Instead, I have

---

[1] John Marshall, Virginia Convention Debates, June 10, 1788, Jensen, ed., *Documentary History*, 9: 1120.
[2] Federalist 10, Rossiter, ed., *Federalist Papers*, 83.

noted why the states should *not* have contributed to the confederation
using public goods theory, then asked why in fact they did. In other
words, I have asked why states paid large portions of their requisitions
when problems of collective action and the lack of governmental enforcement suggest that they should have not. The fact that joint products
encouraged cooperation, despite the weak institutions of the Articles of
Confederation, should not lead us to conclude that institutions are
somehow irrelevant or that previous studies about institutional failures
are misguided. It shows instead that actors can overcome deficiencies in
institutional design, and how they overcome them. Members of Congress
withheld payments to creditors and created the system of indents to
encourage state contributions. They extended the rules of the confederation to make up for deficiencies within its structure. But even they realized that stretching the rules was not enough. They believed a new
institutional design was the only long-term solution to confederative
problems. Joint products may have encouraged cooperation in a system
that did not offer incentives to contribute, but they were not the long-
term solution that the nation required. What the nation needed was a
stronger institutional design.

What remains is a more precise investigation of how these findings
affect our understanding of the American confederation and confederative designs in general. The argument unfolds in three parts. First, I illustrate how the collective action problem affected the Federalist debates.
Federalists and Anti-Federalists toiled over the trade-offs between greater
efficiency and state sovereignty that defined the nation in earlier years.
Second, I explain why a confederation based on civic virtue cannot be
relied on. State and national interests will inevitably conflict even for virtuous politicians. If basing a system on civic virtue implies leaving
enforcement with the states, then other confederations are likely to face
the same problems as found in the American confederation. Finally, I
conclude by suggesting that the private aspects of joint products could
explain why many confederations and international organizations have
partially succeeded. The institutions they adopt are important, but non-
institutional incentives may be encouraging cooperation despite weak-
nesses in institutional design.

THE FEDERALIST DEBATES

The struggle over ratification of the Constitution began shortly after the
Constitutional Convention completed its work on September 17, 1787.
As agreed, the Constitution would be ratified by the assent of nine states
in popular conventions, though all states eventually agreed to ratify it.
To sway popular opinion for or against the Constitution and to affect

the opinions of conventioneers, a variety of authors wrote editorials in broadsides and local newspapers under pseudonyms such as Publius, Brutus, and the Federal Farmer. Nationalists who supported the Constitution seized the label of Federalists, while those who opposed the Constitution were branded Anti-Federalists. These names stereotyped two amorphous groups of authors.

The two sides divided over various issues, but the clearest differences of opinion were in the overall design of the union. Previous unions, calling themselves federations, were actually confederations built on state interests. The Anti-Federalists were familiar with this type of federalism and favored confederative designs. The Federalists favored the Constitution, which proposed a new form of federalism that had never been seen before. Rather than create a confederation of small republics, the Constitution established a government based on the simultaneous authority of the people and the states. Both were represented in the new government and both were able to check the authority of the federal authority. Such a plan was a radical idea for the eighteenth century.[3]

Each camp reached its conclusion by taking different sides on the issue of efficiency versus state sovereignty – though neither camp surrendered the opposing point. The Federalists argued in favor of greater efficiency and claimed that the Constitution would help maintain individual liberty. The Anti-Federalists defended state sovereignty and the use of amendments to improve the efficiency of the central government. Ultimately, the Federalists convinced enough Americans that a government that acted directly upon the people should be preferred. They explained how the goals of the union could change from the promotion of state interests and the protection of state sovereignty to the promotion of individual interests and the protection of individual liberty.

Opening Arguments

One of the first and foremost tasks of the Federalists was to establish the deficiencies of Articles of Confederation in terms of efficiency. For them, efficiency was not the precise concept used by economists today, but it captured roughly the same idea. The Federalists wanted a government that would carry out the will of its constituents and provide mutual gain for all. Federalists cited multiple failures of requisitions under the Articles as evidence of the need for greater efficiency. Eight issues of the Federalist Papers were devoted to the subject in late 1787 with the goal of showing the need for a new design. In Federalist 15 Hamilton argued

---

[3] Main, *Antifederalists*, 120.

that the voluntary nature of requisitions prevented the states from fully complying with requisitions. When one state fell behind, other states would withhold their contributions despite their legal obligations. According to Hamilton, state politicians asked, "Why should we do more in proportion to those who are embarked with us in the same political voyage? Why should we consent to bear more than our proper share of the common burden?" State decision makers would not contribute to requisitions, even when it was in the nation's interest as a whole. If some states signaled their inability or unwillingness to comply with a requisition, other states would withhold their requisitions as well. As Madison saw it, "a distrust of the voluntary compliance of each other may prevent the compliance of any, although it should be the latent disposition of all."[4] The union could not rely on requisitions for raising the men and money it required, even if they did protect state sovereignty.

As the Federalists argued for the need to improve the efficiency of the federal government, the Anti-Federalists objected to the Constitution because of its potential to abuse power and to infringe upon state sovereignty. Consistent with Whig theory, the Anti-Federalists believed sovereign states were the ultimate protector of individual liberty and that state sovereignty would help to give individuals their liberty. "The human mind is too apt to rush from one extreme to another," observed Richard Henry Lee. When the Articles of Confederation were written, "the universal apprehension was, of the too great, not the defective powers of Congress."[5] He was right; people were starting to focus on strengthening the national government at the expense of state sovereignty. Prior to the Revolution, the emphasis was at the opposite extreme. The Anti-Federalists defended the confederation and ultimately the system of requisitions because it preserved the sovereignty of states. Leaving the enforcement of requisitions to the states gave the states power to veto "unfriendly" acts. "We wished to pay with our own consent. – Rather than pay against our consent," wrote Patrick Henry, "by [requisitions] we have triumphed in the most arduous struggle . . . To prevent an arbitrary deprivation of our property, contrary to our consent and inclination."

The Anti-Federalists wanted to protect the nation from the same type of government that the British had created – a central government dictating to the states. "The first thing I have at heart is American liberty; the second thing is American Union," Patrick Henry continued. Unlike the Federalists, who later argued that liberty could be threatened by a majority, the Anti-Federalists believed that aristocratic politicians were

---

[4] Hamilton, Federalist 15, Rossiter, ed., *Federalist Debates*, 112–113; James Madison, Vices of the Political System of the United States, April 1787, Madison, *Writings*, 2: 364.
[5] To George Mason, May 15, 1787, Lee, *Letters*, 2: 421.

the greatest threat to liberty. The Constitution created a national government that was far from the people and allowed national politicians to be less sympathetic to popular interests. They believed national politicians would act according to their own demands, detached from their constituents. For example, "A Democratic Federalist" thought federal judges might decide in favor of a federal constable if he conducted wrongful searches of a person's home: "[W]hat satisfaction can we expect from a lordly court of justice, always ready to protect the officers of government against the weak and helpless citizen, and who will perhaps sit at a hundred miles from the place where the outrage was committed?" The physical distance between state and federal government would alienate politicians from their citizens. According to the Anti-Federalists, it would allow federal politicians to act independent of the people. National politicians would not be immersed in town meetings, and they would be less capable of empathizing with local desires. The idea of a federal army, which could be raised independent of requisitions, would be similarly abused. Merely creating a republic the size of thirteen states would allow government officials to act independent of the people and infringe upon state and individual liberties.[6]

The Anti-Federalists also worried that federal politicians might incorrectly estimate demands for national goods and services, in which case they might create armies that exceeded the demands of the states or force states to pay for goods that they did not desire. "Requisitions were attended with one singular advantage. . . . They secure to the States the benefit of correcting oppressive errors." If the federal government assessed an excessive tax under the Articles of Confederation, the states could veto that tax by consciously withholding requisitions. If the federal government assessed an excessive tax on the people under the Constitution, the states would not have the same check. This was the primary reason that Henry defended requisitions. Requisitions provided an additional check upon the federal government and assured that it would not overestimate state demands. Edmund Randolph called the power of direct taxation the soul of government; Francis Corbin called it the lungs. "Must I give my soul – my lungs, to Congress?" asked Henry. "I tell you, they shall not have the soul of Virginia."[7] Anti-Federalists such as Patrick Henry defended requisitions and the history of requisition payments

---

[6] Virginia Convention Debates, June 7, 1788, Jensen, ed., *Documentary History*, 19: 962, emphasis in original; Reply to Wilson's Speech, A Democratic Federalist, October 17, 1787, Bailyn, ed., *Debate on the Constitution*, 1: 73–74. Also see Storing, *Complete Anti-Federalist*, 1: 30–32, 54–55.

[7] Speeches of Patrick Henry, Virginia Convention Debates, June 7, 1788, Jensen, ed., *Documentary History*, 19: 963, 1045.

because requisitions allowed states, and ultimately individuals, the freedom to determine local destinies.[8]

Rebuttal

The Anti-Federalists objected to the infringement of states' rights and individual liberty as the Federalists had predicted. A Freeman wrote that "important men – men in high posts – men of reputed principles and integrity – object against the Constitution as designed to annihilate the state sovereignties, undermine our rights, and to end either in a corrupt aristocracy or absolute monarchy." Though the Federalists were primarily interested in greater efficiency, they were unwilling to concede the issue of liberty to the Anti-Federalists and did not want to go as far as monarchy. Instead of falsely claiming that the Constitution would do a better job of protecting state sovereignty than the confederation had done, the Federalists countered the state sovereignty issue by changing the goals of the confederation. The new goal of their government was to maintain independence and to protect the liberties of individuals, not states.[9]

The Federalists argued that the states were interdependent, especially in the need for common defense. Without a strong union, state independence could not be maintained. "A government capable of controlling the whole, and bringing its force to a point is one of the prerequisites for national liberty," a "Landholder" wrote. "If we mean to have our natural rights and properties protected, we must first create a power which is able to do it, and in our case there is no want of resources, but only a civil constitution which may draw them out and point their force." The new constitution would improve the defense of the nation and thereby protect state independence. Without an effective general government, the states might be overrun by foreign invaders and lose their sovereignty entirely. "New York's existence as a state," wrote Livingston, "depends upon a strong and efficient government." Federalists argued that it would be better to sacrifice some sovereignty to ensure the independence of the states than to hold on to sovereignty and jeopardize their independence. It was a compelling argument that helped justify their push for a stronger government.[10]

---

[8] Speeches of Patrick Henry, June 9, 1788, Storing, *Complete Anti-Federalist*, 5: 235. Also see Speech of Patrick Henry, Virginia Convention Debates, June 7, 1788, Jensen, ed., *Documentary History*, 19: 1045; Brown, *Redeeming*, 160–164, 203–205.

[9] A Freeman to the People of Connecticut, Connecticut Courant, December 31, 1787, Jensen, ed., *Documentary History*, 3: 518.

[10] A Landholder III, November 19, 1787, Bailyn, ed., *Debate on the Constitution*, 1: 329–330; Livingston's speech at the New York convention, June 19, 1788, *Debates in the Several State Conventions*, 2: 211, quoted in Onuf, "State Sovereignty," 83. Also see Storing, *Complete Anti-Federalist*, 1: 4–32.

Besides, a Freeman argued, "the construction of the senate affords an absolute certainty, that the states will not loose their present share of separate powers. No state is to loose its voice therein without its *own consent.*" States would retain an integral role in the new government and their votes would prevent the federal government from usurping state authority. By "protecting the sovereignty of states," James Iredell claimed, the Senate would serve "as a guardian against any attempt of consolidation." The federal government could not act against a majority of states under the Constitution. States would lose only some of their sovereignty but not all of it. "*Independent revenue and resources* are indubitable proofs of *sovereignty*," wrote a Freeman. "The states will posses many of those which now exist, and which hereafter may be created." States would maintain the independent revenues and local militias that allowed them to self-govern. If the federal government ever attempted to subdue the states through military force, the states could draw upon a well-armed populace to defend themselves. Without such resources, the federal government would have to rely on "mercenaries" to attack the states. The Constitution infringed on state sovereignty, but the Federalists convinced many Americans that the infringement was minor and necessary.[11]

Madison offered yet another defense of individual liberty. He turned a common fear of the detachment of federal officials on its head. He argued that the federal government would do a better job of protecting individual liberty than the states because federal officials would in fact be free of particular interests, just as the Anti-Federalists had claimed. "Extend the sphere and you take in a greater variety of parties and interests; you make it less probable that a majority of the whole will have a common motive to invade the rights of other citizens," he wrote. For Madison, a large republic was good for a nation. It created a more heterogenous population and forced national politicians to take broader views. Public officials who focused on the interests of one faction would be removed from office by coalitions of smaller factions. In Madison's view more factions reduced the possibility of any single faction taking control and reduced the possibility of tyranny from one group. He described the principle to Jefferson: "[W]herever the real power in a Government lies, there is a danger of oppression. In our Governments the real power lies in the majority of the community, and the invasion of

---

[11] A Freeman III, Pennsylvania Gazette, February 6, 1788, Jensen, ed., *Documentary History*, 16: 49–51, emphasis in original; James Iredell's speech at the North Carolina convention, July 28, 1788, *Debates in the Several State Conventions*, 4: 133, quoted in Onuf, "State Sovereignty," 82.

private rights is *chiefly* to be apprehended, not from acts of Government contrary to the sense of its constituents, but from acts in which the Government is the mere instrument of the major number of the Constituents." Madison was one of the first to consider the political benefits of a heterogenous population and pointed out that greater disunity could actually work in their favor. The competition of factions freed representatives from the particular interests of various individuals and protected individual liberties from the majority faction.[12]

This was Madison's theory of pluralism. It was a new idea for a new republic and it provided the Federalists with another means of defending the Constitution. By the time Madison had made his argument public, the goals of the union had significantly changed. The Federalists realized that promoting state interests and protecting state sovereignty were the means to greater ends. The real goal of the union was to promote individual interests and to protect individual liberty, and that was the message they needed carried forward. Though the Constitution partially infringed on state sovereignty, changing the emphasis from states to people, as Madison had done, increased support for their plan.

Just as the Federalists were unwilling to concede the issue of liberty, the Anti-Federalists were unwilling to concede the issue of efficiency. They realized that popular tastes were moving in favor of a more efficient government and tried to defend the Articles of Confederation in their ability to promote common state interests. On this point the Anti-Federalists were less convincing. They fell back on many of the Whig arguments that civic virtue held the union together and could be counted on in times of need. As an Old Whig observed, "We have seen many instances of aid being furnished, even voluntarily upon pressing occasions, which should teach us to rely on the exertions of the states upon occasions of real and not imaginary necessity." Anti-Federalists denied that there was a national crisis and pointed out that states contributed sizable amounts during the war. They tried to downplay the apparent inefficiencies of the confederation and to argue that patriotism gave the system its effectiveness. States did not contribute to requisitions in the past because they lacked the resources needed to comply, not because they lacked the unilateral desire. "I am persuaded that a due consideration, will evince," wrote Samuel Bryan, "that the present inefficacy of the requisitions of Congress, is not

---

[12] Federalist 10, Rossiter, ed., *Federalist Debates*, 83; James Madison to Thomas Jefferson, October 17, 1788, Madison, *Writings*, 5: 272, emphasis in original. Also see Storing, *Complete Anti-Federalist*, 1: 38–40; and Madison, "Vices of the Political System of the United States," April 1787, Madison, *Writings*, 2: 366–368.

owing to a defect in the confederation, but the peculiar circumstances of the times." Presumably, states would contribute more when more resources were available.[13]

But could "Congress, after the repeated unequivocal proofs it has experienced of the utter inutility and inefficacy of requisitions, reasonably expect, that they would hereafter be effectual or productive?"[14] The economy was improving, states were regaining their foreign trade, and state revenues were on the rise. At the same time, specie payments were dwindling and Congress was receiving little more than the indents it had requested. Excludable benefits kept indents flowing but they did not provide revenue for the confederative government. Congress did not receive enough funds to maintain its civil list or to pay off its foreign loans even though the states were becoming increasingly capable of paying. Better times might improve state compliance with requisitions but would not solve the collective action problem that was at the heart of the institutional design.

Not every Anti-Federalist, however, favored the requisitions system in its then current form. Most favored supplementing it with some other form of revenue. Some favored impost revenue while others believed states could be coerced when payments were delinquent. Patrick Henry favored something similar to the coercive powers amendment because it preserved requisitions at the core. States could deliberate on taxes locally before asking their citizens to surrender their property. If they failed to pay, Henry said he was willing to submit the state to an extreme form of punishment. "In case Virginia shall not make punctual payment," he argued, "the controul of our custom houses, and the whole regulation of trade, shall be given to Congress, and that Virginia shall depend on Congress even for passports, till Virginia shall have paid the last farthing." Avoiding abusive taxation was a primary motivation for the War of Independence. Continuing to avoid it was a primary goal of the Anti-Federalists.[15]

The Need for a New Union

Suggesting that Congress receive the power to coerce the states fell into the Federalist trap. The Federalists began turning against the idea in the constitutional convention and were using this proposal to justify direct

---

[13] Essays of an Old Whig, Storing, *Complete Anti-Federalist*, 3: 42; Centinel IV (Samuel Bryan), *Philadelphia Independent Gazaetteer*, November 30, 1787, Jensen, ed., *Documentary History*, 14: 319.

[14] Speech of James Madison, Virginia Convention Debates, June 17, 1788, ibid., 9: 1028.

[15] Speeches of Patrick Henry, Virginia Convention Debates, June 7, 1788, ibid., 19: 963, 1045.

action upon the people. The authors of the American confederation assumed that patriotism and civic duty would encourage state politicians to comply with requisitions and to make the confederation work. The Federalists sternly argued this was not the case. "A bare sense of duty, or a regard to propriety is too feeble to induce men to comply with obligations," wrote John Marshall. "We deceive ourselves if we expect any efficacy from these." By arguing that patriotism and civic duty would not provide enough resources to advance the common interest, the Federalists were free to argue that government required "sanction; or in other words, a penalty for disobedience." Without such penalties, state politicians would act upon their immediate interests and withhold resources from their common interests.

These were the first two steps. Without enforcement, requisitions would fail, but with enforcement requisitions were undesirable. Borrowing from Mason, the Federalists realized that such sanctions could not be applied to the states as collective entities. Sanctions would have to be applied to the people. If Congress coerced the states into compliance, it would have to punish both obedient and disobedient individuals within a state, rather than punish the collective as a distinct entity. According to Hamilton, acting upon states was the "great and radical vice" of the confederation.[16] Government "must carry its agency to the persons of the citizens," he thought. It must apply sanctions to individuals rather than to states.[17]

Hamilton's argument was made plausible by the inadequacies of the requisition system. The refutation of the notion that partial compliance resulted solely from limited resources allowed the Federalists to argue against the requisition system and to push for a national republic that acted directly upon the people. In the eyes of the Federalists, the national government needed to raise revenues and recruit a national army directly if it was going to be effective. It had to have the means of carrying out its tasks. The power of direct taxation, though not the abuse of this power, would allow the national government to provide for the people and for the states. "Every government which is worth having and supporting must have a competent degree of power in it to answer the great ends of its creation," a Freeman wrote. Requisitions were inadequate for the task. Coercing the states was even worse. According to the Federalists, new powers, such as those provided by the Constitution, would allow the federal government to provide public goods more efficiently

---

[16] Federalist 15, Rossiter, ed., *Federalist Papers*, 108; Ostrom, *Political Theory of a Compound Republic*, 36–41.

[17] John Marshall, Virginia Convention Debates, June 10, 1788, Jensen, ed., *Documentary History*, 9: 1121; Federalist 15, Rossiter, ed., *Federalist Papers*, 116.

than occasionally tyrannizing people in a delinquent state. It was a damaging argument for the Anti-Federalists because it convinced many that the Articles could not be repaired without significant infringement on state sovereignty and individual liberty.[18]

The Anti-Federalists had one clear retort. The Federalists had claimed that the nation needed the Constitution to improve its efficiency, but clearly this was not the case. The Constitution was not a necessary solution to the collective action problem. It was one of many institutions that could improve the efficiency of the union. The power to raise import and excise duties, coupled with the current system of requisitions, could have given the federal government ample revenue for years, without reconstituting the union. Alternatively, Congress could have coerced compliance when states failed to comply, as Henry suggested. Certainly, other ideas would have worked as well. Creating a new government that acted directly upon the people was not fully justified by the failures of the confederation. It was only one of many approaches to reform. "My own opinion," wrote Brutus, "is, that the objects from which the general government should have authority to raise a revenue, should be of such a nature, that the tax should be raised by simple laws, with few officers, with certainty and expedition, and with the least interference with the internal police of the state. – Of this nature is the impost on imported goods – and it appears to me that a duty on exports, would also be of this nature." For the Anti-Federalists, the power to tax was the power to destroy. The conditions of the confederation may have warranted the need for reform, but they did not warrant the end of the confederation.[19]

What both sides were struggling with was the fundamental trade-off between liberty and efficiency that has plagued public choice scholars for years.[20] Clearly, "States in [a] confederacy, like individuals in society, must part with some of their privileges for the preservation of the rest."[21]

[18] A Freeman to the People of Connecticut, *Connecticut Courant*, December 31, 1787, Jensen, ed., *Documentary History*, 3: 518; James Wilson's Speech at a Public Meeting, October 6, 1787, Bailyn, ed., *Debate on the Constitution*, 1: 67–68.

[19] Brutus VII, *New York Journal*, January 3, 1788, Jensen, ed., *Documentary History*, 15: 236–239. Arguments for assigning Congress with the power of the impost include Agrippa IX, December 28, 1787, *Debate on the Constitution*, 1: 629. The state ratifying conventions of New Hampshire and Massachusetts, for example, proposed amendments that forbade Congress from levying direct taxes unless imposts and excises were insufficient, and then only if a state failed to pay its requisition. The Virginia and North Carolina conventions stipulated that Congress would be allowed to levy direct taxes only if the entire requisition system did not work (Main, *Antifederalists*, 143–149).

[20] Sen's Liberal Paradox, for example, illustrates the conflict between efficiency, minimal liberty, and a weak social ordering (Sen, *Collective Choice*, 78–88).

[21] James White to Richard Caswell, November 13, 1787, Burnett, ed., *Letters of Members*, 8: 681–682.

The Federalists emphasized the need to protect national borders, to repay federal debts, and to restore the general effectiveness of the union. The Anti-Federalists emphasized the need to defend state sovereignty and to protect individual liberty. Neither wanted to surrender to the other side, but they both had to admit the trade-offs between efficiency and sovereignty that discouraged previous reforms. The Constitution was not necessary for the improved efficiency of the federal government, and the confederation was not necessary for the protection of state sovereignty. A variety of designs were offered and countless more could be proposed – each of which contained its own mix of efficiency and liberty. Choosing among these alternatives was a value judgment that many Americans had to make. After fifteen years of a half-functional confederation, Americans were ready for a more radical design.

A CONFEDERATION BASED ON VIRTUE

Part of the problem stemmed from relying on civic virtue. The Federalists thought that self-interest had always governed human action. "It is the nature of man to pursue his own interest, in preference to the public good," claimed James Wilson. Government needed something more proven and more dependable than civic virtue to enforce its edicts. Any government based on the assumption of a self-abnegating citizenry was destined to fail. As Noah Webster wrote, "virtue, patriotism, or love of country, never was and never will be, till mens' natures are changed, a fixed, permanent principle and support of government." Similarly, Edward Carrington believed that "Man is impatient of restraint, nor will he conform to what is necessary to the good order of Society, unless he is perfect in discernment and virtue, or the Government under which he lives is efficient." Carrington saw the problem as a dilemma: Unless citizens were perfectly virtuous, the government would have to enforce its measures. "The Fathers of the American Fabric," he continued, "seem to have supposed the first of these principles peculiarly our lot, and have chosen it for a foundation. In the progress of experiment the fallacy is discovered, and the whole pile must fall if the latter cannot be supplied."[22]

Early Americans were not uniquely unprincipled. In fact, they may have been the most principled people in U.S. history. They valued honor and the ability to act independently of particular interests. But even the most arduous patriots knew they were incapable of consistently judging

---

[22] James Wilson's Speech in the State House Yard, October 6, 1787, Jensen, ed., *Documentary History*, 2: 171; Webster, "Examination into the Federal Constitution," in Ford, ed., *Pamphlets on the Constitution*, 59; Edward Carrington to Governor Edmund Randolph, December 8, 1786, Virginia, *Calendar of State Papers*, 195.

the greater good by themselves. They could not continually sacrifice their needs, or the needs of their families, for the common interest when others got ahead by fending for themselves. Acting out of self-interest was typical of humans throughout history. Certain sacrifices could be made, but civic virtue could not be counted on to enforce government measures perpetually.

As the empirical and historical evidence presented in earlier chapters suggests, self-abnegation for the common good was not the entire reason for states to contribute to the union. States contributed out of local interests at least some of the time and may have contributed out of local interests all of the time. Contributing large portions of men to the nation's war effort and paying off reasonable portions of the confederation's debt may have appeared to be acts of patriotism and civic duty to contemporaries, when in fact they were nothing more than the pursuit of local interests. This is not to suggest that patriotism or acts of civic-mindedness did not exist, it is merely to suggest that many behaviors traditionally associated with civic virtue may have been localism in disguise.

Showing that states contributed out of local interests is more than a side note for an era characterized by patriotism and civic duty. The authors of the American confederation created a system that depended on individual commitment to the common good and some sense of self-abnegation. They assumed that patriotism and civic duty would encourage states to comply with requisitions and to make their confederation work. Finding that private interests explain a large portion of state contributions undermines the whole precept of basing a confederation on civic duty. If a confederation based on civic virtue failed during the gentlemanly times of the American confederation, then it is likely to fail when virtuous behaviors are less expected.

Conflict for Politicians

The conflict between virtue and particular interests is particularly arduous for state politicians. Just because state delegates sit in a common national assembly to discover national interests does not mean that they will find interests common to them all. When they do, there is no reason to believe that their legislatures will act according to these concerns, particularly when it requires putting the needs of the union before the needs of their constituents. Pleasing local constituents was more important for a legislator's reelection and for maintaining the well-being of his state than sacrificing local interests for the confederation.

This tug-of-war between state and national interests reflects the true inconsistency of a confederation based on civic virtue. How could state politicians advance the interests of their people on one hand then turn around and surrender these interests to the greater good of the confederation on the other? To argue that civic-minded politicians from different states would never face this dilemma implies that there was a single common interest that they would arrive at independently. Georgians could never interpret the confederation's interest differently than the citizens of New York when both sets of people were acting virtuously. In other words, it would be impossible, according to the claim, for Georgians to find protecting themselves from the Indians in the nation's interest, while New Yorkers found withholding state import duties from Georgia's defense in the nation's interest at the same time. The fact that such differences could exist, even if citizens of all states were acting virtuously, implies that delegates would still have problems acting collectively. They could defend the civic interests of their states and find it in their state's unilateral interest to deviate from the common good. In other words, even if the nation achieved perfect virtue, which many realized it could not, there could still be collective action problems between states.

Decentralized Enforcement

The primary failures of the Articles of Confederation resulted from assigning all enforcement powers to the states. State enforcement hindered the executive, judicial, and legislative functions of Congress, in a variety of ways.

Leaving enforcement to the states prevented Congress from raising enough men to fully secure the union. Congress could not curb hostilities with the Indians in the West, dislodge the British from the North, nor open the Spanish blockade of the South. The former affected the price of western lands and reduced federal revenue from its sale. The latter two challenged the nation's ability to defend itself and weakened the country in international affairs.

Without adequate money, the executive function of national finance was also impaired. Congress could not pay the bulk of its domestic and foreign loans and found it difficult to secure new ones. Creditors did not want to invest in federal securities that had been partially paid in the past, and foreign investors did not want to loan money when Congress ignored the bulk of its foreign obligations. The federal government did not pay the vast majority of the debts it owed France or Spain and fell behind in its payments to the Dutch. Not paying the French hampered relations with an important ally and endangered a traditional source of specie.[23]

---

[23] For more on the problems of paying French loans, see James Monroe to James Madison, February 9, 1786, Smith, ed., *Letters of Delegates*, 23: 136–138, esp. n. 3.

Without adequate money from the states, Congress also fell short on the salaries it owed to soldiers of the Revolutionary War. When local courts demanded that veterans pay private creditors on schedule, many veterans felt the pinch and protested. They were unable to pay their mortgages after being stripped of their income during the war. They could not tend to their crops or create wares as they had traditionally done, and they did not receive the money promised for their military services. In some cases this left them without excess income for years. As courts persisted, protests turned into insurrections. Not only did the lack of enforcement power prevent the nation from responding to threats such as Shays' Rebellion, it prevented the nation from raising the revenues needed to pay veterans and avoid the whole problem in the first place.

Leaving enforcement with the states also hampered the judicial functions of Congress. Congress could adjudicate disputes between states, but it could not enforce its judgments. States could violate the verdicts of Congress as they willed, leaving Congress with little more than the ability to recommend an outcome. Congressional verdicts were not taken seriously and Congress became more of an arbitrator than a judiciary.

A less obvious consequence of assigning enforcement powers to the states was its effect on legislative functions, specifically congressional attendance. Grayson wrote, "It is a practice with many States in the Union to come forward & be very assiduous till they have carried some State jobb & then decamp with precip[it]ation, leaving the public business to shift for itself." When Congress lost its effectiveness, through lack of revenue and inability to enforce its measures, states had no reasons to send their delegates. Congress lost its ability to create effective policy and delegates were inclined to stay at home. A delegate from Connecticut wrote, "I cannot see there remains any necessity for keeping up a Representation in Congress, in our present Scituation [sic], all we can possibly do, is to recommend, which is an old, stale device & no better than the wish of a few Individuals relative to publick Concerns." There was no reason for delegates to attend Congress when its recommendations were being ignored. With important business back home, they did not want to attend Congress. The proportion of working days that Congress had a quorum of seven or more states declined by more than 40 percent from the period of 1783–85 to the period of 1786–87, and Congress rarely received the nine states needed to conduct major business in the last three years of the confederation. Poor attendance, precipitated by a lack of federal resources, inhibited Congress's ability to pass legislation.[24]

[24] William Grayson to James Madison, May 28, 1786, ibid., 23: 318; Stephen Mix Mitchell to Jeremiah Wadsworth, January 24, 1787, ibid., 24: 74. For the figures on congressional attendance, see Riker, "Lessons of 1787," 24–27.

Not all of the defects of the confederation can be tied to requisitions, however. Some stemmed from unrelated problems while others came from collective action problems outside the system of requisitions. Consider international commerce, for example. In 1783 Britain closed its ports in the West Indies to American shipping. Congress tried to respond by applying similar restrictions to British ships, but without the explicit power to block British shipping, Congress could not respond as desired. It might have suggested that the states prevent British ships from entering their harbors, but it could not count on states to carry out the measure. If some states reacted to the British embargo by blocking British shipping, British captains would merely sail to a more friendly state. A uniform response to the British was in the interest of every state, but unilateral maintenance of such an embargo was not. States would gain from the additional trade brought by British ships and improve their import revenue by defying it. The confederation's intent of leaving enforcement with the states prevented the states from responding to British commercial policy in kind. This was a typical problem with the Articles of Confederation. Acting independently, the states had no incentive to enforce policies that they mutually desired.

Allowing states to maintain the exclusive power of enforcement weakened Congress's executive, judicial, and legislative functions. It was the underlying cause of many of the problems associated with the Articles of Confederation. Some were a result of the failures of the requisition system. Others were not. Combined, they demonstrated to Americans that their institutions were inadequate for a well-functioning government.

A Change of National Ideology

The events between 1775 and 1787 gave early Americans a taste for confederative government strongly devoted to state sovereignty. The Articles of Confederation protected the autonomy of states at the expense of providing public goods efficiently. With enforcement left to the states, the national government was unable to raise the men and money it requested, it could not regulate international commerce, and it could not prevent the states from feuding over interstate disputes. The ineffectiveness of the Articles of Confederation became increasingly clear as the 1780s progressed. "In our opposition to monarchy, we forgot that the temple of tyranny has two doors," wrote Benjamin Rush. "We bolted one of them by proper restraints: but we left the other open, by neglecting to guard against the effects of our own ignorance and licentiousness."[25] By 1787 the typical

---

[25] Rush, *Selected Writings*, 26.

American was ready to return some power to the central government that they had carefully stripped from the British. The events of the confederation showed them why they should prefer a more efficient government and why they might want to replace the Articles of Confederation.

Ever since the backlash to John Fiske's *The Critical Period in American History*, describing conditions as "critical" or approaching critical, has been taboo. Historians sympathetic to the Anti-Federalist position noticed that Fiske based his work primarily on the rhetoric of the Federalists. The Federalists claimed that the nation was on the verge of collapse and hoped their claims would increase support for the Constitution.[26]

Notwithstanding Federalist claims, there is strong evidence that the economy was improving and that the daily life of the typical American was improving as well.[27] With conditions improving in the states, anything that resembles a critical thesis has come under attack. Though claims of an improving economy are reasonably well supported, the government of the confederation was not improving. In fact, it was becoming decidedly worse. The confederation was not raising the money needed to pay its debt, it could not enforce its resolution of disputes between states, and it could not regulate interstate commerce. Congress could not even raise the money it needed to pay its civil list. A government cannot last long under such circumstances, and in this sense the confederation was not well. There was not an economic nor a military crisis, but the institutions of the confederation needed repair. Problems with congressional institutions became more apparent as time progressed over the 1780s. They hastened men of national prominence to seek a solution, but they also caused a wider number of Americans to take interest in the cause. Events changed popular attitudes toward a stronger national government and made more Americans willing to sacrifice some state sovereignty for a more effective government.

A pure protection of state sovereignty may have seemed reasonable when Americans were attempting to thwart British rule, but after living in a system that did little more than protect state sovereignty, Americans wanted something more. They realized the old system was not working and changed their preferences in favor of a more effective government.

---

[26] For Federalist rhetoric, see Louis Guillaume Otto to Comte de Montmorin, November 26, 1787, Bailyn, ed., *Debate on the Constitution*, 1: 422; and Brown, *Redeeming*, 141–155.

[27] Perhaps the greatest critic of the "critical period" thesis is Jensen, *A New Nation*. Jensen argues that a minority of Nationalists created rhetoric about a critical period to justify their push for a strong National government. For a review article on the critical thesis, see Morris, "Confederation Period." For economic conditions, see Perkins, *American Public Finance*, and Nettels, *Emergence of a National Economy*.

This was part of the reason that they ratified the Constitution in 1788, when similar attempts would have failed five years before. National ideology was not changing on its own. It was shifting as events became worse. The events of the 1780s changed American credos and convinced many that the confederation needed reform. Many Americans were no longer willing to live with institutions that protected liberty with such huge trade-offs in efficiency. They adopted ideology that clarified their positions and chose the Constitution after experiencing failures in the design.

LESSONS FROM THE AMERICAN CONFEDERATION

Ironically, the same localism that contributed to the confederation's failure also contributed to the union's success. In pursuit of private benefits state politicians were driven to contribute when local interests were at stake and to withhold their resources when they were not. They complied with requisitions to protect local lands, to free families from occupation, and to pay local constituents. This localism bound the union together, perhaps more than the patriotism and the sense of the common good that the confederation had been based upon.

Understanding the role of joint products can also help us explain why other confederations and international organizations partially succeed. Regional republics and nation-states contribute to their common concerns not because they have a greater understanding of needs of the whole, but because contributing is in their private interests. One of the reasons that weak institutions seem to succeed is that regional republics and nation-states may not face a pure public goods problem at all. They may be pursuing joint products, and the private benefits from those joint products may encourage them to contribute in much the same way as private benefits encouraged states to contribute during the American confederation. The public benefits from joint products, though valued, provide no incentive for regional republics or nation-states to contribute to their common interests and prevent public goods from being optimally provided.[28]

Consider the United Nations, for example. It has been argued that some countries contribute to U.N. peacekeeping forces to obtain the private benefits from contribution. Almost all nations would like peace

---

[28] For an overview of confederations, see Forsyth, *Unions of States*, and Riker, *Federalism*. For the suboptimal production of joint products, see Sandler, *Collective Action*, 42–44, 59; and Cornes and Sandler, *Theory of Externalities*, 225–272. Changing the technology of supply from a summation of contributions to the contribution of the weakest link, for example, may encourage optimal contributions, but in most cases the production of joint products remains suboptimal.

in Cambodia, Bosnia, and other places of international unrest, but this does not mean that they are willing to contribute to obtain that peace, particularly when other states free-ride. Such benefits are nonexcludable and provide no incentive for nations to contribute. Nor do nations contribute because their citizens are more virtuous than citizens in other countries. Many nations simply contribute to obtain excludable, private benefits from contributing. Soldiers from Pakistan, Nigeria, and India, for example, receive higher pay for serving with the U.N. than their governments can afford. Perhaps this is why these countries consistently volunteer national forces. It is cheaper for them to maintain and train their divisions at the expense of the U.N. than to train their soldiers at their own expense. Certainly, soldiers would appreciate the higher wages if they received the difference. Contributing forces to the U.N. allows nations to maintain a standing army at only a fraction of the full cost. These unilateral interests may be part of the reason nations voluntarily contribute soldiers to the U.N.[29]

Perhaps similar factors can explain national compliance with requisition in the European Union. More than half of E.U. revenue comes from value-added taxes, but a remaining quarter comes from requisitions. Roughly 80 percent of the total is spent on agricultural subsidies and regional development programs. Is it possible that countries which gain more agricultural and regional development subsidies have a greater propensity to pay their requisitions than those that do not? Such behavior would certainly be consistent with the interest of recipient states. It would also be consistent with the theory of joint products.[30]

International organizations, such as the Organization of African Unity (OAU), in contrast, may fail to obtain contributions from member states because they cannot provide the same type of private benefits that the U.N. does. The OAU does not provide higher salaries for soldiers than member states and may not provide other private benefits. The public aspects of providing peace in Africa provide no incentive for countries to unilaterally contribute to common interests even when regional peacekeeping is desired. Further research will indicate whether the relationship between state compliance and private benefits holds in other confederations and international organizations as well.

The authors of the American confederation clearly designed a system that favored the protection of state sovereignty over the promotion of

---

[29] Bobrow and Boyer, "Maintaining System Stability." For budgeting, apportionment of forces, and greater problems with U.N. peacekeeping, see Kazimi, *Financing U.N. Peacekeeping Operations*, 1–47, and Berdal, "Whither UN Peacekeeping?"

[30] For rough budget information, see McCormick, *European Union*, 215–220.

common state interests. In doing so, they created institutions that did not overcome a natural collective action problem among states. States were left with few institutional incentives to contribute to the union, and they withheld their resources as might be expected from any organization based on voluntary compliance.

Framers of future confederations and international organizations should not rely on the private aspects of joint products to bind their unions together. Without knowing how many private benefits will be produced, framers will not know whether private aspects will encourage sufficient provision. In other words, unions may produce enough public benefits to justify their existence, but they may not produce enough private benefits to overcome the natural collective action problems inherent in the provision of public goods. Even if private aspects can encourage regional republics and nation-states to contribute to their central governments, the public aspect of joint products will almost always ensure that goods are suboptimally supplied. Joint products can encourage contributions among actors, but they will rarely encourage actors to contribute as much as they demand.

Framers of future unions should seek strong institutional designs that promote common state interests while still providing other goals of the union, such as protecting state sovereignty. The value-added tax used by the E.U. may be an example. The E.U. receives a fixed percentage of the value-added tax assessed in each nation and retains only minimal control over how much each nation assesses. Value-added taxes provide the E.U. with most of its revenue, while still protecting state sovereignty. Whether this institution produces efficient outcomes or is the best at protecting national sovereignty is worthy of further investigation. The ultimate decision about which institutional design is "best" depends on the effectiveness of each institution as well as subjective valuations about the importance of efficiency and sovereignty. Many constitutional designs, such as the ones examined in Chapter 7, improve efficiency at the expense of state sovereignty. Others, such the Articles of Confederation, protect state sovereignty at the expense of efficiency. Determining the proper constitutional design depends on the values of participants as well as each institution's ability to fulfill its goals.

If statesmen want to promote an efficient production of public goods, they should seek strong institutional designs rather than allow each state to contribute according to its immediate aims. Problems of collective action can prevent states from contributing enough resources to produce the goods that they demand, and confederations that rely on the private aspects of joint products will not obtain all the goods that their member states desire. Unless lawmakers can manipulate private incentives to encourage cooperation or enforce compliance, requisition systems should be avoided. They will not provide incentive for states to adequately contribute to their common affairs and may leave unions chronically underfunded. With the adoption of requisition systems by the Commonwealth of Independent States, the U.N., and the E.U., finding the right solution is an increasingly modern concern.

Appendix: Olson's Collective Action Game

A number of simplifications help create a model of continuous, pure public goods. First, assume that states purchased the amount of a public good between zero and infinity that maximized their monetary net benefits. Second, set aside states that opposed the purchase of a good or received negative benefits from its provision. This will help to show that all the states could benefit from a public good but still choose to free-ride. Third, assume that states have complete information and each state's payoff function is common knowledge. State 1 knows state 2's payoffs, state 2 knows that 1 knows this, and so on. Complete information simplifies the analysis and makes the model's empirical prediction more precise. Finally, assume that each state has unlimited resources to apply toward the purchase of public goods. Although the final assumption is clearly unrealistic, it helps to show that the free-rider problem is independent of ability to pay. Even with unlimited resources, states still find it rational to withhold their contributions. Combined, these assumptions create a continuous payoff function that reflects the decision to pay in an institution-free setting.[1]

---

[1] In addition to these assumptions, I implicitly assume that each state legislature made its decision as a unitary actor. Although this assumption is frequently criticized as unrealistic, the assumption does not assume that members of the legislature have the same preferences or that Arrow's impossibility theorem is somehow denied. It merely suggests that each state legislature creates an actionable agenda through some type of political process. This political agenda is then representative of the legislature's interest. In other words, the analysis starts after state legislatures have determined their actionable goals, in much the same way that historians refer to a "state's interest" in their descriptions of historical events.

THE PROVISION OF PURE PUBLIC
GOODS IN AN INSTITUTION-FREE SETTING

More precise formalism helps illustrate the game theoretic prediction for an institution-free setting. Let x be the amount of the public good supplied from zero to infinity; $B_i(x)$ be the benefits state i receives from x; $B(x)$ be the total benefits gained by all states from x (in this case $B(x) = \Sigma_i B_i(x)$); and $C(x)$ be the cost of providing the good. Each of these terms is a function of the continuous variable x, rather than the simple variables written in the text. The following assumptions outline a game for continuous pure public goods.

1. Continuous choice: Each state i chooses $x_i \in X$ where $X = [0, \infty]$. Note: $x = \Sigma_i x_i$.
2. Complete information.
3. Payoff: $V_i(x) = B_i(x) - C(x)$
4. Payoffs are continuous and well behaved.[2]
   a. $B_i(x)$ is monotonically increasing and twice differentiable, with $B_i''(x) < 0$.
   b. $C(x)$ is monotonically increasing and twice differentiable, with $C''(x) \geq 0$.
   c. When no state contributes, $x = 0$, $B_i(0) = 0$, and $C(0) = 0$.
   d. $B'(0) > C'(0)$.
   e. $\lim_{x \to \infty} B_i'(x) < C'(x)$.
5. Social valuation: $V(x) = B(x) - C(x)$

More general assumptions could be employed, but these five guarantee that a social optimum exists and that it is unique.[3] Mathematically, the social optimum corresponds to the point where $B'(x) = C'(x)$.[4] This is the amount provided at point x^o in the two state society depicted in Figure A.1. At this point, the slope, or tangent, of the aggregate benefit curve equals the slope of the cost curve, corresponding to the condition of marginal aggregate benefits equaling marginal costs. It is also the point

---

[2] Assumptions 4a and 4b ensure that each state's payoff function (and the social valuation function) have unique optimums. This simplifies the analysis. Assumption 4c prevents the social optimum from already being obtained before a state makes its decision – in effect, giving it something to choose. Assumption 4d guarantees that the social optimum exists and that it is greater than zero, while assumption 4e guarantees that each individual's optimum and the social optimum is less than infinity.

[3] In this context, the social optimum corresponds with a utilitarian notion of optimality. Although this optimum is an element of the Pareto set, it is not a unique element.

[4] This condition is derived by taking the partial derivative of V with respect to x and setting the result equal to zero in the equation $V(x) = B(x) - C(x)$. The second-order condition is met by assumption.

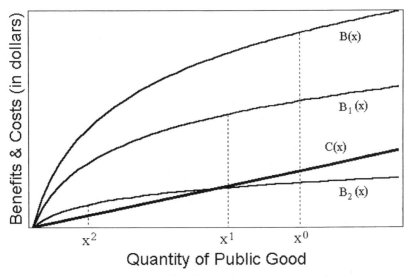

Figure A.1. The provision of public goods in an institution-free setting.

where the difference between $B(x)$ and $C(x)$ is the greatest. This is the best that the states can do as a union. Producing any other amount of the good would sacrifice potential benefits and make at least one state worse off.

Consider what would happen if states were not organized into a union. Under such conditions, the best that a state can do is to purchase the amount of public good that maximizes the difference between its benefits and costs. This corresponds to the point where $V_i(x)$ is maximized.[5] Any other provision leaves room for a state to gain valuation from purchasing more of the good or from purchasing less. In the two-state society depicted in Figure A.1, the best that state 1 can do, or its rational provision, is marked x^1. Similarly, the rational provision for state 2 in a nonstrategic setting is marked x^2. Let's call these points the nonstrategic bliss points (NBPs) for state 1 and state 2, respectively.[6] At these

---

[5] Assuming $V_i(x) = B_i(x) - C(x)$, the stated first-order condition is derived by taking the partial of V_i with respect to x and setting the result equal to zero. The second-order condition is met by assumption. Olson, *Logic*; Frohlich and Oppenheimer, *Modern Political Economy*; Mueller, *Public Choice II*.

[6] As used here a bliss point is the most preferred outcome in an actor's unconstrained preference order (Varian, *Intermediate Microeconomics*, 42–44). In a nonstrategic setting this is the point where marginal state benefits equal marginal costs. I call this point the nonstrategic bliss point to differentiate it from the more preferred alternatives that can be obtained when the contributions of others are introduced.

points, the slope (or tangent) of $B_i(x)$ equals the slope (or tangent) of $C(x)$ for each state. This corresponds to the first-order condition of marginal state benefits equaling marginal costs at the individual optimum. When no other state contributes, a state that purchases this amount receives the most benefit for the buck.

When each state is allowed to consider the actions of other states, however, a suboptimal amount is purchased for the group. This follows because it is not rational for all states to purchase at their NBPs.[7] In Figure A.1, neither state 1 nor state 2 is willing to purchase an amount that would give it the social optimum, x^o, in combination. State 1 prefers to purchase x^1 units of the public good and state 2 prefers to take advantage of 1's generosity by providing zero. This is because state 2 receives a greater payoff by consuming its portion of the benefits at 1's NBP, $B_2(x^1)$, without paying any of the costs, than it would by paying $C(x^2)$ and getting $B_2(x^1 + x^2)$ in return. In other words, $B_2(x^1) > B_2(x^o) - C(x^2)$. Likewise, state 1 is not affected by 2's indolence because state 1 would provide x^1 even if state 2 were not around. When strategic behavior is introduced, this is the Nash equilibrium of the two-player game.[8] State 2 contributes nothing and state 1 contributes x^1 – a suboptimal amount for the group.

In other words, the pursuit of local interest prevents states from providing optimal, or efficient, amounts of the goods that they commonly desire. Even when all states agree that the optimal provision makes them better off, they still have incentive to withhold their contribution. This is because a state gains from the provision of the public good, but gains even more if it obtains the good without paying. Since public goods are nonexcludable, the large state purchases the public good, while the small state free-rides on the good's provision. Without institutions or political entrepreneurs to solve the collective action problem, suboptimality is predicted for disunified states. States would not purchase what they demanded.[9]

---

[7] To show that the good is suboptimally supplied, compare state i's marginal benefit at the national optimum $B_i'(x^o)$, with state i's marginal benefit at its individually rational response. If a rational state contributed the optimal amount, then $B'(x^o) = C'(x^o) = B_i'(x)$ in equilibrium. But from the condition for social optima we know that $B_i'(x^o) = C'(x^o) - B'_{-i}(x^o)$. Unless all the other states combined gained zero marginal benefits from the public good (which they cannot by assumption), the amount provided in equilibrium is less than the social optimum (see Mueller, *Public Choice II*, 17–21).

[8] An outcome is in Nash equilibrium if and only if no state has a unilateral incentive to deviate from the amount it purchases (see Myerson, *Game Theory*, 91, for a more precise definition).

[9] Frohlich and Oppenheimer define a political entrepreneur as "an individual who invests his own time or other resources to coordinate and combine other factors of production to supply public goods" (*Modern Political Economy*, 68). We can imagine that these

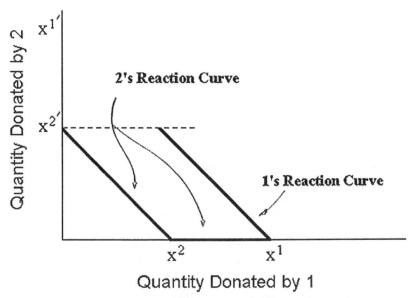

Figure A.2. Reaction curves.

Specific predictions about how much of the public good will be produced can be obtained by an analysis of state reaction curves. A reaction
curve illustrates a state's best response to contributions made by other
states. To set up the game, imagine that we could know each state's benefits from a public good and could order the thirteen states from smallest
to largest. In this context, "smallest" means the state that receives the least
benefit from the good, or more precisely has the smallest x^i associated with
its NBP, while "largest" is the state that has the largest quantity of the
good associated with its NBP, or the largest x^i.

Figure A.2 summarizes the "best responses" for the largest and the
second largest states. Analyzing the best responses for the two largest
states alone illustrates the Nash equilibrium for the entire group. Here the
x-axis denotes quantities of the good purchased by the largest state, state
1, while the y-axis denotes quantities of the good purchased by the second
largest state, state 2. Heavily shaded lines are the reaction curves for state
1 and state 2, respectively. State 1's reaction curve denotes its best response

types of entrepreneurs, or similar outside influences, would induce cooperation in an
"institution-free" setting. However, there is no evidence that this type of entrepreneur
existed in the context of the confederation, and, as I use the term, an "institution-free"
setting does not include outside influences.

to the quantities purchased by state 2, while state 2's reaction curve denotes its best response to the quantities purchased by 1. Each state's NBP is marked along the axes as x^1 and x^2, respectively.

No state would be willing to contribute when others donated more than their NBP. This is because additional purchases cost more at the margin than they produce in benefits. If state 1 purchased x^2 units or greater, the best response for state 2 would be to go no further and purchase nothing. Any additional purchase made by state 2 would exceed state 2's NBP. If, however, state 1 purchased less than x^2, the best response for 2 would be to contribute the amount which brought the total contribution back up to its NBP. The first point gives the reaction curve its horizontal region between x^2 and x^1 on the x-axis, while the second connects x^2 and $x^{2\prime}$ by a straight line.

State 1's reaction curve can be drawn similarly. If state 2 buys any amount of the public good between zero and $x^{2\prime}$ inclusive, the best response for state 1 is to donate the amount that brings the total back up to 1's NBP. Since state 2 has no incentive to purchase beyond its own NBP, 1's reaction curve is cut off by the dotted line at $x^{2\prime}$. The intersection of these two curves marks the equilibrium. This is the point where the largest state purchases its NBP, x^1, and the second largest state purchases nothing. There are no other equilibria for this two-player game, though the equilibrium can manifest itself in different behaviors.

In fact, if we extend the analysis to n players and note that no state has any incentive to produce beyond its NBP, it is easy to see that this equilibrium applies to all thirteen states as well. No state would ever purchase more than its own NBP, and the largest state would always be willing to cover the difference needed to bring the total up to its own NBP. If the largest state does this, smaller states have no incentive to contribute. This produces an equilibrium where the largest state contributes at its NBP while everyone else contributes nothing.

If total costs exceed each state's benefit against the depiction of Figure A.1, the good continues to be suboptimally supplied and the equilibrium still holds. Only this time the equilibrium appears somewhat trivial. The largest state does not find it in its unilateral interest to purchase any of the good and contributes at its NBP of zero. The smaller states contribute nothing as well. Any positive contribution produces negative returns for a state; therefore, all states would withhold their resources despite the net benefits they could gain from mutual cooperation. Under these conditions, the game becomes a classic prisoners' dilemma, where every state has a dominant incentive to defect even though they could gain from mutual cooperation.

Finally, there is one other set of equilibria for the game. If there is more than one "largest" state, in other words two or more states that share the largest x^1, then any division that brings the total back up to the NBP shared by the largest states is in equilibrium. More specifically, if the NBP shared by the largest states is at x^1 and there are only two "largest" states, then the equilibria for these two actors are $\alpha[0] + (1 - \alpha)[x^1]$ for one of the states and $(1 - \alpha)[0] + \alpha[x^1]$ for the other state, where $\alpha = [0, 1]$. This means that one state contributing one quarter of the NBP while the other contributing the remaining three quarters is just as much in equilibrium as the two splitting the burden fifty-fifty. Neither state has incentive to deviate from the contributions within this set. Of course, these equilibria can be extended to cases where more than two states share exactly the largest x^1. In which case, the states tied for the largest will split the contribution and all other states will contribute zero.

These are the only equilibria for the complete information game. No state contributes to the treasury; the state that benefits the most contributes at its NBP while all other states contribute nothing; or the states that share the greatest benefit jointly contribute their NBP, while all others contribute nothing. Considering that the latter case may be quite rare, we now have a very precise prediction to use in this book. Barring ties for the "largest" state, one or no states should contribute to the purchase of public goods. Since Congress usually purchased continuous public goods, this prediction should apply to the requisitions of Congress.

The Provision of Pure Public Goods under the System of Requisitions

To show that the Articles of Confederation did not have an effect on the decision to contribute, we need to go one step further. We need to consider what happens when states contributed money to the national treasury rather than purchase public goods directly. The difference between an institution-free setting and the Articles can be established by comparing rational decision-making without the Articles to rational decision-making with the Articles. If there is no difference, the Articles do not have an effect. If there is a difference, the direction of the effect will have to be determined. Rational decision-making in an institution-free setting was developed in the previous section. Rational decision-making under the Articles requires additional assumptions.

Let y be the amount of money contributed by all states from zero to infinity. The amount of public good actually supplied, x^*, can be then derived from the total amount of money received from the states using the inverse of the cost function, $x^* = S(y) = C^{-1}(y)$. Finally, the variable π_i is the proportion of costs assigned to state i in a requisition, where $\pi_i \in [0, 1]$ and $\Sigma_i \pi_i = 1$.

Under the Articles, Congress determined the amount of goods needed for a requisition and estimated their cost, $C(x^r)$, based on the market price. The total cost was then apportioned among the states according to a set distribution, $\{\pi_i C(x^r)\}_{i=1\ldots 13}$ with each state receiving a share of the costs, $\pi_i C(x^r)$. In the best-case scenario, Congress would have the insight and ability to apportion costs according to each state's Lindahl tax share. This is the "best" division of the costs based on each state's marginal benefit at the social optimum. If Congress could get each state to pay this amount, an optimal amount of the good would be provided. However, even in the best-case scenario, a state would be unmotivated to pay its share.

The following assumptions define the public goods game under the Articles and illustrates the point.

1. Continuous choice: Each state i chooses $y_i \in Y$ where $Y = [0, \infty]$. Note: $y = \Sigma_i y_i$.
2. Complete information (as before).
3. Payoff: $V_i(x) = B_i(x) - y_i$.
4. Payoffs are continuous and well behaved (as before).
5. Social valuation: $V(x) = B(x) - y$

This game is exactly the same as the one developed in the previous section, except this time a state chooses the amount to pay, y_i, which is reduced from its payoff function. In other words, the choice variable is on the y-axis, not the x-axis. This reflects the practice of pooling money prior to purchasing the good. As before, a rational state would try to maximize its net benefits by paying the amount that gave it the greatest benefit for the buck. It would choose y_i to maximize its payoff function V_i. Surprisingly, this produces the same first-order conditions as found in the institution-free setting. Taking the partial derivative of V_i with respect to y_i, the necessary condition for the unconstrained optimum of V_i is obtained, where

$$\frac{\partial V_i}{\partial y_i} = \frac{\partial B_i}{\partial x}\frac{\partial S}{\partial y_i} - 1$$

is set equal to zero, or

$$B_i'(x) = C'(x).^{10}$$

---

[10] Recognizing that $B_i(x) = B_i[S(y)] = B_i[C^{-1}(y_i + y_{-i})]$, the payoff function can be written as $V_i(y_i, y_{-i}) = B_i[C^{-1}(y_i + y_{-i})] - y_i$ from which the first-order condition can be derived as follows:

$$\frac{\partial V_i}{\partial y_i} = \frac{\partial B_i}{\partial x_i}\frac{\partial S}{\partial y_i} \cdot 1 - 1 = \frac{\partial B_i}{\partial x_i}\frac{1}{C'(x)} - 1$$

setting the equation equal to zero: $B_i'(x) = C'(x)$. The second-order condition is met by assumption.

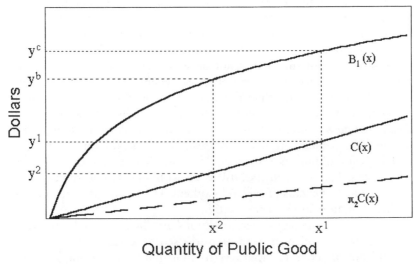

Figure A.3. Rational provision of public goods under the Articles.

This suggests that a state maximizes its payoff by contributing where its marginal benefits equal marginal national costs – not the marginal costs assigned to it in a requisition nor the marginal cost of its donation. This is because the amount assigned to a state in a requisition is not the amount a state actually pays. A state actually pays y_i, which must buy a single unit of the good before it can purchase additional units. Since a state pays the entire cost of each additional unit, marginal costs of the whole good are relevant to its decision.

Graphical techniques help illustrate the result (see Fig. A.3). Here the x-axis depicts the quantity of the good purchased, while the y-axis depicts costs and benefits in dollar amounts. The cost and benefit functions for the smaller state 2 are drawn as before, only this time the graph is enlarged and read backward. Under the Articles, states were assigned a proportion of the total costs through a requisition. This is marked by the dashed line $\pi_2 C(x)$, but as we shall see, this assignment was irrelevant to a state's decision.

In this situation a state has to figure out how much money to donate based on the amount of additional public benefit its contribution would produce. If other states contributed zero and state 2 donated y^2, Congress would purchase x^2 units of the good. This is because the inverse of the cost function determines how much of the good can be purchased from the total dollars donated. The quantity x^2 gives state 2 y^b worth of benefits for a net benefit of $y^b - y^2$. Without other contributions, this is the best that state 2 can do, and it is exactly the same amount as found in the institution-free setting.

When other states contribute, state 2 continues to act as if there were no institutions. If state 1 contributed y^1 toward the good and state 2 paid nothing, then x^1 of the good would be produced through the inverse of the cost function. We do not know how much this would benefit state 1 (because its benefit function is not drawn), but we do know that this donation would give state 2 y^c dollars of benefit at a cost of zero. This amount is much greater than the amount it could gain by donating at y^2, particularly when we consider that state 2 contributes nothing to obtain the new amount. State 2 would be unwilling to donate any amount that pushed national purchases beyond its NBP and would gain only by withholding its resources. The best that state 2 can do when others contribute beyond its NBP is to withhold its contribution and free-ride on the benefits provided by others. This is the same outcome as predicted in an institution-free setting.

The fact that the first-order conditions are the same under the Articles as they are under an institution-free setting suggests that the Articles did not affect state incentives to contribute toward public goods. Pooling resources prior to the purchase of a good may have helped states coordinate policies, but it gave them no reason to contribute their share. States that attempted to purchase public goods through the system of requisitions faced the same type of free-rider problem as they would without the system. One or no state would contribute and a suboptimal provision would result.[11] The consistently high levels of payment made during the confederation could not be explained by the Articles of Confederation. They had to be explained by something else. Joint products could be the answer.

---

[11] Comparing the individual optimum to the national optimum under the Articles shows that the public good is again suboptimally supplied. Recognizing that $B(x) = B[S(y)] = B[C^{-1}(y_i + y_{-i})]$ and that $y = y_i + y_{-i}$, the social valuation function can be written as $V(y) = B[C^{-1}(y)] - y$ from which the first-order condition can be derived by taking the partial derivative of V with respect to y. This gives

$$\frac{\partial V}{\partial y} = \frac{\partial B}{\partial x} \frac{\partial S}{\partial y} \cdot 1 - 1 = \frac{\partial B}{\partial x} \frac{1}{C'(x)} - 1$$

setting the equation equal to zero: $B'(x) = C'(x)$. The second-order condition is met by assumption. If a rational state contributed the optima amount, then $B'(x^o) = C'(x^o) = B_i'(x)$ in equilibrium. But from the condition for the social optimum, above, we know that $B_i'(x^o) = C'(x^o) - B_{-i}'(x^o)$. Unless all the other states combined gained zero marginal benefits from the public good (which they cannot by assumption), the amount provided in equilibrium is less than the social optimum.

Glossary

bills of credit paper currency issued in anticipation of future tax receipts.

bills of exchange paper drafts drawn on foreign loans made in specie. When France lent the United States money in specie, for example, the actual coin remained in France, while American commissioners drew from it using bills of exchange. These bills usually maintained their face value.

certificates paper drafts issued by various departments of the Continental army, similar to an IOU for conscripted supplies.

civic virtue "The willingness of the individual to sacrifice his private interest for the good of the community," patriotism, or love of country (Wood, *Creation of the American Republic*, 68).

collective action problem when actors have no unilateral incentive to contribute to their common interests. In the words of Mancur Olson, "Though all of the members of the group have a common interest in obtaining this collective benefit, they have no common interest in paying the cost of providing that collective good" (*Logic*, 21).

debt sinking putting current income into a sinking fund.

efficiency (loosely) the ability to satisfy mutual interests or demands.

final settlement the settling of unpaid debts between Congress and the states or Congress and individual citizens. Regarding debts between Congress and the states, many states incurred expenses on behalf of the union that Congress would not credit without adequate documentation and testimony. The process of obtaining this evidence and settling the state accounts lasted from roughly 1782 to 1793. Regarding debts between Congress and individual citizens, final settlement liquidated Congress's debts to unpaid soldiers, certificate holders, and staff officers through a similar procedure. Since records of debts to individuals were poorly kept, this process continued for roughly the same period as the settlement of state accounts.

free riders   actors that shirk their responsibility by not contributing to a group.

impost   a duty on imported goods secured by the importer at the time of importation.

indent   a note issued to holders of loan office certificates in payment for interest due. The name comes from an indentation on the left side of the note designed to prevent counterfeiting.

joint product   a good containing multiple aspects of publicness. As used here, a joint product is a good that produces both public and private benefits.

loan office certificates   public bonds sold to individual investors in return for interest. Loan office certificates were named after the loan offices that distributed them.

nonexcludable good   a good that cannot be feasibly excluded from an actor (state) if it is provided for other actors (states).

nonrival good   a good whose quantity is not reduced when an actor (state) consumes it.

nonstrategic bliss point (NBP)   the point that maximizes a state's net benefits when no other state purchases the public good and the state's budget is unlimited.

"old money"   federal currency issued between 1775 and 1780, also referred to as "Continentals."

Pierce's certificates (military certificates)   promissary notes issued by the federal government to pay the salaries of Continental soldiers. The name comes from Paymaster General John Pierce, who signed the certificates.

private good   a good that is both excludable and rival.

public debt   the debt a government or a nation owes to individual creditors. The public debt does not include loans borrowed from other governments. The bulk of public debt during the confederation was based on loan office certificates, certificates, and Pierce's certificates.

public good   a good that is both nonexcludable and nonrival.

requisition a request for money from the states, similar to an unenforced tax on the states for confederative goods and services.

sinking fund a fund set up for the purpose of redeeming long-term debts when they mature. Money within a sinking fund is usually invested to produce returns that can be applied toward interest due on the public debt.

sovereignty the degree of self-determination or political control that a state maintains.

specie gold and silver coins used as a medium of exchange. During the eighteenth century, specie was usually more valuable than paper currency with the same face value.

Tory a member of one of the two major, conservative parties in Great Britain. American Tories sided with the British during the war.

Whig American Whigs sided with the American revolutionaries during the war, championing democratic government and popular rights. They initially supported the idea of a republic based on civic virtue.

References

Adams, Samuel. 1968. *The Writings of Samuel Adams*. Ed. Harry Cushing. New York: Octagon Books.

Allen, W. B., and Gordon Lloyd, eds. 1985. *The Essential Antifederalist*. New York: University Press of America.

Anderson, William G. 1983. *The Price of Liberty: The Public Debt of the American Revolution*. Charlottesville: University Press of Virginia.

Appleby, Joyce. 1992. *Liberalism and Republicanism in the Historical Imagination*. Cambridge, MA: Harvard University Press.

Bancroft, George. 1900. *History of the Formation of the Constitution of the United States of America*. New York: D. Appleton and Company.

Bailyn, Bernard. 1967. *The Ideological Origins of the American Revolution*. Cambridge, MA: Harvard University Press.

1990. *Faces of Revolution: Personalities and Themes in the Struggle for American Independence*. New York: Alfred A. Knopf.

Bailyn, Bernard, ed. 1993. *The Debate on the Constitution*. 2 vols. New York: Library of America.

Banning, Lance. 1987. The Practicable Sphere of a Republic: James Madison, the Constitutional Convention, and the Emergence of Revolutionary Federalism. In Richard Beeman, Stephen Botein, and Edward C. Carter, eds. *Beyond Confederation*, pp. 162–187. Chapel Hill: University of North Carolina Press.

1995. *The Sacred Fire of Liberty: James Madison and the Founding of the Federal Republic*. Ithaca: Cornell University Press.

Beard, Charles. 1935. *An Economic Interpretation of the Constitution of the United States*. New York: The Free Press.

Becker, Robert A. 1980. *Revolution, Reform, and the Politics of American Taxation, 1763–1783*. Baton Rouge: Louisiana State University Press.

Beloff, Max. 1989. *The Debate on the American Revolution, 1761–1783*. New York: Sheridan House.

Berdal, Mats R. 1993. *Whither UN Peacekeeping?* Adelphi Paper 281. London: Brassey's.

Bezanson, Anne. 1951. *Prices and Inflation during the American Revolution*. Philadelphia: University of Pennsylvania Press.

Boatner, Mark Mayo. 1973. *Landmarks of the American Revolution*. Harrisburg, PA: Stackpole Books, Inc.

Bobrow, Davis B., and Mark A. Boyer. 1997. Maintaining System Stability: Contributions to peacekeeping operations. *Journal of Conflict Resolution* 41 (6): 723–748.

Boucher, Jonathan. [1797] 1967. *A View of the Causes and Consequences of the American Revolution*. New York: Russell and Russell.

Brown, Robert E. 1965. *Charles Beard and the Constitution: A Critical Analysis of "An Economic Interpretation of the Constitution."* New York: W. W. Norton.

Brown, Roger H. 1993. *Redeeming the Republic*. Baltimore: Johns Hopkins University Press.

Brunhouse, Robert. 1971. *The Counter-Revolution in Pennsylvania, 1776–1790*. New York: Octagon Books.

Burnett, Edmund, ed. 1936. *Letters of Members of the Continental Congress*. 8 vols. Washington, DC: Carnegie Institution.

——— 1964. *The Continental Congress*. New York: Norton.

Cain, Michael J. G., and Keith L. Dougherty. 1999. Suppressing Shays' Rebellion: Collective Action and Constitutional Design under the Articles of Confederation. *Journal of Theoretical Politics* 11 (2): 233–260.

Cappon, Lester J., ed. 1976. *Atlas of Early American History: The Revolutionary Era, 1760–1779*. Princeton: Princeton University Press.

Carp, Wayne E. 1984. *To Starve the Army at Pleasure*. Chapel Hill: University of North Carolina Press.

Clinton, George. 1899–1914. *Public Papers of George Clinton: First Governor of New York*. Albany: State of New York.

Cochran, Thomas C. 1932. *New York in the Confederation*. Philadelphia: Pennsylvania University Press.

Connecticut. 1945. *Public Records of the State of Connecticut, 1785–1789*. Ed. Leonard Labaree. Hartford: State of Connecticut.

Cornes, Richard, and Todd Sandler. 1996. *The Theory of Externalities, Public Goods, and Club Goods*. 2nd ed. New York: Cambridge University Press.

Crosskey, William Winston, and William Jeffrey, Jr. 1981. *Politics and the Constitution in the History of the United States*, vol. 3: *The Political Background of a Federal Convention*. Chicago: University of Chicago Press.

Davis, Joseph. 1977. *Sectionalism in American Politics, 1774–1787*. Madison: University of Wisconsin Press.

Dickinson, John. 1801. *Political Writings of John Dickinson*. Wilmington, DE: Bonsal and Niles.

Dougherty, Keith L. 1997. Collective Action under the Articles of Confederation: The Impact of Institutional Design on the Provision of Public Goods. Ph.D. dissertation. University of Maryland, College Park.

——— 1999. An Empirical Question in the Federalist Debates (working paper).

——— 2000. A Public Choice Comparison of U.S. Constitutions (working paper).

Dougherty, Keith L., and Michael J. G. Cain. 1997. Marginal Cost Sharing and the Articles of Confederation. *Public Choice* 90: 201–213.

Dworkin, Gerald. 1989. The Concept of Autonomy. In John Christman, ed., *The Inner Citadel*, pp. 54–62. New York: Oxford University Press.

Farrand, Max, ed. 1936–1987. *The Records of the Federal Convention of 1787*. 4 vols. New Haven: Yale University Press.

Ferguson, James E. 1961. *The Power of the Purse*. Chapel Hill: University of North Carolina Press.

Fiske, James. 1888. *The Critical Period of American History, 1783–1789*. Boston: Houghton Mifflin.

Ford, Paul Leicester, ed. 1881. *Pamphlets on the Constitution of the United States, Published during Its Discussion by the People, 1787–1788*. Brooklyn, NY.

Forsyth, Murray. 1981. *Unions of States: The Theory and Practices of Confederations*. Leicester: Leicester University Press.

Franklin, Benjamin. 1962. *The Papers of Benjamin Franklin*. Ed. Leonard W. Labaree. New Haven: Yale University Press.

1970. *The Writings of Benjamin Franklin*. Ed. Albert Henry Smyth. New York: Haskell House.

Freedman, Eric M. 1993. Why Constitutional Lawyers and Historians Should Take a Fresh Look at the Emergence of the Constitution from the Confederation Period. *Tennessee Law Review* 60 (4): 783–839.

Freer, Robert. 1988. *Shays Rebellion*. New York: Garland Publishing, Inc.

Frohlich, Norman, and Joe Oppenheimer. 1978. *Modern Political Economy*. Englewood Cliffs, N.J.: Prentice-Hall.

Gonzales, R., and S. L. Mehay. 1991. Burden Sharing in the NATO Alliance: An Empirical Test of Alternative Views. *Public Choice* 68: 107–116.

Greene, Evarts B., and Virginia D. Harrington. 1966. *American Population before the Federal Census of 1790*. Gloucester, MA: Peter Smith.

Hamilton, Alexander. 1962– . *The Papers of Alexander Hamilton*. Ed. Harold C. Syrett. New York: Columbia University Press.

Hammond, Bray. 1957. *Banks and Politics in America*. Princeton: Princeton University Press.

Hampshire Gazette. 1786. Northampton, NH: William Butler.

Hannum, Hurst. 1990. *Autonomy, Sovereignty, and Self-Determination*. Philadelphia: University of Pennsylvania Press.

Hansen, Laurna, James C. Murdoch, and Todd Sandler. 1990. On Distinguishing the Behavior of Nuclear and Non-Nuclear Allies in NATO. *Defense Economics* 1: 37–55.

Hart, Levi. 1775. *Liberty Described and Recommended*. Hartford, CT: Eben Watson.

Helderman, L. C. 1938. The Northwest Expedition of George Rogers Clark, 1786–1787. *Mississippi Historical Review* 23 (3): 317–334.

Hening, William W., ed. 1823. *Statutes at Large: A Collection of All the Laws of Virginia*. Richmond: George Cochran.

Henry, Patrick. [1891] 1969. *Patrick Henry: Life Correspondence and Speeches*. Ed. William Wirt Henry. New York: Burt Franklin.

Hoffert, Robert W. 1992. *A Politics of Tensions: The Articles of Confederation and American Political Ideas*. Boulder: University Press of Colorado.

Holt, J. C. 1992. *Magna Carta*. New York: Cambridge University Press.

Hopkins, Stephen. 1765. A Vindication of a Late Pamphlet Entitled, The Rights of Colonies Examined. . . . *The Providence Gazette and Country Journal*, January 23, p. 1, col. 1.

Isaac, R. Mark, Kenneth F. McCue, and Charles R. Plott. 1985. Public Good Provision in an Experimental Environment. *Journal of Public Economics* 26: 51–74.

Jefferson, Thomas. 1904–1905. *The Works of Thomas Jefferson*. Ed. Paul L. Ford. New York: G.P. Putnam's Sons.

1950– . *The Papers of Thomas Jefferson*. Ed. Jullian P. Boyd. Princeton: Princeton University Press.

Jenkins, William Summer, comp. 1949– . *Records of the States of the United States of America*. Washington, DC: Library of Congress. Microfilm.

Jensen, Merrill. 1965. *The New Nation: A History of the United States during the Confederation 1781–1789*. New York: Alfred A. Knopf, Inc.

1970. *The Articles of Confederation*. Madison: University of Wisconsin Press.

Jensen, Merrill, ed. 1976– . *The Documentary History of the Ratification of the Constitution*. Madison: State Historical Society of Wisconsin.

Jillson, Calvin, and Rick K. Wilson. 1994. *Congressional Dynamics: Structure, Coordination, and Choice in the First American Congress, 1774–1789*. Stanford: Stanford University Press.

Kammen, Michael. 1986. *The Origins of the American Constitution: A Documentary History*. New York: Penguin Books.

Katcher, Philip R. 1973. *Encyclopedia of British Provincial and German Army Units, 1775–1783*. Harrisburg, PA: Stackpole Books.

Kazimi, M. R. 1988. *Financing the U.N. Peacekeeping Operations*. Delhi: Capital Publishing House.

Ketcham, Ralph, ed. 1986. *The Anti-Federalist Papers and the Constitutional Convention Debates*. New York: Mentor Books.

King, Rufus. 1894. *Life and Correspondence of Rufus King*. Ed. Charles K. King. New York: G. P. Putnam's Sons.

Knox, Henry. 1960. *Microfilms of the Henry Knox Papers*. Boston: New England Historic and Genealogical Society.

Ledyard, John O. 1995. Public Goods: A Survey of Experimental Research. In John H. Kagel and Alvin E. Roth, eds., *The Handbook of Experimental Economics*, pp. 111–194. Princeton, NJ: Princeton University Press.

Lee, Richard Henry. 1914. *The Letters of Richard Henry Lee*. Ed. James Curtis Ballagh. New York: Macmillan.

Lesser, Charles H. 1976. *The Sinews of Independence: Monthly Strength Reports of the Continental Army*. Chicago: University of Chicago Press.

Lister, Frederick K. 1996. *The European Union, the United Nations, and the Revival of Confederal Governance*. Westport, CT: Greenwood Press.

Lodge, Henry Cabot, et al., eds. 1925. *Warren-Adams Letters*. Boston: Massachusetts Historical Society.

Luenberger, David G. 1995. *Microeconomic Theory*. New York: McGraw-Hill.

Lutz, Donald. 1990. The Articles of Confederation as the Background to the Federal Republic. *Publius* 20 (Winter): 55–70.

Madison, James. 1900–1910. *The Writings of James Madison.* Ed. Gaillard Hunt. New York: G. P. Putnam's Sons.

— 1962–1989. *The Papers of James Madison.* Eds. William T. Hutchinson and William M. E. Rachel. Chicago: University of Chicago Press.

— 1966. *Notes of Debates in the Federal Convention of 1787.* Ed. Adrienne Koch. Athens: Ohio University Press.

Main, Jackson Turner. 1961. *The Antifederalists: Critics of the Constitution.* Chapel Hill: University of North Carolina Press.

— 1973. *Political Parties before the Constitution.* Chapel Hill: University of North Carolina Press.

Marks, Frederick W. 1973. *Independence on Trial: Foreign Affairs and the Making of the Constitution.* Baton Rouge: Louisiana State University Press.

Mason, George. 1970. *The Papers of George Mason.* Ed. Robert Rutland. Chapel Hill: University of North Carolina Press.

Massachusetts. 1787. *Session Laws, January 21–February 14, 1787.* Boston: Adams and Nourse. Evans #20496.

— General Assembly. 1786. *Massachusetts Resolves.* Boston: Adams and Nourse. Evans #19793.

— General Assembly. 1787. *Resolves of the General Court, January 30–March 10, 1787.* Boston: Adams and Nourse. Evans #20514.

Matson, Cathy D., and Peter S. Onuf. 1990. *A Union of Interests: Political Economic Thought in Revolutionary America.* Lawrence: University of Kansas Press.

McCormick, John. 1996. *The European Union: Politics and Policies.* Boulder, CO: Westview Press.

McDonald, Forrest. 1958. *We the People.* Chicago: University of Chicago Press.

McLaughlin, Andrew. 1935. *A Constitutional History of the United States.* New York: D. Appleton-Century Co.

— 1969. The Articles of Confederation. In Leonard W. Levy, ed., *Essays on the Making of the Constitution,* pp. 44–60. New York: Oxford University Press.

Middleton, Lamar. 1938. *Revolt U.S.A.* New York: Stackpole Sons.

Minot, George R. [1788] 1971. *History of the Insurrections in Massachusetts in 1786 and of the Rebellion Consequent Thereon.* Reprint. New York: Da Capo Press.

Monroe, James. 1898. *The Writings of James Monroe.* Ed. Stanislaus Hamilton. New York: G. P. Putnam's Sons.

Montesquieu, Charles de Secondat. 1989. *The Spirit of the Laws.* Eds. Anne M. Cohler, Basia Carolyn Miller, and Harold Samuel Stone. New York: Cambridge University Press.

Monthly Review or Literary Journal. 1776. Vol. 54. London: R. Griffiths.

Morgan, Edmund S. 1959. *Prologue to Revolution: Sources and Documents on the Stamp Act Crisis, 1764–1766.* New York: Norton and Company.

— 1988. *Inventing the People: The Rise of Popular Sovereignty in England and America.* New York: W. W. Norton.

Morrill, Dan L. 1993. *Southern Campaigns and the American Revolution.* Baltimore: Nautical and Aviation Publishing Co.

Morris, Richard B. 1956. The Confederation Period and the American Historian. *William and Mary Quarterly* 13 (April 1956): 140–156.

1987. *Forging of the Union, 1781–1789*. New York: Harper and Row.

Morris, Robert. 1975– . *The Papers of Robert Morris*. Eds. James Ferguson et al. Pittsburgh: University of Pittsburgh.

Mueller, Dennis. 1989. *Public Choice II*. New York: Cambridge University Press.

Murdoch, James C., and Todd Sandler. 1984. Complementarity, Free Riding, and the Military Expenditures of NATO Allies. *Journal of Public Economics* 25: 83–101.

Myerson, Roger. 1991. *Game Theory*. Cambridge: Harvard University Press.

Nettels, Curtis P. 1962. *The Economic History of the United States*, vol. 2: *The Emergence of a National Economy, 1775–1815*. New York: Holt, Rinehart and Winston.

Nevins, Allan. 1924. *The American States during and after the Revolution*. New York: Macmillan.

New York. *Journal of the Assembly, 1780*. Boston: Adams and Nourse. Evans #16907.

Journal of the Assembly, 1787. New York: Loudons. Evans #20576.

Journal of the Senate, 1787. New York: Loudons. Evans #20577.

North, Douglas C. 1990. *Institutions, Institutional Change, and Economic Performance*. New York: Cambridge University Press.

Olson, Mancur. 1965. *The Logic of Collective Action*. Cambridge, MA: Harvard University Press.

1982. *The Rise and Decline of Nations: Economic Growth, Stagflation, and Social Rigidities*. New Haven: Yale University Press.

Olson, Mancur, and Richard Zeckhauser. 1966. An Economic Theory of Alliances. *Review of Economics and Statistics* 48: 266–279.

Onuf, Peter S. 1983. *The Origins of the Federal Republic: Jurisdictional Controversies in the United States, 1775–1787*. Philadelphia: University of Pennsylvania Press.

1988. "State Sovereignty and the Making of the Constitution." In Terence Ball and J. G. A. Pocock, eds., *Conceptual Change and the Constitution*, pp. 78–98. Lawrence: University of Kansas Press.

Ostrom, Elinor. 1990. *Governing the Commons: The Evolution of Institutions for Collective Action*. New York: Cambridge University Press.

Ostrom, Vincent. 1987. *The Political Theory of a Compound Republic*. Lincoln: University of Nebraska Press.

Patterson, Stephen E. 1993. The Nationalist Reaction to Shays' Rebellion. In Robert A. Gross, ed., *In Debt to Shays: The Bicentennial of an Agrarian Rebellion*, pp. 101–118. Charlottesville: University Press of Virginia.

Peckham, Howard. 1974. *The Toll of Independence: Engagements and Battle Casualties of the American Revolution*. Chicago: University of Chicago Press.

Pennsylvania. 1780. *Session Laws, May 10, 1780*. Philadelphia: Dunlap. Evans #16931.

1853. *Pennsylvania Archives*. Ed. Samuel Hazard. Philadelphia: Joseph Severns and Co.

Pennsylvania Gazette. 1784–1787. Philadelphia: Hall and Sellers.

Perkins, Edwin J. 1994. *American Public Finance and Financial Services, 1700–1815.* Columbus: Ohio State University Press.

Pitkin, Timothy. [1817] 1980. *A Statistical View of the Commerce of the United States of America.* Reprint. New York: Goldsmith's Kress Library of Economic Literature. No. 21731. Microfilm.

Rakove, Jack N. 1979. *The Beginnings of National Politics: An Interpretive History of the Continental Congress.* New York: Alfred Knopf.

1982. The Legacy of the Articles of Confederation. *Publius* 12 (Fall): 45–65.

1988. The Collapse of the Articles of Confederation. In Jackson Barlow, Leonard Levy, and Ken Masugi, eds., *The American Founding*, pp. 225–245. New York: Greenwood Press.

Reed, Joseph. 1847. *Life and Correspondence of Joseph Reed.* Ed. William B. Reed. Philadelphia: Lindsay and Blakiston.

Reid, John Phillip. 1987. *Constitutional History of the American Revolution: The Authority to Tax.* Madison: University of Wisconsin Press.

1991. *Constitutional History of the American Revolution: The Authority to Legislate.* Madison: University of Wisconsin Press.

1993. *Constitutional History of the American Revolution: The Authority of Law.* Madison: University of Wisconsin Press.

Rhode Island Historical Society. 1827–1902. *Rhode Island Historical Society.* 15 vols. Providence: John Miller.

Riker, William. 1964. *Federalism: Origins, Operation, Significance.* Boston: Little Brown.

1987. The Lessons of 1787. *Public Choice* 55: 5–34.

1996. *The Strategy of Rhetoric.* Eds. Randall L. Calvert, John Mueller, and Rick K. Wilson. New Haven: Yale University Press.

Roche, John P. 1961. The Founding Fathers: A Reform Caucus in Action. *American Political Science Review* 55 (4): 799–816.

Rossiter, Clinton, ed. 1961. *The Federalist Papers.* New York: Mentor.

Rush, Benjamin. 1947. *Selected Writings of Benjamin Rush.* Ed. Dagobert Runes. New York: Philosophical Library.

Samuelson, Paul A. 1954. The Pure Theory of Economic Expenditure. *Review of Economics and Statistics* 36: 386–389.

Sandler, Todd. 1992. *Collective Action: Theory and Applications.* Ann Arbor: University of Michigan Press.

1993. The Economic Theory of Alliances. *Journal of Conflict Resolution* 37: 446–483.

Sen, Amartya. 1970. *Collective Choice and Social Welfare.* San Francisco: Holden-Day.

Smith, Paul et al., eds. 1976– . *Letters of Delegates to Congress, 1774–1789.* 23 vols. Washington, DC: Library of Congress.

South Carolina. House of Representatives. 1788. *Debates Which Arose in the House of Representatives of South Carolina on the Constitution Framed for the United States by a Convention of Delegates Assembled at Philadelphia.* Charleston: City Gazette Printing Office. Evans #21470.

Spaulding, E. Wilder. 1932. *New York in the Critical Period, 1783–1789.* New York: Columbia University Press.

Staples, William. [1870] 1971. *Rhode Island in the Continental Congress, 1765–1790.* Reprint. Reuben A. Guild, ed. Providence: Providence Printing Co.

Stokey, Edith and Richard Zeckhauser. 1978. *A Primer for Policy Analysis.* New York: W.W. Norton.

Storing, Herbert, ed. 1981. *The Complete Anti-Federalist.* Chicago: University of Chicago Press.

Studenski, P., and H. Krooss. 1963. *Financial History of the United States.* New York: McGraw-Hill.

Szatmary, David P. 1980. *Shays' Rebellion: The Making of an Agrarian Insurrection.* Amherst: University of Massachusetts Press.

Thorpe, Francis N., comp. 1909. *The Federal and State Constitutions: Colonial Charters and Other Organic Laws.* Washington, D.C.: Government Printing Office.

Tocqueville, Alexis de. 1988. *Democracy in America.* Ed. J. P. Mayer, trans. George Lawrence. New York: Harper Collins.

United Nations. 1992–95. *Yearbook of the United Nations.* Vols. 45–48. Boston: Martinus Nijhoff Publishers.

United States. *Papers of the Continental Congress.* Record Group 360, M-247. Washington, DC: National Archives. Microfilm.

Statement of the Accounts of the United States of America, during the Administration of the Board of Treasury, November 1, 1784–September 12, 1789. Record Group 39, M-1014, roll 23. College Park, MD: National Archives.

Statement of the Financial Affairs of the Late Confederated Government, 1781 to 1789. Peter Force Papers, Series 8D, reel 54, entry 121.2. Washington: Library of Congress.

1785. *Statement of the Accounts of the United States of America, during the Administration of the Superintendent of Finance, February 20, 1781–November 1, 1784.* Philadelphia: Robert Aitken. Record Group 39, M-1014, roll 23. College Park, MD: National Archives.

1791. *Statement of the Receipts and Expenditures of Public Monies during the Administration of the Finances by Robert Morris.* Philadelphia. Evans #23922.

1910–37. *Journals of the Continental Congress, 1774–1789.* Eds. Worthington Chauncey Ford, et al. 34 vols. Washington, DC: Government Printing Office.

Bureau of the Census. 1989. *Historical Statistics of the United States, Colonial Times to 1970.* Washington, DC: U.S. Department of Commerce.

Treasury Department. 1832. *American State Papers.* Washington, DC: Gales and Seaton.

Varian, Hal R. 1987. *Intermediate Microeconomics: A Modern Approach.* New York: W. W. Norton.

Virginia. 1787. *Journals of the House of Delegates, October 16, 1786–January 11, 1787.* Richmond: Dixon and Holt. Evans #20840.

1928. *Official Letters of the State of Virginia.* Ed. H. R. McIwiane. Richmond: Virginia State Library.

1967. *Journals of the Council of the State of Virginia.* Ed. George H. Reese. Richmond: Virginia State Library. Evans #20840.

1968. *Calendar of Virginia State Papers from January 1, 1785 to July 2, 1789.* Vol. 4. Reprint. Ed. William P. Palmer. New York: Kraus Reprint Corporation.

Warren, Joseph P. 1905. The Confederation and the Shays Rebellion. *American Historical Review* 11 (1): 42–67.

Washington, George. 1938. *The Writings of George Washington.* Ed. John Fitzpatrick. Washington, DC: United States Printing Office.

1995. *The Papers of George Washington, Confederation Series.* Eds. W. W. Abbort et al. Charlottesville: University of Virginia Press.

Weslager, C. A. 1976. *The Stamp Act Congress.* Newark: University of Delaware Press.

Wood, Gordon S. 1969. *The Creation of the American Republic, 1776–1787.* New York: W. W. Norton.

Wright, Robert K. 1983. *The Continental Army.* Washington, DC: Government Printing Office.

Zuckert, Michael P. 1986. Federalism and the Founding: Toward a Reinterpretation of the Constitutional Convention. *Review of Politics* 48 (2): 166–210.

Index

Adams, Samuel, 17, 128
American Confederation, 2–4, 6, 20; see also Articles of Confederation
American Revolution, see Revolutionary War
American State Papers, 94
Annapolis Convention, 142–4, 157
Anti-Federalists, 7, 11–13, 50, 93, 146, 163–70, 172–3, 178; see also Federalists
Articles of Confederation, 11, 13–14, 41, 50, 73, 99–100, 104, 125, 147, 155, 163, 175, 189; Article II, 4, 28–9; Article III, 4, 28; Article IX, 27; Article VI, 109; Article VIII, 4–5, 27, 59; Article XIII, 137, 154; proposed amendments, 68, 103, 130, 132, 138–9, 142, 144–5, 153; purpose, 7, 17, 21, 23, 25, 31–4, 37, 45, 131, 165, 169, 177, 181; ratification procedures, 156, 159; see also coercive powers amendment; conditional direct taxation amendment; impost, amendments; sovereignty; taxation

Bailyn, Bernard, 153
Beard, Charles, 153
Becker, Robert, 12
bills of credit, 52; defined, 193; see also "old money"
bills of exchange, 54–55; defined, 193

Bowdoin, James, 112, 115, 120–2
Braxton, Carter, 17
British threat to states, 90–2, 98, 106–7, 116, 129, 165, 175, 177; strength report, 88
Brown, Roger, 12, 42n.8
Bryan, Samuel, 169

Cappon, Lester J., 90
Carrington, Edward, 116, 173
certificates, 58, 82, 94; defined, 193
civic virtue, 6, 19, 169, 173–4; defined, 193
civil list, 80, 170, 176, 178
Clark, George Rogers, 75, 111–12
Clinton, George, 68, 122–3
coercive powers amendment, 132–4, 136–7, 152, 154
coinage, see currency; specie
collective action game, 41, 183–92
collective action problem, 35, 36n.3, 152, 177, 181; defined, 193
conditional direct taxation amendment, 137–40, 152
confederations and international organizations, 2–3, 15, 179–80
Congress, 1–3, 6, 27–30, 36, 44, 47, 54, 60–2, 66, 74–6, 81–2, 84–8, 94, 98, 106–8, 110–11, 113, 115–16, 121–2, 157, 170, 176; see also Articles of Confederation; debt; loans; requisition

Connecticut, 12, 80, 92, 105–6, 114–16, 120, 126
Constitution, 128, 130–1, 133, 140, 149, 152–3, 158, 160–2, 166, 169, 179; Article I, section 8, 150; Article VII, 151; Article VII, section 1, 150; Article VII, section 5, 150–1; ratification, 159
Constitutional Convention, 135, 145, 156, 163
Continental Army, 8, 10, 14, 35, 39, 46–8, 50, 69, 74, 86–7, 92, 98, 106, 109, 113, 125–7, 160; distance from, 84, 88–90, 105; payment of veterans, 82, 176
Continental Congress, 4, 23, 45; first, 22; second, 51, 104
"continentals," *see* "old money"
Corbin, Francis, 166
currency, 26–7, 52–3, 56–8; *see also* "old money," specie

Dane, Nathan, 109, 143
Day, Luke, 122
debt, 3, 7–8, 14, 35, 47, 50, 52, 59, 62, 69, 76, 78, 80, 85–6, 94, 96, 101, 103, 119, 178; domestic, 2, 10, 48, 70, 93, 98, 109, 175; foreign, 2, 61, 77, 81–2, 99; *see also* loans
debt sinking, defined, 193
Dickinson, John, 32
Duane, James, 17, 135

efficiency, 164–5, 169, 172, 179, 181; defined, 193
Ellsworth, Oliver, 51, 159

Federalist Papers, 147, 164
Federalists, 7–8, 10, 12, 14–15, 50, 63, 165, 167, 170–3, 178; *see also* Anti-Federalists
final settlement, defined, 193–4
Finney, Captain, 111–12
Fiske, John, 178
France, *see* loans, French
Franklin, Benjamin, 6, 119, 151

free riders, 3, 41, 50, 52, 66, 69, 76, 102, 104–7, 124, 180, 183, 186, 192; defined, 193
French and Indian War, 24, 45–6

Galloway, Joseph, 45
Georgia, 12, 44, 47, 162, 175
Gerry, Elbridge, 146, 151, 159
Gorham, Nathaniel, 159–60
Grayson, William, 11, 72, 109–10, 138, 176

Hamilton, Alexander, 1, 7–8, 14, 53, 59, 64–5, 94, 101, 136, 142, 147, 153, 156, 165, 171
Hancock, John, 128
Harmar, Josiah, 109–11, 114, 118, 126
Hartford convention, 133
Hazen's Regiment, 94
Henry, Patrick, 108–11, 165–6, 170, 172
Holland, *see* loans, Dutch
Howell, David, 5, 19, 61
Humphries, David, 116, 122
Huntington, Samuel, 115

impost, 60–1, 70–1, 125, 138, 153; amendments, 132, 134, 137, 152; defined, 194
indent, 77–8, 82, 98, 100–1, 170; defined, 194; out of state, 80
Indians, 26–7, 102, 104, 109, 111, 113, 115, 118, 129, 175; Shawnee, 105, 108, 112; Wabash, 105, 107, 112, 117
Intolerable Acts, 131
Iredell, James, 168
Irvine, William, 144–5

Jackson, Henry, 115, 121–2, 125
Jay, John, 30, 139–40
Jefferson, Thomas, 29, 145, 154, 157–8, 168
Jensen, Merrill, 153
Johnston, Samuel, 59
joint product, 13, 47–8, 50, 66, 163,

179, 181, 192; argument, 85, 102, 104; defined, 194; model, 127; theory of, 14–15, 35, 49, 180

Jones, Joseph, 84

Katcher, Philip R., 88

Kentucky, 108–11, 113, 118

King, Rufus, 72, 80, 112, 121, 123, 138, 151

Knox, Henry, 104, 111–13, 115, 121–2

Lansing, John, 71, 146, 149

Lee, Richard Henry, 17, 22, 110, 129, 156, 165

Lesser, Charles H., 90

liberty, 131, 138, 167–9, 172

Lincoln, Benjamin, 120–1

Lindahl tax share, 190

Livingston, Robert, 167

loan office certificates, 54, 56, 58, 76–7, 94, 98–9; defined, 194

loans, 80, 170, 175; Dutch, 56, 80; French, 56, 80; from private businessmen, 115; Spanish, 56, 80; *see also* debts

local interests, 13, 19, 45, 50, 66, 82–3, 174, 179, 186

Locke, John, 20

Logan, Benjamin, 111–12

Logic of Collective Action, 34

Madison, James, 6, 17, 46, 59, 81, 123–4, 130–2, 134–5, 140, 142, 146–7, 149, 151, 153–4, 156–62, 165, 168; "Notes on Ancient and Modern Confederacies," 141; pluralism, 169; "Vices of the Political System of the United States," 145

Main, Jackson Turner, 131

Marshall, John, 162, 171

Martin, Alexander, 146

Martin, Luther, 11, 146, 149, 151

Maryland, 120, 155

Mason, George, 146–7, 149, 171

Massachusetts, 92, 123–6, 132–3,

143, 155, 158, 162; Shays' Rebellion, 38–9, 74–5, 81, 101, 103–7, 112, 114–15, 119–21

McLaughlin, Andrew, 6

Mercer, John F., 103, 146

Monroe, James, 72, 109–10, 137

Montesquieu, Charles de Secondat, 19, 149

Morris, Gouverneur, 53

Morris, Robert, 27, 51–2, 59, 61–4, 73–4, 76–7, 98–100

Nash equilibrium, 186–9

national defense, 4, 9–10, 25, 27–8, 35, 40, 85–6

Nationalists, 59, 76, 129–30, 146

Nevin, Alan, 56

New Hampshire, 64, 106, 114, 126, 162

New Jersey, 56, 65–6, 72–3, 80, 137, 142–3

New Jersey Plan, 147–50

New York, 46–7, 56, 64–6, 92–3, 104, 106, 122–3, 126, 137, 144, 155, 175; 1780 attack on New York City, 67–9, 133; 1783 impost amendment, 71–3

nonexcludable good, 2, 4, 8–10, 101, 186; defined, 194

nonrival good, 8–10; defined, 194

nonstrategic bliss point (NBP), 185–9, 192; defined, 194

North Carolina, 12, 75, 143

Northwest territory, 75; *see also* Indians

"old money," 57–8; defined, 194; *see also* currency; specie

Olson, Mancur, 34, 40–1, 183

Otis, James, 20

Parsons, Eli, 122

Paterson, William, 147–9, 159

Pennsylvania, 23, 67, 71–2, 82, 92, 119–20, 143, 155

Pierce's certificates (military certificates), 94, 155; defined, 194

Pinckney, Charles, 72, 123, 137
pirates, 27; Barbary, 2, 129
Pitt, William, 24
pluralism, Madison's theory of, 169
postal service, 26–7
private benefits, 9, 14, 35, 46–8, 66,
    87–9, 92, 94, 101, 105, 107, 127,
    179–80; hypothesis, 49–50, 84–7,
    98
private good, 47, 84; defined, 194;
    rival, 9
private interests, 9, 179
public benefits, 14, 41, 107, 183–4,
    186, 188, 191–2; of debt
    reduction, 96–8; nonexcludable,
    47, 82, 84, 87, 109, 180;
    nonexcludable and nonrival, 35
public bonds, 54, 97
public debt, 62, 84, 95; defined, 194;
    see also debt
public good, 10, 18, 25, 37, 49–50,
    59, 81, 106, 181, 183–7, 191–2;
    defined, 194; excludable, 9, 83;
    jointly private and public, 69; pure,
    40, 84, 101, 189; theory of, 8,
    34–5, 41–2, 44, 83, 102, 163; *see
    also* nonexcludable good
public interests, 18, 25, 74, 106

Randolph, Edmund, 34, 116–17,
    145, 148, 156–60, 166
Reed, Joseph, 93
requisition, 1–5, 7, 10, 12–14, 18,
    23–6, 32, 34, 38, 42–4, 51–3,
    58–9, 67, 84, 134–6, 138, 141,
    146, 148, 152, 166, 171, 177, 180,
    189–92; for debt payments, 81,
    119; defined, 195; for men, 87–9,
    105, 116, 119; for money, 54, 62,
    77–9, 87, 95, 97, 101–2, 105, 115,
    118, 124, 126; payments to
    Canadian regiments, 82, 99;
    settlement of state accounts, 73,
    76; in supplies, 57
Revolutionary War, 1–3, 13, 17,
    25–6, 36, 52–4, 56, 58–60, 74, 86,
    103, 131, 176

Rhode Island, 19, 60–1, 71, 73, 106,
    114, 124, 126, 132, 160
Riker, William, 146
Root, Jesse, 134
Rush, Benjamin, 131, 177

Secretary at War, 27, 104, 110, 112
Secretary of Foreign Affairs, 27
Shawnee, *see* Indians, Shawnee
Shays, Daniel, 103, 122
Shays' Rebellion, 14, 19, 38, 50, 81,
    101, 104–7, 112, 116–18, 120–1,
    123–4, 126–9, 176
Sherman, Roger, 141
sinking fund, defined, 195
Smith, Melancton, 11
South Carolina, 22, 123, 158
sovereignty, 18, 25, 28, 31–3, 60,
    131, 137–8, 147, 153, 161, 167,
    177–8, 180–1; defined, 195
Spain, treaty, 139; *see also* loans,
    Spanish
Spanish blockade, 2, 129, 140, 175
specie, 55, 62–4, 71, 77–8, 81–2, 97,
    100–1, 124, 170, 175; defined, 195;
    see also currency; "old money"
Stamp Act, 6, 23, 131
Stamp Act Congress, 21–2
state militia, 26, 103–4, 120–1,
    123–5
state sovereignty, *see* sovereignty
Superintendent of Finance, 27, 59, 63

taxation, 20–2, 24, 37, 53, 106, 172;
    direct, 139–40, 148, 153, 166,
    171; regressive, 12; *see also*
    specie
Tocqueville, Alexis de, 19
Tory, 47, 65, 67; defined, 195
Townshend Act, 21, 24
Tupper, Benjamin, 132

Varnum, James Mitchell, 134–5
Virginia, 39, 61, 68, 75, 81, 92,
    101, 141–3, 162; and Indian
    attacks, 104–6, 108–9, 116–20,
    123–4, 126

Virginia Plan, 130–1, 145–7, 149–50, 156–7, 159, 161

Wabash, *see* Indians, Wabash
Wadsworth, Jeremiah, 116
War of Independence, *see* Revolutionary War
Warren, James, 133–4
Washington, George, 54, 145–6, 151, 157–8; during Revolutionary War, 1, 6, 56, 66–9, 90, 133–4

Webster, Noah, 173
Wheeler, Adam, 122
Whig, 5, 11, 14, 18–20, 32, 165, 169; defined, 195
Whipple, Joseph, 64
Wilson, James, 17, 149, 159, 173
Witherspoon, John, 29, 133–4
Wood, Gordon, 5, 153

Yates, Robert, 146